Resistance in Psychotherapy

Thomas Abel

Resistance in Psychotherapy

The Eight Forms – Clinical Approaches and Meaning in the Therapeutic Process

Springer

Thomas Abel
Berlin, Germany

ISBN 978-3-662-72662-4 ISBN 978-3-662-72663-1 (eBook)
https://doi.org/10.1007/978-3-662-72663-1

Translation from the German language edition: "Widerstände in Psychotherapien" by Thomas Abel, © Springer-Verlag GmbH DE 2025. Published by Springer Berlin Heidelberg. All Rights Reserved.

This book is a translation of the original German edition "Widerstände in Psychotherapien" by Thomas Abel, published by Springer-Verlag GmbH, DE in 2025. The translation was done with the help of an artificial intelligence machine translation tool. A subsequent human revision was done primarily in terms of content, so that the book will read stylistically differently from a conventional translation. Springer Nature works continuously to further the development of tools for the production of books and on the related technologies to support the authors.

This Springer imprint is published by the registered company Springer-Verlag GmbH, DE, part of Springer Nature.
The registered company address is: Heidelberger Platz 3, 14197 Berlin, Germany

Contents

Introduction

1

> People suffer from psychological or physical problems, seek treatment, long for change, but at the same time, from the very beginning, do a great deal to slow down or even prevent any change, sometimes even the recognition of their issues. Some end therapy as soon as the first improvements are achieved or the problem is understood. This applies not only to psychotherapy but to all of medicine.

Using studies, statistics, an image, touching scenes from a fairy tale, and a patient's dream, I would like to provide, at the beginning of this book, an initial understanding of the seemingly bizarre phenomenon of resistance, which is much more than mere laziness or defiance on the part of patients, before I define what resistance is and what forms it can take.

The painting "Wanderer above the Sea of Fog" by Caspar David Friedrich, created in 1818 and long lost, by a gifted painter of landscapes of longing, which inspired the cover of this book, places us as therapists in a surprisingly immediate way into an everyday therapeutic situation. We have before us a man who is just taking the first step on a longer journey, his foot searching for support. He wants to reach a distant summit, but fog-shrouded chasms, valleys, and as yet unseen dangers separate him from it. Only a few rocks, with or without trees, protrude from the veils of mist. It is a figure seen from behind, inviting us to view the world and the path ahead from his perspective. Much like in this painting, in psychotherapy we try to see the inner and outer world of a patient and the life path ahead of them from their point of view. They will be able to tell us clearly where they want to go. But the path to their therapeutic goals lies in the fog: they do not know how to get there—if they did, they would not have come to us, but would have gone alone. They also do not know what chasms or nearly insurmountable cliffs lie ahead, whether they will have to cross raging rivers or protect themselves

T. Abel, *Resistance in Psychotherapy*, https://doi.org/10.1007/978-3-662-72663-1_1

from dangerous animals or people. That is why, although they are very willing and motivated to begin their journey through their inner landscapes, they also have legitimate and understandable fears, which are expressed in the red color of the jacket. At the beginning, but also repeatedly along the way, after each danger has been overcome, they will ask themselves whether they will be able to master and survive the next inner abyss. The fears in the therapeutic process, which flare up anew after every significant emotional insight, after every change, lead to moments when the patient does not want to go on, does not want to continue, perhaps even wants to turn back, because at least they know the evils and dangers of the regions they come from, and because they have previously managed to cope with them, albeit with much suffering and effort. As therapists, we are trained mountaineers, but we do not know the exact path through the specific chasms that lie ahead of our patients. For us, too, the fog will only lift bit by bit, revealing the next few meters. Perhaps this perspective can help us not to see emerging resistance in psychotherapy merely as unwillingness or lack of motivation on the part of our patient, but also to empathize with the underlying fears and thus help to overcome them step by step.

▶ Some patients say at the end of therapy that it was the fog that was unsettling—the not knowing, not having any idea what would come their way on the stretch of life's journey that is psychotherapy, what would await them next after overcoming a fear or an inner abyss. Others say that without the fog, they might never have dared to embark on the journey at all—if it had been clear to them at the start, that is, not fogged over, through which rocky gorges or raging streams they would have to pass to reach their goal in the end. Both are quite understandable and can help us to accept the many resistances that arise during psychotherapy with understanding and to help our patients overcome them.

1.1 Defenders and Explorers

▶ Studies show that in all larger and smaller groups—from families, therapy groups, school classes, work teams, sports teams, all the way up to the entire society of a country—there is a division: a progressive, forward-looking third of people who desire and drive change; a conservative, preserving third who fear the new and do everything to keep things as they are or once were; and an undecided third who sometimes lean one way, sometimes the other, or stay out of it altogether.

In the USA, these camps correspond to the Democrats and the Republicans; in other democratic countries, there are similarly reform-oriented and conservative parties, with undecided or swing voters in between. Governments alternate between being formed by one camp and then, a few years later, by the other, then again by the first, and so on, so that there is always a back-and-forth between progress and preservation. A recent study at the University of Münster by Back et al. (2024) empirically investigated these processes in 5000 people from Germany, Sweden, France, and Poland. The authors hold professorships in psychology, sociology, and political science—a good mix for bringing together very different perspectives. They called the group interested in change "explorers," and those who want to preserve the status quo "defenders." What is reflected in society and in all groups also exists within each individual. Depending on whether the explorer or the defender predominates in a person, they belong to one group or the other. If both are balanced, they belong to the last third. In every patient, but also in every therapist, there are explorers who want to set out into unknown territory, and defenders who would rather keep everything as it is. At the beginning of psychotherapy, we often focus more on the explorers. In this book, however, the defenders should also have their say, along with the many good reasons why they exist.

1.2 Compliance in Somatic Medicine

> In somatic, body-related medicine, resistance is a frequently underestimated phenomenon. The term compliance—which also encompasses resistance—refers to adherence to therapy, cooperativeness, and participation of patients and their social environment in medical treatment, and relates to taking medication, following diets, or making lifestyle changes, such as reducing risk factors like smoking, overweight, or lack of exercise.

According to a 2003 report by the World Health Organization (WHO), only 50% of patients demonstrate sufficient compliance. In other words, only half of patients implement what they have discussed with their physician, while the other half do so only partially or not at all. Intended or unintended non-compliance, i.e., insufficient implementation of the treatment plan, can, depending on the underlying disease, be associated with increased mortality risk, more symptoms, and reduced quality of life. Some hospital admissions are caused by poor implementation of treatment plans. Studies have identified poor communication in the physician-patient relationship as an important factor for inadequate adherence to therapy (see Härter et al., 2005). For this reason, in English-speaking countries, the term compliance is increasingly being replaced by adherence, which focuses more on shared decision-making between patients and providers, aiming to replace the still common asymmetrical, paternalistic relationship between them.

On the patient side, regularly taking medication—and even more so, changing one's lifestyle—requires a great deal of effort, strength, and perseverance. At the beginning of January, with good New Year's resolutions to eat less, smoke less, or drink less alcohol, and to exercise more, many people manage quite well for a few days. By mid-January, however, old patterns have usually reestablished themselves and everything is back to the way it was. When it is medically important and necessary for patients to make such changes, they need their physician to explain why it is necessary, to encourage them that it is not easy but achievable, and to regularly check whether the agreed measures are actually being implemented, in order to achieve sufficient compliance.

On the physician's side, however, there are also some fundamental aspects that contribute to poor compliance among their patients. One of these is depicted in the play "Cat on a Hot Tin Roof" by Tennessee Williams. In it, the doctor hastily takes his leave of his patient "Big Daddy" immediately after telling him the fatal diagnosis of already widely metastasized colon cancer, from which he would soon die. Essentially, he left him alone with his fear of death, instead of helping him cope psychologically with illness and death. Certainly, much has changed in medicine since 1955. Nevertheless, feelings of powerlessness and fear on the part of physicians still often prevent them from adequately supporting patients when the possibilities of medication, surgery, or radiological treatments have been exhausted. As in the play, it is then left to families to accompany the patient through the next steps, which certainly does not contribute to good compliance.

A second aspect concerns the amount of time required in a conversation to explain to the patient the necessity of changing their lifestyle. In the case of early type 2 diabetes mellitus, for example, which now affects 8.5% of the population—currently 61 million people in Europe alone—a third of those affected could manage without medication. Through dietary changes, weight reduction, regular exercise, and abstaining from alcohol and nicotine, the body's cells would, after a few months, absorb more sugar again, resulting in a lasting reduction in blood sugar levels. However, this requires, especially immediately after diagnosis, counseling and ongoing conversations to support patients in making and maintaining these changes, as seen in the TV documentary series "The Nutrition Docs." Most physicians, however, do not devote this much time, but instead quickly prescribe antidiabetic medication. Even if not the entire third could permanently change their lifestyle, it is still a pity for the many people who could have succeeded but were given medication right from the start. Studies have also shown that another third of patients with type 2 diabetes have no compliance for a year or longer, i.e., they do not take their medication at all and do not change their lifestyle (see Kaleta et al., 2023). Adherence to therapy plays a central role, especially for people with diabetes, in order to prevent serious consequences such as cardiovascular disease, kidney failure, blindness, or neuropathies as much as possible. Internal resistance to accepting the illness, but also to following the treatment measures discussed with the physician, leads to this non-compliance. Convenience on the part of the patient, who does not want to change, but also on the part of the physician, who does not have the conversation or keeps it too short, are likely the main reasons.

Conclusion

Many other examples could be named. In any case, lack of adherence to therapy—that is, resistance to treatment—should receive more attention in many medical practices.

1.3 Prevalence, Care Situation, and Psychotherapy Methods

> According to epidemiological studies, mental illnesses are the second most common diseases after infectious diseases.

According to a "Study on the Health of Adults" by the Robert Koch Institute, 27.8% of the adult population in Germany are affected by a mental illness each year, which, at 17.8 million people, corresponds to the population of North Rhine-Westphalia. Across the entire European Union, up to 164.8 million people are estimated to be affected (see, for example, Jacobi et al., 2014; Plass et al., 2014). Anxiety disorders, affective disorders such as depression, and addiction disorders—especially due to alcohol and medication dependence—are the most common. About half of those affected have several diagnoses at the same time, especially anxiety disorders and depression. The prevalence of 27.8%, i.e., the frequency of fully developed mental illnesses within a 12-month period, varies across sociodemographic groups: young people, those with lower social status, and those living in metropolitan areas are more frequently affected. One in three women and one in four to five men were recorded as ill, with women tending more toward anxiety disorders and depression, and men more toward aggression and addiction disorders. However, the impression that mental disorders are women's diseases is incorrect. Women are more likely to seek psychosocial support, while men, due to the way they deal with psychological problems, often remain untreated and are therefore sometimes not captured in statistics. Men sometimes end up in the legal system, for example through violence, criminal acts, or debt due to addiction. When men have mental disorders, they are more likely to direct their aggression outward, toward others, rather than inward, toward themselves, which would lead to depression.

According to the Federal Criminal Police Office's report on gender-based crimes against women, 360 femicides were committed in Germany in 2023, meaning that almost every day a woman was murdered, usually by a man. Every three minutes, women or girls are victims of domestic violence, 68% of which is perpetrated within families or partnerships. When violence is directed against one's own body, it results in suicide. According to the Federal Statistical Office, 28 people take their own lives every day, totaling 10,119 in 2022, of whom 75% are men. Fortunately, these numbers have declined, perhaps also thanks to improved psychotherapeutic care: in 1980, 50 people per day took their own lives.

Of the aforementioned 17.8 million recorded people with a mental illness, most do not seek psychotherapy. Of these, only 3.4 million, or 19%, sought the healthcare system for their psychological complaints in the previous year; most, namely 16%, received outpatient treatment, 2.3% received inpatient treatment, and 3.5% used services from complementary institutions (such as counseling centers or self-help groups). Even when four or more mental health diagnoses are present, only 40% of those affected seek treatment, even though the comprehensive and diverse suffering caused by mental disorders must be particularly great in these cases.

In Germany, the Scientific Advisory Board for Psychotherapy assesses which methods are classified as scientifically recognized and effective. These currently are:

1. Psychodynamic therapy, which is subdivided exclusively in Germany into analytic and depth psychology-based therapy
2. Systemic therapy
3. Behavioral therapy
4. Client-centered therapy, which is indeed effective but has not yet been approved for funding by statutory health insurance, as its effectiveness in the area of anxiety disorders, according to a 2017 report by the Scientific Advisory Board, could not be sufficiently demonstrated. However, as mentioned above, anxiety disorders and affective disorders are the most frequently treated mental illnesses.

Therapy forms 1 to 3 are available as benefits of statutory health insurance to all people in Germany. Poorer and younger individuals, who have a higher prevalence of mental illness, can thus access psychotherapy, whereas in most other countries they would not be able to afford it due to private financing. In this respect, the provision of outpatient psychotherapy in Germany is among the best worldwide. Perhaps psychotherapy is so well funded and supported by the community of solidarity in Germany—almost more so than anywhere else in the world—because, in light of the crimes of National Socialism, we have inflicted far more horrific traumatization on people than any other nation. To a significantly lesser extent, the USA has also killed millions of indigenous people, and Russia or China millions of regime opponents, often in camps. However, the engagement with historical guilt and the resulting need for reparation is less pronounced there than in Germany, which leads to many consequences, presumably including much poorer societal funding for psychotherapy.

From 2032, the approval process for psychotherapy in Germany will be fundamentally changed. There is concern that there will be noticeable cuts in the approved quotas and that extending therapies will become more difficult, so that we may lose some of what we have achieved in recent decades. Although shorter psychotherapies initially save money, we already know from the ever-shorter stays in psychiatric hospitals about the "revolving door effect," whereby patients are discharged from the hospital more quickly than before, but also have to be readmitted more quickly because their illness is only temporarily improved, not adequately treated, and aftercare is not sufficiently organized. In the long term, this does not save money; rather, it tends to increase costs—already in inpatient care, and presumably in the future also in outpatient therapy.

Unfortunately, far too few psychotherapists are licensed in Germany: in 2023, according to the Federal Medical Register, there were 33,715 psychological psychotherapists, of whom 7703 were child and adolescent psychotherapists, plus 5912 medical psychotherapists, making a total of 39,627 psychotherapists. This represents 21% of all outpatient physicians and psychotherapists. If we consider the 31,924 psychotherapists for adults, and 3.4 million adults seeking treatment, each therapist would have to treat

106 patients per year. This would only be possible if all therapists offered 35 treatment hours per week over 45 weeks, and each patient received only 2 consultation hours and 12 hours of acute treatment. This does not happen, as it would not be sufficient for most patients. Already, 77% of treatments are short-term therapies of 24 hours due to this enormous pressure—twice as extensive as would be mathematically necessary to provide care for all those seeking therapy. And even this usually leads only to short-term symptom relief. Patients have to wait an average of 142 days, or just under 5 months, even for these short-term therapies (cf. Deutscher Bundestag, 2023), so that their disorders become chronic and are often compounded by additional mental illnesses such as addiction disorders.

Part of the problem discussed here is systemic, because the government still does not base the number of licenses for psychotherapists on actual need, despite several attempts, but rather on the fear that the whole thing could become too expensive. Perhaps there is also resistance to the very painful realization for society and those in government that, in such a highly developed, prosperous industrial nation as ours, such a large number of people are mentally ill.

A further significant shortage of psychotherapists will result from the reform of the Psychotherapists Act, which came into force on 01.09.2020. This reform aligns the further training of psychotherapists with that of medical specialists. However, as funding is still completely unresolved and the responsible federal states do not wish to assume it, legal proceedings are underway, the outcome of which is, of course, uncertain. As things stand, many of the previous training centers will either not offer reformed training at all or, if they do, only in a greatly reduced form (for example, 5 instead of the previous 80 colleagues), so that there will be little new blood. Accordingly, the future adequate provision of psychiatrists and psychotherapists in Germany is highly endangered (Deutscher Bundestag, 2023).

In the still very many cases where psychotherapy does take place despite all difficulties, compliance and resistance play a very decisive role. There are well-researched and practice-proven concepts for this, which are presented in this book. Presumably, psychotherapy is also the second most effective form of treatment in medicine—with symptom improvement rates of 60–87%—significantly ahead of many medications, surpassed only by vaccinations and some antibiotic medications, because it has developed a differentiated concept of resistance and its management. Steinert and Leichsenring (2017) compiled 3000 studies worldwide on the effectiveness of psychotherapy, of which 44 were filtered according to strict criteria, such as the use of randomized controlled trials (RCT), the current gold standard of efficacy research. According to this, the treatment of the following disorders is considered:

- effective, as demonstrated by two or more RCTs: depressive symptoms, social phobia, post-traumatic stress disorder, somatoform disorders (irritable bowel, pain), bulimia, anorexia, and borderline disorders;

- probably effective, as demonstrated by one RCT: dysthymia, complicated grief, generalized anxiety disorder, panic disorder, binge eating disorder, and opioid dependence.

Other mental disorders not listed here are also treatable effectively, but there are "only" naturalistic studies for these, which were conducted in real-world settings, i.e., in psychotherapy practices during ongoing operations. The appearance of borderline personality disorders as a moderate to severe mental illness among the syndromes proven to be effectively treatable is remarkable. On the one hand, this is certainly due to the now very sophisticated and well-structured treatment methods developed for this purpose, such as transference-focused psychotherapy (TFP), mentalization-based therapy (MBT), and dialectical behavior therapy (DBT). On the other hand, I suspect it is also due to the specific type of resistance in these patients: they have too little resistance, and what they do have is rather crude and easily recognizable. In Chapters 2 and 3.2, I will describe much of this in the context of framework resistances and primitive defense mechanisms. Provided we feel up to the task of working with these patients and can handle their resistance, therapy often achieves impressively rapid and profound changes.

Conclusion
At the moment, we do not even want to imagine what would happen if the 81% of people with mental illnesses who currently do not seek treatment were to overcome their resistance and seek therapy, when we are not even able to care for those who already overcome their resistance.

1.4 "How Good That Nobody Knows...": Fear of Being Recognized

▶ People who seek therapy have, on the one hand, the desire to be understood, to be recognized in their problems and personality, and thereby to receive help. At the same time, however, they are deeply afraid of this, so that the start of psychotherapy is repeatedly postponed. When they finally do begin therapy, they find it difficult to truly show themselves and open up.

The conflict between the wish to be understood and the fear of it seems as old as humanity itself. In the folk tale "Rumpelstiltskin," passed down from generation to generation and told to the Brothers Grimm by the Hassenpflug sisters in 1811—who wrote it down and published it for the first time in 1812 as tale number 55 in their collection of Children's and Household Tales—this conflict is vividly depicted. In the final part of the tale, Rumpelstiltskin appears before the queen three times and challenges her to guess his name. On the one hand, he wants to be recognized for what he is. On the other hand, he does everything he can to prevent her from guessing his name. In therapy, we therapists find ourselves in the role of the queen. We try to find out and guess who is sitting in front of us. We ask: "Are you called Kunz? Are you called Heinz?" Time and again, we hear the answer "No!"—which sounds relieved, even though the patient has come to us precisely to be recognized. The messenger, who in the tale wanders through the forest—symbolically, the world of feelings—could represent our therapeutic experience, our knowledge of our own wounds and fears, or perhaps a good textbook from which we have learned something about what can be found in forests. As soon as we guess the name with this help, the following happens in the first written version of the tale: "The devil told you that! screamed the little man, ran away angrily, and never came back again." The therapy is broken off at the very moment the patient feels recognized. In unfavorable cases, she leaves with the impression that therapy is the devil's work and never seeks out a therapist again. This can happen, for example, if we bypass resistance too early—say, in the third session—using a good messenger and address aspects of the patient too quickly that are associated with much shame, guilt, or fear. In later, more familiar versions, the shame is even more pronounced, as Rumpelstiltskin tears himself in two and sinks into the ground: "'The devil told you that!' screamed the little man and, in his rage, stamped his right foot so deep into the earth that he sank in up to his waist, then seized his left foot with both hands and tore himself in two."

A look at what Rumpelstiltskin does in the forest, in the depths of his emotional home, before being unmasked, helps us to sense the concerns with which many patients come to us for treatment. He jumps around his hut by a fire and calls out: "Today I bake, tomorrow I brew, the day after tomorrow I'll fetch the queen's child; oh, how good it is that nobody knows that my name is Rumpelstiltskin!" (cf. Dettmering, 1999, pp. 205 f.). After Rumpelstiltskin first tries in vain to satisfy his needs through baking and brewing—perhaps through food or alcohol addiction—he hopes to receive the queen's child from the therapist, i.e., something alive that can grow and develop within him, something needy that he can care for, something he perhaps was never allowed to be himself. At the same time, he does not want to be recognized in his shame-laden problems and imperfections.

For some patients, such a child is completely sufficient—some forever, others for a certain time. In my work at a day clinic, some told me they only wanted to get rid of their panic disorder, but did not want to talk about current relationships or their life history. After just a few hours of behavioral therapy following Schneider and Margraf (2014), the panic had completely subsided, and they said goodbye to me, relieved and happy. Others wanted to learn more about themselves after all. One patient, whose panic had largely subsided, came to her therapy session, but placed her anxiety diary and her glasses on the table in tears and asked, somewhat annoyed, whether she could not talk about her marital problems here for once, instead of always just about the anxiety diary and her exercises. In the initial interview, she had strictly refused to discuss her marital situation. Now I was allowed to learn more about the shame-laden marital conflicts and her own part in them. Had I told her too early what her name probably was, she would certainly have run away and discontinued treatment. We should therefore take resistance to uncovering work in therapy very seriously and consider it in our indication decisions. If the fear and shame of being recognized are too great, psychodynamic methods are rather contraindicated. Behavioral therapy or systemic approaches might be more suitable for giving Rumpelstiltskin something to hold in his hands, something that can grow and thrive in and with him.

A special kind of Rumpelstiltskin, whose name psychotherapy searched for a long time, is bulimia. Although it has probably existed for a long time, and although it occurs in 4% of the population—four times as often as anorexia—it was not discovered until 1979. At first, it was considered a subtype of anorexia, thus hiding behind a false name. Even when it was included in the ICD, it was not really given the right name, because bulimia is derived from the Greek words "bous" for ox and "limos" for hunger, meaning "ox hunger." But this name expresses only half the symptomatology, namely the ravenous consumption of food, not the subsequent self-induced vomiting, the discussion of which is always particularly embarrassing for patients, as they associate it with disgust and shame. These feelings cause the resistance to showing oneself, which in this case even led for a long time to a widespread disorder not being discovered at all and then being misnamed. When the 20% of patients, after an average of 4–7 years, finally dare to enter therapy and reveal their symptoms, the treatments are very successful, as shown in the overview in the previous section. Often, however, they only leave their fire in the lonely forest, where they bake and vomit, when serious side effects occur, their teeth and hair fall out, and they can no longer hide their suffering, or when other diagnoses arise, such as suicidality and depression, with which they are more willing to show themselves than with their eating-purging addiction.

Conclusion

In any case, it is important to sense, feel, and gently address the patient's fear of being recognized—even though she had the courage to enter our consultation room.

1.5 "That's Way Too Hot For Me!"—Resistance in the Initial Dream

With a slight expansion of an earlier work (Abel, 2013, pp. 147 f.), I would like to present the initial dream of a patient whom I will call Yvonne, her first dream, which she already brought to the preliminary sessions. It expresses wishes and longings that she associates with the therapy, but also great fears, which became recognizable as resistance:

Example

"I am in a house underground, as if it had sunk into the sand. Only at the very top is there a window to the outside, just above ground level. I open it a crack and look out. There I see a beautiful blue sea, with the sun shining on it, and many happy people running around, sitting, swimming, or playing something on the beach. It's all way too much for me. The sand reaches up to my window. I touch it. It's totally hot. That's way too hot for me. So I close the window again and go down into the cool depths of my house."

In this dream, even without knowing more about Yvonne, resistance is already quite clearly recognizable. Something is "way too much" and "too hot" for the patient. She is drawn to what she sees outside, but another force prevents her from opening the window further, looking longer, or even going out to join the other people and have fun with them. The outward gaze represents a reversal into its opposite; in fact, it is about looking inward, which is what the upcoming therapy calls for. There, the patient sees many happy people, with whom she associates wishes to be happy herself, to be exuberant, to play childishly, but also to be in the warmth of the sun and the sand, i.e., to feel the warmth of human relationships. At the same time, the people on the beach were naked, which the patient left unmentioned in her dream narration and only shared during our discussion about the dream. So it is also about phallic wishes, about eroticism, about seeing and being seen, admiring and being admired, sexuality and the relationship between the sexes, which in the dream is a joyful, playful one, just as the patient never experienced in her family of origin, nor in her later relationships, which is why she longs for it all the more. The sand reminded her of the desert, Africa, then of her parents' stays in Angola when she was 10 and 14 years old, each lasting a year. Her brother, eight years younger, was taken along, while the patient had to stay with her grandparents in the GDR. She only learned about this the day before their departure. This meant a sudden, painful, almost unmanageable experience of loss for the patient. Moreover, it represented a narcissistic injury in a double sense: For her father, she was apparently not so important and attractive that he would have taken her along as well. For her mother, the brother seemed worthy of her care and protection, but not her. The dream thus also deals with the theme of being excluded, being left alone in the dark and cold, with the hurt and abandonment associated with it, but also with the wishes for belonging. All of this is too hot for her. She cannot bear the sight, does not want to perceive the wishes and conflicts she might see within herself. Therefore, she retreats into a lonely self-sufficiency. Interestingly, she goes down in her house, as if into the basement, which she—like the darkness in the house—associated with a sinking of her mood, with depression. The cold embodies the opposite of the desired warmth, but also a state of emotional freezing, as the patient often experienced. Depression and being cut off from feelings were indeed a reason to seek therapy, but on the other hand, they were still more bearable than what lay behind them. Therefore, these symptoms served as defense. In the therapeutic relationship with me, they manifested as resistance. The patient reported in the initial phase that on her way to the sessions, she still had many feelings, which seemed to be switched off, as if frozen, as soon as she entered the practice, but returned when she left. In the dream, it is thus quite clearly depicted what was happening in the patient during the sessions, how she withdrew from her wishes, fears, and conflicts into a cool, lonely way of speaking, characterized by rationalizations and isolations.

Working through this resistance enabled the patient to gradually share more feelings with me and to approach the frightening wishes of her dream. Without my actively addressing the resistance, she would probably have continued to speak withdrawn, cool, and without feelings for many more sessions, without anything changing. In the worst case, the window would have remained closed for the entire therapy, and the patient would have achieved nothing. ◀

Conclusion
Reich (1933) therefore emphasized that addressing resistances always takes precedence over addressing content.

1.6 Resistance: Definition, Origin, and Development of the Concept

▶ By resistance, we mean defense operations that arise in the course of treatment and hinder it if they are not recognized, discussed, and reduced (cf. Thomä & Kächele, 2006).

In psychodynamic approaches, there is the assumption of the unconscious and the conscious as the tip of the iceberg. Cognitive scientists do not speak of the unconscious, but rather of implicit mental processes. Both mean that the patient usually does not carry out the defense operations intentionally and deliberately, and often does not even know or sense what she is currently trying to avoid.

The patient primarily seeks help from the therapist. Resistance is secondary, and is the result of significant distress: the achieved equilibrium guarantees the patient safety and stability. Resistance is meant to maintain it. Psychotherapy represents an intervention in the psychological homeostasis. This triggers insecurity, self-doubt, and fear, and endangers the previous self-concept. The adaptation that was found was, after all, the best possible solution to the conflicts. Now it is threatened.

Even in the word "psychoanalysis," the work on resistance is reflected: the Greek word "lyse" or "lysis" means dissolution or solution in the sense of being dissolved. "Alyse" is the negation of this, the taming of chaos, in our context the control of psychological chaos by defense mechanisms. An "An" before "alyse" is a second negation. "An" is the opposite of "A," namely the systematic dissection of what holds things together, of that which tames chaos, i.e., the defense that had previously laboriously held the unstructured psyche together before lysis. Out of fear of the chaos of lysis, the "A" opposes the "An." Defense mechanisms cannot simply be dissolved; instead, they confront us as resistance to our systematic attempts at dissection in psychotherapy.

Freud already dealt with the phenomenon of resistance in 1895 in the *Studies on Hysteria*. He first used the term resistance in describing the treatment of his patient Elisabeth von R. in 1892. He understood her not-knowing as a not-wanting-to-know of internal, unbearable ideas. Later, he explained that a force opposes memory, corresponding to the force that originally led to repression, and thus also to symptom formation. This force is meant to keep the repressed content unconscious. Defense and resistance are thus related phenomena: resistance is defense as it appears to us in the therapeutic process. Ultimately, the discovery of resistance led to the abandonment of hypnosis, as Freud found that the communication of memories brought to light under hypnosis could often not be accepted by patients after the hypnosis was lifted and usually increased resistance. Hypnosis was therefore replaced by work with and on resistance. Greenson (1973) considers this paradigm shift to be the beginning of psychoanalysis. Reich (1933) formulated the technical principle that working through resistance takes precedence over working through content.

▶ Today, the four cornerstones of psychoanalysis are considered to be an understanding of the unconscious, resistance, transference, and countertransference.

In Germany, they are even enshrined in law in § 16 of the Psychotherapy Guidelines. Here are some excerpts:

> "§ 16a Depth Psychology-Based Psychotherapy:
>
> (1) Depth psychology-based psychotherapy comprises etiologically oriented therapy forms with which the unconscious psychodynamics of currently active neurotic conflicts and structural disorders are treated, taking into account transference, countertransference, and resistance. ...
>
> § 16b Analytical Psychotherapy: Analytical psychotherapy comprises those therapy forms that, together with the neurotic symptomatology, treat the neurotic conflict material and the underlying neurotic structure of the patient, and in doing so initiate and promote the therapeutic process with the help of transference, countertransference, and resistance analysis, utilizing regressive processes."

In the regulations for systemic and behavioral therapy, the term resistance or anything comparable is not yet present, as an understanding of this phenomenon is only gradually developing here in its early stages. Schulte (2014) distinguishes, from a behavioral therapy perspective, three forms of resistance, which are listed in Sect. 1.7 under the forms of resistance and correspond to structure-specific resistances and resistances through defense mechanisms from psychodynamic approaches.

Within the various schools of psychoanalysis, the concept of resistance occupies a very different position. Among Jungians, the concept has essentially not found its way into the theoretical framework. In individual psychology, the "safeguarding tendencies" (Adler, 1912) serve to preserve the neurotic lifestyle. Insofar, it has a concept of resistance and how to deal with it. In Melanie Klein's work, projection replaced repression as the prototypical defense mechanism. The importance of resistance to repression diminished. Technically, the Kleinian approach operates behind the back of resistance, because access to unconscious fantasies and affects seems possible directly through anxieties. These reach the therapist's unconscious directly via projection and projective identification, who contains them and returns them to the patient in a digested form. Resistance disappeared from Kleinian terminology. At most, it appears as negative transference, which is interpreted early on as an attack on the analyst—on their thinking, knowledge, and understanding (cf. Thomä & Kächele, 2006, p. 140, as well as Abel, 2011b). In Kohut's self psychology, the extent of resistance depends on the current behavior of the analyst. Resistance primarily serves to avoid renewed empathic injuries.

▶ For König (1995), what matters most is an optimal level of resistance. Therapy can be slowed down, made more difficult, or rendered impossible by too much or too little resistance.

1.7 Forms of Resistance

Following the revision of the theory of anxiety and in the context of the structural theory, Freud (1926) in *Inhibition, Symptom, and Anxiety* classified resistances according to the agencies ego, id, and superego, with the first two categories being considered ego resistances:

1. Repression resistance
2. Transference resistance
3. Superego resistance
4. Id resistance
5. Resistance due to secondary gain from illness

What Freud (1926) described as repression, but at other times also called defense, was further differentiated by his daughter. In her work *The Ego and the Mechanisms of Defense*, Anna Freud (1936) described a whole series of defense mechanisms and the resistances they cause, for example, regression resistance, isolation resistance, projection resistance, resistance through undoing, or through turning against the self. In this respect, it makes sense to replace the term repression resistance and to speak of resistances through defense mechanisms.

Glover (1955) compiled some "gross resistances," which today can be considered frame resistances. König (1995) differentiated structure-specific resistances that are related to the specific character structure of a person. In Erikson (1970) and Adler (1912, 1933) we find an identity resistance, which, however, coincides with the resistance of schizoid personality structures described by König (1995) and is therefore subsumed by me under that category.

Furthermore, countertransference resistances are identified, which on the one hand concern the perception and reception of what the patient communicates to the therapist, and on the other hand the personality structure of the therapist. König (1993) describes in detail what therapists with different character structures are able to perceive and understand well in their patients, but also where they develop resistances to something the patients wish to convey. Due to the therapist's own fears, needs, or feelings of shame, she may be unable to sense and take in the patient's wishes or drive impulses. Sandler (1999, 2001) addressed the therapist's willingness to assume roles: this concerns her readiness to take on feelings of the patient with which she is to be projectively identified, especially when these evoke erotic desire or destructive impulses in her, which her ego ideal or superego might reject.

Finally, there are also special types of resistance in therapy groups, which Bion (1962) already pointed out, as well as others after him, and resistances in couple and family therapies. These are presented in the manuals of the respective approaches and cannot be described here for reasons of space.

In the meantime, the concept of resistance has also been adopted and adapted from psychoanalysis by other forms of therapy. Schulte (2014), for example, develops a behavioral therapy perspective that overlaps with the psychoanalytic view. He distinguishes three forms of resistance:

1. Resistance as a trait: Resistance is a personality trait, as people differ in how strongly they are provoked into it when something is expected of them that they cannot imagine. It corresponds to the personality trait of reactance. In studies, men have shown stronger reactance than women.
2. Resistance as current behavior (state): Reactance as a personality trait influences the occurrence of resistance in the current situation.
3. Disorder-related resistance: Resistance can be a consequence of the disorder itself. For example, the inactivity of a depressed patient will manifest as reduced engagement in therapy.

I use a classification of resistances that combines all these aspects, which will guide the subsequent chapters of this book:

1. frame resistances
2. resistances through defense mechanisms
3. transference resistances
4. Shame and guilt: superego resistances
5. The familiar: id resistances
6. resistances due to secondary gain from illness
7. personality structure-specific resistances
8. countertransference resistances

The case examples in the following chapters are either patients from my own practice or those presented to me by colleagues in supervision. They have been disguised, mostly blended with other, similar patients to prevent identification. The first names given are, of course, pseudonyms. Some passages have been taken from my earlier publication (Abel, 2013) in an expanded and slightly modified form.

2 Frame Resistances

On the one hand, these are resistances against the external framework of treatment, such as missing sessions, arriving late, dropping out of therapy, or a destructive, treatment-endangering approach to suicidality or substance use. On the other hand, these resistances concern the internal framework, the regulatory system that dictates to the patient what she should and may do in therapy and what she may not. In addition to the prohibition of violent outbursts in the therapy room, this mainly involves phenomena such as silence, falling asleep, or not following the basic rules, such as free association in psychodynamic approaches or the handling of exercises in behavioral therapy.

2.1 External frame resistances

▶ The more severe and complex the symptoms, and the more the self is impaired toward a personality disorder or even psychotic personality organization, the more we must expect gross violations of the external framework of treatment. That is why, in specialized treatment approaches, such as those for borderline patients, very detailed agreements about the framework and how to handle its violations are specified (see, for example, Yeomans et al., 2017). This allows the external framework to be largely maintained, and its violations can be clearly identified and discussed as resistance to therapy.

The therapy contract creates an external framework with certain possibilities, conditions, and boundaries within which the therapeutic process can unfold and in which both the patient and the therapist can feel safe, protected, and comfortable. The patient, her personality structure, and her symptoms determine what we include in the agreement about the framework conditions. With all patients, we must make arrangements regarding the

T. Abel, *Resistance in Psychotherapy*, https://doi.org/10.1007/978-3-662-72663-1_2

cancellation of therapy sessions, cancellation fees, or our telephone availability. Depending on the symptoms and issues, other regulations may be added, such as those concerning suicidality, violence, addiction, or eating disorders. We should take plenty of time for this and formulate the agreements as precisely as possible, either in writing as a therapy contract or verbally, which is often sufficient. In any case, I note verbally made agreements in the patient's file so that I can refer to them if necessary. It is best to agree on the therapy contract already during the preliminary discussions, partly because it clarifies the external framework of treatment and how to handle its violations. On the other hand, patients at the beginning of therapy are still experiencing a high level of distress and thus have a strong motivation for change, making them more willing to accept the rules than they might be later on.

▶ Already during the preliminary discussions, therapists should explain the external framework of treatment, make binding agreements with the patient, and only begin treatment if a mutually acceptable agreement has been reached.

2.1.1 Missing sessions and cancellation fees

▶ If the patient cancels a therapy session at short notice or fails to appear without excuse, the therapist cannot reassign the appointment or bill it to an insurance company or, in the case of self-paying patients, to the patient herself. This results in a financial loss for the therapist.

That is why a cancellation policy is negotiated before the start of every therapy. According to this, the patient commits to paying a cancellation fee if she does not cancel the therapy session in time, for example, 48 hours before the start of the session. This time frame is often used because it is legally secure. Other deadlines are therefore not illegal, but have simply not yet been tested in court. However, I would not sue for a cancellation fee, but rather end the treatment if the patient refused to pay the agreed cancellation fee. 48 hours is sometimes also an inconvenient deadline: if, for example, the therapy session is scheduled for Monday morning at 9 a.m., the patient could cancel until Saturday at 8:59 a.m. If the therapist even receives the message over the weekend, she will not be able to reassign the appointment on Monday morning and will incur a financial loss. In this respect, it is better to agree on two working days, so that the patient would have to cancel by Thursday at 8:59 a.m. Sometimes I also negotiate longer cancellation periods, such as one week or 14 days. This can prevent a patient who is angry with me during a therapy session from canceling the next session, which would otherwise happen quite often with borderline patients, as they become angry with the therapist very quickly and express their anger in action, such as by canceling sessions. It should also be discussed whether a cancellation fee is due if the patient or her child becomes ill and she cannot attend. In the case of a sick child, an online session could be considered, so that the patient can be near her sick child and still attend her therapy session. If the patient herself is only mildly ill, she could still come to the session, so that the session would only have to be canceled in the case of more serious illness. In these cases, some therapists waive the cancellation fee. If such cancellations become frequent, the patient would have to provide a medical certificate to prove the severity of her illness, as she would in any case have to see a doctor, be treated, and receive a sick note.

It becomes tricky with migraine patients. They argue that they are familiar with their regularly occurring migraine attacks, that they have to lie down in a darkened room for half a day, and therefore would not go to their doctor specifically, and, moreover, that they cannot leave the house during a migraine attack. In addition, these attacks only announce themselves shortly beforehand, so they cannot cancel sessions two working days in advance. If we accept this argument and do not agree on a cancellation fee for such cases, we open the door wide to framework resistances, because the patient could then cancel any session at will, citing a migraine attack, regardless of whether she actually had one or not. It is advisable not to waive the cancellation fee in these cases, because then the patient will only cancel if she really has a migraine attack, and sometimes even comes to the session despite a migraine if it is not too severe. This gives us the opportunity to discuss psychosomatic aspects of the migraine, such as what is currently giving the patient a headache in therapy, or what insights or changes the migraine attack is preventing or making more difficult. Discussing this resistance often leads to the migraine attack being reduced or sometimes disappearing altogether, because the patient is able to express what is frightening her in therapy and which topics she is not yet ready to approach. If she does not come but cancels the session due to migraine, we must discuss these aspects in the following session. The cancellation fee is helpful in this respect, because patients get annoyed about having to pay it, even if they otherwise quickly ward off any form of aggression. The anger that is somatized in the headache can show itself at this point and becomes discussable. Part of the psychological conditions underlying the psychosomatic illness migraine is brought into therapy and changed by the cancellation fee and the feelings it triggers, instead of continuing to be warded off somatically, remaining outside, and leading to frequent missed therapy sessions and, for us, to financial losses and frustration. Our frustration is worth mentioning because it can become a countertransference resistance, especially if we ward it off and do not feel it. If we allow ourselves to feel the frustration, it is not easy to address it with the patient, because she will argue that she cannot help her migraine attack, that she suffers greatly from it, and would much rather come to the therapy session. Therefore, she cannot understand why we are annoyed. By charging a cancellation fee and thus avoiding financial losses, our frustration will be greatly reduced. Any remaining frustration should be made conscious so that it does not become a countertransference resistance, and should be understood as the patient's anger, which she unconsciously, subtly communicates to us, i.e., with which she projectively identifies us. In sect. 3.2.5 on projective identifications, I describe how we can return this anger to the therapeutic relationship in a contained and marked way, so that it no longer paralyzes us as resistance, but becomes accessible for processing.

The amount of the cancellation fee should be set slightly below the remuneration for a therapy session. In Germany, statutory health insurance funds paid €116.62 for a therapy hour in January 2025, so a cancellation fee of up to €115.00 would be possible. I usually do not go lower than that. If patients have only very low incomes, they can also pay the cancellation fee in small installments. In our negotiations, we keep in mind that the cancellation fee should ideally never be incurred during the entire course of therapy, provided the patient handles appointments responsibly and conscientiously, and that the amount of the cancellation fee helps ensure that resistance does not manifest through missed sessions, but rather in other ways, such as arriving late. In my 30 years of outpatient psychotherapeutic practice, I have only very rarely had to charge a cancellation fee, because sessions were attended very regularly and resistance shifted from the framework into the therapeutic process itself. Nevertheless, the topic is, of course, a sensitive one. As the saying goes: "Friendship ends when it comes to money!" Many therapists are reluctant to discuss this topic, especially since it must be clarified during the initial consultations, when we barely know our patients and often have not yet established a solid working relationship. Therapists find it difficult not to appear caring and helpful, but instead to demand something, to claim something for themselves, to appear strict, to reveal that they do not speak with their patients solely out of warmth, but also earn their livelihood this way. From supervision, I know that some agree to very low cancellation fees of €30 or €40 and implement the negotiated conditions very leniently or sometimes not at all. The main form of learning for humans is identification, imitation. How are patients supposed to learn to claim their rightful share in life if their therapist, whom they internalize and allow to become a role model, appears very yielding, cannot articulate legitimate financial claims, and cannot take anything for herself from the other party? If modeling through the therapist does not work, we can prescribe 100 hours of behavioral exercises to formulate claims with attachment figures or to demand something, or we can discuss the patient's rational, emotional, and etiological reasons for why she cannot take anything for herself, without achieving anything. However, if we face the process of negotiating the cancellation policy, we sometimes already get caught up in emotional whirlpools during the initial consultations, which, in my experience, lead to clarifying important matters and, precisely through mutual honesty and openness, deepen the working relationship with the patients. When we stand up for our interests as therapists, we become figures of identification, role models who help the patient to negotiate for her own interests without guilt. Not once have I experienced a case where such discussions prevented treatment from taking place. It has probably also contributed to the fact that I have very rarely been confronted with therapy dropouts, because clear and differentiated framework conditions and negotiating their implementation shift the resistance more into the therapy itself, where it can be discussed more effectively.

Example

An example will illustrate how quickly we can find ourselves in deep abysses when negotiating the cancellation policy. Lilly, a 30-year-old, very friendly and sad patient, laughed at me with great contempt during the third initial consultation when I mentioned €110 as a cancellation fee, and said: "So little? I work as a high-class prostitute and charge €400 an hour. Most of my clients talk to me for 55 minutes about all their problems at work and with their wives. Then they remember that they are officially here for something else, and we quickly have sex. Basically, I do the same as you, but I earn much, much more than you! I can easily pay you €200 or €300, otherwise I would feel like I was at Aldi." Hatred, disgust, devaluation, and shame, which the patient usually associated with herself and her life, she now directed at me. The parallels between psychotherapeutic work and prostitution confused and shamed me at first, until my inner figures of identification came to my aid, such as Joseph Sandler (1999, 2001) with his concept of reversed roles. Now I was in the role of the used and soiled prostitute, and the patient in the role of the devaluing client, pretending not to care that he can only satisfy urgent, otherwise unmet needs and act out drives for horrendous sums of money. Since she had noticed my confusion, I reflected back to her, in a very attenuated and marked way, that she had just put me in the role of the prostitute, the role she usually occupies in her work, so that I felt a little of the shame she probably experiences much more intensely and frequently every day. We were able to have a deep emotional conversation about how much she would actually like to give up her current profession, that she would like to find a different place in life through therapy, and how difficult that was for her for various reasons. Finally, we also talked about the differences between our professions, for example, that in psychotherapy, fulfilling wishes for security, familiarity, and acceptance is only a small part, but much more about becoming aware of longings, needs, and intentions, which are then not to be fulfilled in therapy, but rather outside in her relationships, or in individual cases, to be mourned as unfulfillable. In the end, our goal is for her not to need me anymore, which is not something her clients would be interested in. We also found differences regarding money, because, apart from the cancellation fee, I am paid by the health insurance. This, in turn, is financed by the majority of our society, a community in which there is much good, but also dark areas where the kinds of psychological problems arise that brought her to me—in her case, sexual abuse and emotional neglect by her parents, which were neither prevented nor stopped by her family or the youth welfare office called in by neighbors. We all pay money so that people can be helped who sometimes suffer terrible things right next to us, in the dark areas of our society, and thus belong to the 27.8% of our population who develop mental illnesses. Perhaps it is a form of reparation for what we did not notice in time or could not prevent. In any case, it makes a difference whether a client pays for something, or a community that could not prevent something. The very intelligent and well-read patient discussed these connections with me with great interest and was ultimately able to accept that she herself would only have to pay €110 if she failed to notify me late or not at all that she was canceling an appointment. ◀

To ease the therapist's conscience, it should be noted that more and more medical practices with appointment systems now have cancellation policies. At some online restaurant reservations, I was also informed that I would have to pay slightly less than the menu price if I did not cancel 24 hours in advance. Some flight bookings must be canceled several weeks in advance to get a refund. Even my hairdresser told me that cancellation fees are becoming common in his industry in the USA and also in Germany, which I very much supported. Perhaps this will help some therapists feel less uneasy, as if we were doing something extraordinary by charging cancellation fees.

Conclusion
Not always, but not so rarely either, we and our patients plunge into such psychological abysses. However, avoiding these abysses by foregoing a cancellation policy or by making very vague agreements, by setting very low cancellation fees, or by not enforcing what has been agreed upon, leads to important issues being kept out of therapy and makes missing therapy sessions an attractive way for patients to express their resistance.

2.1.2 Delays as Resistance

▶ Delays on the part of our patients are sometimes the result of problems with traffic or public transportation, but most often they are an expression of resistance. The more the mental illness tends toward a personality disorder or psychosis, the more drastic the delays become, as patients use them to regulate their fears of closeness.

Delays of 20 or 25 minutes occur more frequently in the early stages of therapy for early disorders. Occasionally, patients may even arrive 45 minutes late, leaving only 5 minutes for the therapy session. Even though important and pressing matters are often discussed in this shortened time, we should address the delay each time and clarify which topics the patient is currently trying to avoid in therapy. It is often the case that, especially after emotionally intense sessions, patients are late to the next appointment out of fear of continuing or deepening the topic that was started. When patients learn to express these fears in words at the beginning of the session and, together with the therapist, weigh how deeply they want to engage with feelings and conflicts in that session, they no longer need to regulate this resistance through being late. Some therapists add a few minutes at the end of the session to make up for the delay, but this does not help to understand the underlying resistance.

Example

I would like to draw attention to easily overlooked, minimal delays, such as with Bea, a patient with anorexia whose appointment began at 5:00 p.m., but who always rang the bell at 5:02 p.m., even though she had already been in the vicinity of my practice half an hour before the appointment. After thinking several times that I shouldn't be so petty, I addressed these delays with her. She told me, very agitated, how angry her mother would get if she arrived too early, because her mother would not yet be finished preparing for the meeting. But even if she arrived on time, her mother would look at her with great annoyance, which Bea experienced with deep shame, feeling unwanted—a fundamental feeling in her life—as well as an existential sense of guilt for stealing time from others, especially her parents, for whom she was an "accident," and for being a burden. She wanted to avoid at all costs experiencing me as annoyed when she arrived for her session. I interpreted the resistance as an attempt to avoid unpleasant feelings. She was surprised when I addressed the resistance to experiencing positive feelings, such as feeling welcome or seeing me pleased if I smiled at 5:00 p.m. when she arrived at the practice. She was not familiar with such feelings in her relationships, so her basic experience was to sneak through life, to "make herself small," just to avoid standing out unpleasantly and being a disturbance once again. Only when she took the risk of arriving at 5:00 p.m., and later, like most other patients, at 4:57 p.m., and found me not annoyed but pleased, was she able to give up the resistance to experiencing these pleasant feelings of acceptance, as well as the deep sadness associated with having always been too much, especially within her closest family circle, for many years. ◀

▶ Major, but also minimal, delays usually represent a resistance to becoming aware of and changing important emotional attitudes toward life and other people, and should therefore be addressed early on.

2.1.3 Telephone Contacts and Messages Between Therapy Sessions

▶ Whether and in which cases the therapist is available to the patient by phone or email between therapy sessions should also be agreed upon in the therapy contract.

Some therapists are not available to their patients outside of therapy sessions at all, fearing this could be exploited or that patients might intrude into their private lives. Especially at the beginning of therapy, when patients are just learning to cope with conflicts and intense emotions, this can lead to crises to which they may respond with substance use, intentional or unintentional self-injury, psychosomatic disorders, and much more. I have found it effective to offer patients during the initial consultations the option to call me in an emergency on a mobile number between 9 a.m. and 9 p.m., including weekends or during my vacation. This does not apply to acute suicidality, which will be discussed in the next chapter. Beyond that, patients themselves decide what they consider an emergency. Simply reflecting on whether they are currently in an emergency, and if so, what they would say to me if they called, usually initiates a process of reflection and introspection about what is going on, so that they may sit in the kitchen with the phone in hand for an hour, but most of the time do not call and resolve the emergency themselves. We then explore this further in the next therapy session. As a result, I am ultimately called very rarely, at most once a year across all patients in my practice. In such cases, I may not be able to talk immediately, but we arrange a specific time. Since I know the patient and they do not have to recount their entire history as they would with a crisis service, the calls are often brief but help prevent escalations with minimal effort, avoid symptom exacerbations, accidents, or hospital admissions, which would otherwise be costly for both the patient and the healthcare system, and could also negatively impact or interrupt the psychotherapeutic process.

Other ways for the patient to contact their therapist include emails or voice messages, though I make it clear that I do not respond to these unless the patient asks a specific question. I usually do not read or listen to longer messages until the next therapy session. The acute event in an emergency would then be stored in the email, like in a container. This gives us a very immediate impression of a conflictual situation, perhaps more directly and openly than the patient could convey a few hours or days later in the next therapy session, when their defenses have stabilized again and much is less accessible. In this way, sensitive material can enter therapy by bypassing resistance. Emails sent in distress cannot be taken back. Of course, unique forms of resistance can develop here, which we would need to address if necessary—for example, if patients were to flood us with so many emails that we could no longer read all the texts during therapy sessions, let alone discuss and process them. We would then need to address this resistance through flooding and clarify which of the submitted material is particularly important and what we want to focus on. Especially for patients with personality disorders, this variation from the classic setting, in which everything is supposed to be addressed only in the therapy session itself, can be very helpful, as these patients are often initially unable to hold onto sensitive material until the next session and instead react with acting out or symptom exacerbation.

Example

Kai came to me for treatment for borderline disorder, so at the beginning of therapy he found it difficult to hold onto strong fears, such as fear of being alone, feelings of helplessness, or anger, until the next therapy session. Especially when there were arguments in his on-off relationship, but also during conflicts at work or with friends, he was often on the verge of calling me. With his mobile phone in hand, he would sit in his kitchen, thinking about what he wanted to say to me, what I would probably ask, what I might say, which in turn triggered reflection and emotional processing in him. He often sat like this for an hour, instead of, as he used to, leaving the apartment, wandering the city, going to clubs, or using drugs. The inner dialogues with me became easier and more differentiated, with an increasingly clear inner image of me sitting across from him, looking at him thoughtfully or kindly. At some point, he compared it to the film "Becoming a Winner" by director Soleen Yusef, which is about eleven-year-old Mona, who fled from Syria to Berlin-Wedding with her seven-member Kurdish family and, initially speaking little German, has to find her way in a completely new and often difficult world. In particularly conflictual situations, Mona briefly retreats inwardly into memories of her aunt Helin, who in her Kurdish homeland runs toward her, waves, smiles at her, sometimes hugs her, or says something encouraging. This gives Mona strength and confidence to return to the real, external situation and face confrontations and other difficult situations. What Kohut (2016) called a selfobject—something that, for many people, remains with us for life as an encouraging presence from an early, supportive relationship with mother, father, or grandparents, for Mona from her relationship with Aunt Helin, but which is usually lacking in people with early developmental impairments—is portrayed in this film as movingly and vividly as almost nowhere else. At the film's premiere at the 2024 Berlinale, the director said that it depicts her own story and that Mona is the real name of her aunt, who for her embodies the meaning of Aunt Helin. Kai felt that through our conversations, but also his inner dialogues with me on the kitchen chair, I had become his Aunt Helin—a selfobject that would accompany him through his life even after the end of therapy. In reality, he called me only once in the four years of our therapy, when he was sitting by a lake on a Saturday and suddenly a woman collapsed and lay lifeless in the grass. As a physician in training, he was able to successfully resuscitate her while others called an ambulance. The feelings of fear of death, proximity to death, helplessness, and despair, which he had never experienced so intensely during resuscitations in his clinical work, overwhelmed him so much that even an inner conversation with me did not help, so he called me. I had a few minutes for him, so I could listen to his experience and share his feelings. Listening and sympathy (translated as compassion)—that was all that was needed. Instead of panicking and escalating, he calmed down and we were able to process everything else in the next session. ◀

Conclusion

Ultimately, every therapist will decide for themselves whether their patients may call or contact them by other means between sessions. It is important to me to discuss this during the initial sessions and to include a mutual agreement in the therapy contract. In my experience, this often saves us detours and escalations and is rarely actually used. Should we ever get the impression that a patient is taking advantage of it and calls us constantly about every little thing, we would need to address and limit it in therapy.

2.1.4 Suicidality as Resistance

> If suicidal thoughts, suicidal fantasies, or suicide attempts are part of the patient's symptom profile, they will intensify in the initial phase of therapy because all the new experiences, the discussion of problems, and the taking of the case history destabilize the internal equilibrium. But even after that, this part of the symptomatology will persist for some time and become a form of resistance if we have not negotiated helpful framework agreements.

Here, too, it applies that the agreements made in the preliminary discussions regarding the handling of suicidality should be all the clearer and more detailed, the more the patient's personality organization tends toward borderline or psychosis. Suicidal thoughts or fantasies must be communicated at the beginning of the session so that it can be clarified in which situation and with which emotional conflict they have occurred. If they are only brought up at the end of the session, this constitutes resistance, because existential issues have been kept out of the treatment—issues that are likely underlying the suicidality, such as intense self-directed hatred, unbearable states of anxiety, separations, or excessive closeness that cannot be tolerated, and much more. By addressing suicidality, these issues can come into awareness and be discussed, but only if they are not disclosed just before the end of the session. Therefore, suicidal impulses that are not addressed at the beginning of the session should be named as resistance, and their underlying causes explored.

Suicide attempts must not be made at any point during therapy. The patient has chosen life by starting therapy, in order to understand and change important things for and in her life. She is not in therapy to die; she is responsible for her survival, not the therapist. An agreement that has proven effective is one based on Yeomans, Clarkin, and Kernberg (2017). It stipulates that the patient either goes directly to the emergency room of a hospital or contacts the crisis service or emergency doctor by phone if she notices that she will soon no longer be able to control her suicidality and is therefore at risk of attempting suicide. If the crisis service cannot resolve this in conversation, they will admit the patient to a hospital. The advantage of the crisis service is that the patient can reach them at any time, easily, via her phone, and get help quickly. The disadvantage is that she is often asked many questions about difficult aspects of her current situation and life history, which can be more upsetting and increase suicidality rather than calm her. In this respect, we consider whether it might be better for the patient to go directly to the hospital in such situations. If the patient has previously been in a psychiatric hospital, we can ask her to speak with the senior physician who was responsible for her at that time, if she wishes, with a brief letter or call from us to support her request. In this conversation, it should be agreed that the patient will present herself at the hospital emergency room if her suicidality becomes uncontrollable. Usually, in such cases, the senior physicians make a clear note at the front of the patient's file, indicating that she should be admitted to a specific ward if she presents with suicidality. This note is intended to prompt the on-duty doctor to send the patient to the designated ward without discussing the current symptomatology in detail, which would only further destabilize her and increase her suicidality. Likewise, no current case history is taken upon admission, and certainly no biographical history. In my experience, patients are then transferred to the appropriate ward within minutes of reporting to the emergency room, where it is assessed the next day how much support they still need or whether outpatient care can continue. This saves the often sleep-deprived and inexperienced junior doctors a lot of effort, and spares the patients upsetting conversations and waiting that could further increase their suicidality. The patient should carry important phone numbers and addresses with her several times over—not just once in her mobile phone, which often breaks or runs out of battery at a critical moment, but also on a slip of paper in her wallet and another in her skills pouch, which she always has with her. The therapist and patient should take as much time as needed in the preliminary discussions until both feel, in light of the patient's previous experiences, that these measures will reliably prevent a suicide attempt.

- The final step is to agree that the patient must adhere to these arrangements. If she nevertheless attempts suicide, the therapy is thereby terminated.

Example

With my patients, this agreement has so far prevented any suicide attempts, so I have never had to terminate treatment. It was common, however, for patients to take out their slips of paper at home in the evening and pick up the phone, only to pause and reflect on whether they really were about to lose control over their suicidality, whether there truly was no other help than to call the agreed number, and what had actually happened to bring them into such distress. This triggered a process of thinking and feeling, making different emotions and conflicts clearer. Instead of calling the crisis service or the hospital, patients often preferred to call a friend, where they could cry or vent briefly, enabling them to hold out until the next therapy session. Sometimes, however, admission to the hospital was necessary, from which the patient could be discharged after a day or two because the suicidality quickly subsided in the safe, familiar environment.

A supervisee of mine had not made a suicide agreement with a patient, so the patient would often mention as she was leaving that she might kill herself when she got home. Time and again, she actually made suicide attempts of varying severity, after which she was sometimes only briefly treated in the emergency room, sometimes had to stay in the hospital for a few days. The hospital staff already knew the patient from her many short stays. She caused a lot of trouble for the staff because she also tried to regulate everything through suicidality there. After being discharged from the hospital, the patient continued her therapy. However, the therapist became increasingly afraid to address sensitive topics, as the patient would more and more quickly make allusions to her suicidality, which might arise if a certain topic was brought up or explored further.

These allusions were made through a look, a gesture, words, or threats at the end of the session. Eventually, nothing conflictual could be discussed anymore, because the looming suicidality had become a form of resistance. The therapist articulated her fear: "If the patient really does kill herself after today's session, I will feel guilty for the rest of my life and wonder whether I really had to address this issue, or whether I should have left it alone. Then she would surely still be alive. Maybe after a suicide, her mother will sue me for underestimating her daughter's suicidality, like my colleague, and I will have to deal with it for years." Only after working through this in supervision did the therapist point out the massive resistance to her patient, which the patient could also understand. After emotional negotiations, they were able to introduce the suicide agreement described above, so that the resistance shifted from suicidality to milder areas and there were no further suicide threats or attempts. ◀

2.1.5 Self-Injurious Behavior

▶ In self-injurious behavior, abbreviated as SIB, there is a conscious, voluntary, and direct destruction of body tissue, primarily the skin, but without suicidal intent.

There are various forms:

- Cutting, scratching, or slashing the skin with sharp or pointed objects, especially on arms and legs, using razor blades, knives, scissors, or shards of glass
- Hitting the head with the hands or banging the head against the wall
- Punching hard objects with the fist
- Hitting one's own body with arms, legs, or objects
- Pulling out hair
- Biting accessible parts of the body, including the insides of cheeks and lips
- Burns or scalds, for example by holding the hand on a hotplate or in a candle, or extinguishing cigarettes on the skin
- Chemical burns to the body
- Severe forms of nail-biting with painful nail injuries or tearing out nails
- Tying off body parts

Diagnostically, SIB is coded in ICD-10 under R45.88, and in ICD-11 under the disorders where it most frequently occurs, such as 6A06.1 Stereotyped Movement Disorder with Self-Injury, 6D11.5 Borderline Pattern, or 6B65 Partial Dissociative Identity Disorder. Furthermore, ICD-11 has introduced the independent diagnosis of non-suicidal self-injury under MB23.E. In earlier versions of the Diagnostic and Statistical Manual of the American Psychiatric Association (APA), it was, similar to the ICD, listed as a symptom of various disorders. In 2013, "nonsuicidal self-injury" (NSSI) was included for the first time as its own diagnostic category in Section 3 of the 5th edition of the DSM-5, and appeared in 2018 in the German version as Non-suicidal Self-Injurious Behavior (NSSV). Particularly interesting here is Category B:

> "The individual engages in the self-injurious behavior with one or more of the following expectations:
>
> 1. to obtain relief from a negative feeling or cognitive state
> 2. to resolve an interpersonal difficulty
> 3. to induce a positive emotional state
>
> Note: The desired relief or response occurs during or shortly after the self-injury, and the individual may display patterns of behavior that suggest dependence in the sense of repetitive occurrence."

Replacing psychologically painful feelings and thoughts with physical pain (point 1), or convincing others of one's suffering or manipulating them through openly visible self-injuries (point 2), is generally the best known.

The third point, that injuries can trigger positive feelings, may be surprising. This is related to the fact that, in particular, skin injuries cause the brain to release endorphins. These are endogenous morphines, that is, opioids produced by the body itself, which are generated in the pituitary gland and hypothalamus in all vertebrates. They offer the evolutionary advantage of alleviating fear and triggering euphoric, courageous, and powerful feelings when animals are fleeing and sustain skin injuries from branches or stones, or when a person receives scratches on their arms and legs while defending themselves against a pursuing predator. Instead of freezing in terror at the wound, the blood, and the proximity to death, the opioids induce relaxation and courage, erase panic, and enable us to continue fighting or fleeing. Patients from the above-mentioned disorder groups often experience intense anxiety. Instead of taking external morphines in the form of medication or drugs, they inflict self-injuries so that endogenous opioids are released and the same effect occurs. This is why the DSM-5 note asks us to be aware that there is also a risk of dependence here. Some patients cut themselves very regularly and frequently over years, so that their arms and legs are covered with old and new scars.

▶ During psychotherapy, SIB can become a significant resistance, because it is easier to alleviate or eliminate internal, psychological pain and interpersonal problems through external, physical pain, rather than feeling the internal conflicts and working through them in therapy. Therefore, it is important to include in the therapy contract at the very beginning of treatment that SIB should be quickly reduced, by having the patient repeatedly try to postpone it and find various alternatives, so that she can bring the painful feelings into therapy, where she should address them right at the start of the session.

In skills training, patients are offered various alternatives, for example. Instead of cutting their forearm with a razor blade, they can knead a spiky massage ball, snap a rubber band against their wrist, put chili powder on their tongue, suck on chili candies, put peas in their shoes and walk up and down stairs, place ice packs on their forehead, or do other things that produce strong stimuli or mild pain, but do not leave permanent scars. As the skills training progresses, many other options are introduced, so that patients develop abilities to cope internally with painful feelings, fears, and self-doubt, enabling them to endure these until the next therapy session without resorting to SIB.

Example

Lena usually inflicted cuts on her arms and legs with a razor blade several times a week, and sometimes burns with a lighter. At least twice a month, the wounds were so severe that she went to the emergency room to have them dressed. She still wore short dresses in the summer, so her scars were openly visible. She injured herself when she was dissociated, to return to reality, when she was angry at herself, but also when she was angry at someone else but did not want or was unable to say so, and often when she was very sad, lonely, or full of fear. Then, inner peace would set in, anger, fear, or sadness would disappear, replaced by a warm, relaxed, secure feeling. In therapy sessions with me, she dissociated more frequently at the beginning when discussing sensitive topics, could hardly speak or think, and would have preferred to cut herself. Sometimes she tried to scratch her arm with her fingernails, but I would then give her an ice pack to hold to her forehead, or an ammonia vial to smell. In the skills training she did alongside individual therapy with me, she learned many more techniques to gradually reduce and replace SIB. She always carried chili candies, an ammonia vial, a spiky massage ball, and a rubber band in a skills pouch, so she could use skills in difficult situations instead of cutting herself. The intense and often exaggerated scrubbing of her kitchen was something she had discovered as helpful for herself, and later also reading, painting, talking with a friend from her support group, or speaking with me in her mind. She often shared, however, that in the past, cutting had worked faster and more intensely against all sorts of things, whereas now she always had to think of something, which required more effort and often took longer, and then was somewhat less effective than SIB had been before. Until patients have acquired more mature defense mechanisms after one or two years of therapy and can experience and cope with their conflicts internally, they are in this intermediate stage. They need our understanding and a lot of encouragement to persevere through this difficult process of change with these aids, instead of reverting to the familiar SIB. ◀

Conclusion

Self-injurious behavior helps patients in a pathological way to alleviate or eliminate painful inner experiences through external pain, manipulation of others, and the activation of endogenous opioids, so that these experiences are kept out of therapy. In order to prevent NSSI from becoming a form of resistance, we should help the patient to reduce it gradually—not by forbidding it, but by helping her find substitutes, initially through skills, later in conversation with us, and eventually in an internal dialogue with herself.

2.1.6 Scarification, Tattoos, Piercings

> Through various modifications of their bodies, patients want on the one hand to express something, but also to drown out and soothe something else through the associated pain. Both become a form of resistance if the psychological content that is to be displayed or dampened on the skin does not enter therapy, but instead one body modification after another is created.

Scarification, or scarification, derived from the Latin "scarificatio"—meaning scratching, cupping, or scar tattooing—refers to the creation of decorative scars in the skin. It is a body modification deeply rooted for centuries in the traditions of some peoples. It is used for clan affiliation and as body adornment, especially by ethnic groups with dark skin, since tattoos are not easily visible on them, and sometimes also for the initiation of girls and boys at the threshold of marriageable age. In Western countries, scarification has found its way into some subcultures as a form of distinction from other groups and as adornment. In cutting, the skin is incised with a scalpel; in branding, it is burned with an electrocautery device, with slow and repeatedly disrupted wound healing being important, depending on how thick the resulting scars are intended to be. The procedure is very painful, even when performed in professional studios, as is the wound healing process.

A tattoo is an image, symbol, pattern, or text that is injected into the second layer of skin with ink, pigment, or other coloring agents using one or more needles. It is an ancient tradition in all cultures on all continents. The 5300-year-old glacier mummy Ötzi already had 61 tattoos, mainly dots, lines, and figures. Crusaders sometimes wore crosses on their foreheads. Today, tattoos primarily serve as adornment, for attractiveness, protest, or distinction.

A piercing, derived from the English "to pierce," involves inserting jewelry in the form of rings or bars through the skin and underlying fat or cartilage tissue, for example on the lips, ears, nipples, navel, or in the genital area. The oldest evidence of piercing is 7000 years old. Like scarification or tattoos, it serves as adornment, as an expression of something, or as a marker of subcultural distinction.

All these and other body modifications are usually not performed by the individuals themselves, but rather more or less professionally in specialized studios. The procedures themselves, as well as the week following them, are associated with significant pain. Nevertheless, they have become very widespread in Western culture.

During ongoing psychotherapy, body modifications are a form of resistance for several reasons:

1. Similar to self-injurious behavior, the intense and prolonged pain experienced during the creation of body modifications triggers the release of endorphins in the brain, which have an analgesic, pain-relieving effect, but also a psychologically calming, comforting, and sometimes even euphoric effect. Patients who frequently undergo scarification, piercings, or tattoos during ongoing therapy may be attempting to alleviate or suppress painful feelings that arise in therapy, so that they do not have to feel them. As a result, these feelings may not be consciously experienced or adequately processed in therapy.
2. Body modifications always symbolically express something of the patient's experience, which they have inscribed or burned into their bodies instead of first addressing and examining it in therapy, so that by the end of treatment it might become something important, an insight and deeply felt statement inscribed on their body.
3. Patients' experiences often change significantly over the course of psychotherapy. Something that is emotionally important at a certain stage of treatment, that "gets under the skin" and is tattooed or scarified, may be perceived very differently a few months later. Piercings can be removed, but tattoos and scarifications remain visible on the body for a lifetime, even if they represent an experience long past. Many patients regret at the end of therapy that they had something tattooed or scarified at the beginning that no longer fits them at all. Therefore, we should address this at the start of treatment and ask patients to discuss any wishes for body modification in therapy beforehand if possible.

▶ We should not simply shrug off desired or performed body modifications, but address them promptly, discussing which issues the patients are trying to avoid and what consequences these modifications may have.

Example

Cindy is 21 and already has numerous piercings in her ears, tongue, nose, between her eyebrows, on her nipples, navel, and in her vagina when she comes to therapy. She also has tattoos, such as a snake that winds across her entire back, from there over her abdomen to below her navel, and numerous smaller ones on her arms and legs, like the name of her first boyfriend, the image of a deer with a child's foot in its mouth, or one of a burning, sinking ship. In the second therapy session, following our agreement, she brings up that she would like to get scarifications in the near future. During the conversation, she became very sad and cried. Someone had put this spirit into this body. Life did not feel right. Her body was hybrid, because her father was Asian and her mother German. It was beautiful, but should become even more beautiful. More important, however, was the question of whether there was something inside her, a hidden soul, an identity. It felt like a gray, empty, blank sheet on which she wanted to paint something. She decided for her soul, not for the one chosen for her. She decided whether she was a good person or not. I replied that she was here in therapy to discover her identity, but that she would not find it, no matter how much she changed her body. This intervention made her angry, but also thoughtful. Some time later, she began working in a bookstore, reading a lot, painting a lot, and in the process discovering much about herself, which she explored and clarified further in therapy, so that she was able to forgo further body modifications. ◀

2.1.7 Substance Use and Addiction

▶ The misuse or dependence on substance-related or non-substance-related addictive agents represents a significant form of resistance, as patients turn to them for comfort, reassurance, or encouragement, instead of finding access to the associated feelings in therapy or addressing the question of what makes this access difficult for them.

A moving and sensitively researched case report about Max, who died at 19 from a heroin overdose, appeared in the magazine *Der Spiegel* (32/2024). Regarding his first inpatient withdrawal treatment, it states:

> "From the discharge report, end of May 2020: 'The approved measure was terminated early on medical advice.' Max H. had obtained drugs and distributed them to fellow patients in the clinic. He had also taken benzodiazepines, the anesthetic ketamine, and alcohol again. He was 'unable to sufficiently consolidate his motivation for therapy.'" (Klovert, 2024, p. 36)

On the one hand, he wanted to become abstinent during inpatient therapy and learn to cope with life without drugs. On the other hand, resistance apparently set in soon after the start of treatment, as he secretly used drugs himself and even supplied them to others. The same article illustrates how much faster and more intensely drugs can lead to a desired state than psychotherapy ever could: "Taking heroin is like a warm coat that hugs you from behind, says Max's friend. 'Suddenly everything is okay, you are completely content with yourself and need nothing else.'" (Klovert, 2024, p. 37). Working in therapy on oneself, on one's relationships with others, and on the internal handling of one's own feelings in order to be content with oneself, to internalize good, supportive relationships with caring people as a warm coat that hugs us from behind and carries us through life, is much more lengthy and complex than using drugs. We have to dare to try new things in relationships, overcome our inner resistance to risky things, accept and process disappointments before we have gone through this process. The perplexity about how it is even possible to achieve an emotionally deep, reciprocal love relationship is expressed by Capital Bra and Samra in a song with the words: "All I know is: you can't buy love, and life is too short not to smoke."

The word "Trauung" (wedding) was derived in Middle High German from "trauen" (to trust), because it takes a lot of courage to enter into a love relationship in which we confide in another person and should handle their trust with care. I would broaden the deep meaning of the word "Trauung," because not only marriage or partnership is a risk, but every love relationship, every friendship, and of course every relationship with a therapist to whom the patient opens up and entrusts herself with many hopes and wishes. This process is always associated with great fears. That is why the temptation is always very great to turn to drugs instead of daring to fight through the process of change. The danger that resistance to psychotherapy will develop is always present, so we must constantly keep an eye on it and address it.

▶ In Germany, it is sensibly prohibited by psychotherapy guidelines to conduct psychotherapy in cases of acute addiction as long as the patient is not yet living abstinently. If a dependency on alcohol, drugs, medication, or on gaming on the computer, smartphone, or in arcades has been diagnosed, but also work addiction, the patient must complete addiction treatment before starting psychotherapy. This can be inpatient, partial inpatient, or outpatient. Afterwards, she must join a self-help group in her area of addiction and attend it regularly. In some cases, longer outpatient aftercare programs are also recommended in addiction treatment, such as outpatient addiction therapy groups, which in Germany are usually financed by pension insurance providers, so that the patient can attend them in parallel with outpatient psychotherapy, which is paid for by health insurance.

In therapy, we should regularly inquire whether the self-help groups and aftercare are really being attended regularly. If the patient only attends irregularly or not at all, she is at risk of relapse. In preliminary discussions, we should agree that psychotherapy will be suspended in such cases until the patient resumes regular attendance. We should also include in the therapy contract that the patient will immediately inform us of any relapses, whether they have occurred or were just barely avoided, so that the triggers and the associated feelings and fantasies can be discussed in therapy and alternative ways of dealing with these conflicts can be found. In the case of substance-related addictions, after a relapse, inpatient detoxification may also be necessary before outpatient psychotherapy can be continued and the relapse processed. This, too, should be agreed upon in the written or verbal therapy contract. For substance-related addictions, I recommend an agreement whereby the therapist can at any time, without giving a reason, ask the patient to visit her general practitioner before the next session to have a blood or urine test performed and to bring the results to the session. If the test shows use of the addictive substance, but the patient had previously claimed not to have used, we would immediately terminate psychotherapy, because we cannot work with patients who lie to us in such a serious way. With these agreements, relapses among addicts are very rare. Otherwise, we would risk that patients, in the sense of resistance, use substances secretly instead of addressing and working through the current conflicts and problems in therapy.

It is more difficult with non-substance-related addictions, where relapses cannot be detected by blood or urine tests and withdrawal symptoms are much less specific. In these cases, we can discuss with the patient what options she can think of to prove non-use to us. I am always surprised at what patients are willing to do and what they come up with. Some things can be checked by looking at the screen time on a smartphone, which shows when and how often an app is used, such as a game associated with the addiction. One of my patients handed his game console over to his uncle and brought me a written confirmation from him, as well as a purchase receipt for an older, used laptop, with which he could create texts for his training, answer emails, but not install games. Of course, we cannot achieve one hundred percent certainty with these agreements. However, they show the patient how important abstinence is to us, and they show us how seriously the patient is thinking about this issue and how willing she is to work on herself and with us in the spirit of psychotherapy and change.

In the case of work addiction, we cannot demand abstinence; instead, as with eating disorders, we rely on logs of how many hours were worked on which day. But even with these forms of addiction, addiction treatment is necessary before starting psychotherapy, and attending a self-help group in parallel with psychotherapy. These groups greatly relieve and enrich psychotherapy. They have rules for dealing with addiction and talking about it, which are checked and monitored, so that patients have less opportunity to evade them. Participants in these groups are very sensitive to recognizing when others are cheating or lying to circumvent agreed rules, often better than non-addicts could, such as therapists, because they very empathetically recognize in others their own tendencies to trivialize or conceal addiction.

If there is no dependency, but only abuse of addictive substances, such as alcohol or cannabis, or harmful use of gaming or work, we should agree with the patient in the preliminary discussions that she will keep a diary of the abuse and bring it up at the beginning of each therapy session. We also agree that the patient will significantly reduce the abuse within a manageable period of time; otherwise, we would terminate psychotherapy. For example, the patient could aim to reduce from drinking three or four glasses of wine three or four times a week in the evening to a maximum of two glasses twice a week within half a year. If at all possible, it would of course be best if the patient could aim to completely abstain from the addictive substance during the course of psychotherapy and to inform the therapist of any rare use that could not be avoided despite all efforts, and discuss it with her.

If we are not sure whether there is abuse or already dependency, we can involve addiction counseling centers or clinics' diagnostic services for support. If the patient abstains from an addictive substance, we must not lose sight of the great danger of addiction substitution during the course of therapy. The strong feelings and anxieties that were previously dampened by the addictive substance can now, through displacement, be alleviated by another form of abuse or another addiction.

Example

Florian, a patient of mine, was dependent on Tavor®, a benzodiazepine that enhances the effect of the inhibitory neurotransmitter gamma-aminobutyric acid, so that anxiety signals are perceived less strongly or not at all by the receptors, and the nerve cells become less responsive to incoming stimuli. As a result, the medication leads to a feeling of deep relaxation and security within minutes, without anxiety or aggression. Due to its high potential for dependence, Tavor® tablets should not be taken for longer than three weeks. However, Florian had been taking it daily for three years, by then 10 mg, twice the maximum dose. He wanted to undergo psychotherapy because, despite the medication, he continued to suffer from anxiety and flashbacks at times, due to years of sexual trauma inflicted by his mother. Through therapy, he hoped to process his traumatic experiences, be free from anxiety, and then gradually discontinue Tavor®. I told him that I could only treat him if he first underwent inpatient detoxification, remained abstinent from Tavor® thereafter, and subsequently joined a self-help group for people with medication dependence. I offered to start our psychotherapy immediately after his discharge from the detox clinic, with four sessions per week, to provide sufficient space to address and process the intense anxiety we expected after discontinuing the medication. In the initial sessions, I taught him basic skills and imaginative techniques for anxiety reduction, to show him that there were alternatives to medication for alleviating anxiety. This helped him find the courage to undergo inpatient detoxification. We arranged everything so that, upon his discharge from the clinic, his health insurance had approved coverage for psychotherapy and the four appointments with me were available. Since the various supportive elements of trauma therapy quickly led to a reduction in his anxiety levels, we were able to reduce the number of sessions to three, and later to two per week. There were no relapses, which I also verified through two requested laboratory tests. There was a brief and minor shift of his addiction to alcohol, but we were able to address this quickly through drinking diaries and by working through the underlying reasons for his alcohol use. Florian became increasingly adept at regulating his anxiety and processing his traumatic experiences, so that even several years after the end of psychotherapy, he led a fulfilling life with loving relationships and no longer used Tavor®. ◀

▶ With well-considered framework conditions that are negotiated with the patient in a differentiated and clear manner, addiction or substance abuse does not, or only to a very minor extent, become a form of resistance in psychotherapy.

2.1.8 Psychotropic Drugs and Resistance

▶ Psychotropic drugs influence certain metabolic processes in the brain, thereby having a significant impact on emotions, thought processes, and our processing of experiences.

Of the seven groups, antidepressants, antipsychotics (neuroleptics), and mood stabilizers (prophylactic agents for mood episodes) are particularly important. Their development and introduction in the second half of the 20th century was a blessing, especially for the treatment of severe mental illnesses such as bipolar, manic-depressive disorders, affective, schizoaffective, and schizophrenic psychoses. They can also be very helpful at times in the treatment of moderate mental disorders (personality disorders) and mild (neurotic) disorders. By now, they are among the most frequently prescribed medications. Unfortunately, they are not only prescribed by psychiatrists and neurologists, but also by specialists of all disciplines, who often lack sufficient knowledge about their effects and side effects. Psychiatrist colleagues of mine, who regularly and intensively pursue continuing education, repeatedly tell me how difficult it is to keep up to date with this group of medications, which is constantly and rapidly changing. Psychological psychotherapists, who cannot prescribe psychotropic drugs themselves, should ask patients who have been prescribed such medications by their general practitioner or gynecologist to have them selected in the future by a psychiatrist, and to maintain regular communication with that psychiatrist.

For example, the psychotherapist should know in advance if a patient who has been depressed for some time is prescribed an antidepressant by her doctor. In some cases, these medications improve drive within the first few days, but not yet mood. As a result, patients continue to feel down and sad, but now suddenly have the energy to commit suicide, from which the lack of drive had previously protected them. We therefore need to be very vigilant when an antidepressant is started, and offer the patient more frequent contact, either in person or by phone, during the first two weeks.

In recent years, a second pattern of use has developed and seems to be spreading increasingly. According to the Federal Center for Health Education, the use of illegal drugs among 12- to 17-year-olds has fortunately decreased from 6% in 1997 to 1% in 2019. In contrast, however, the use of anxiolytic and pain-relieving medications purchased on the illegal drug market—such as tilidine, codeine, tramadol, and benzodiazepines—has worryingly increased. It is important that we are informed about this consumption and monitor it closely, because these medications are being used precisely for the purposes that psychotherapy is actually intended to serve.

In addition to their often very supportive function, psychotropic drugs can, due to their emotion-dampening effect, become a form of resistance in two ways:

1. Anxiety, sadness, depression, and anger are dampened by psychotropic drugs to varying degrees. This is very helpful in a crisis, but in longer-term outpatient psychotherapy it can also be a hindrance, because the patient may no longer feel these emotions at all or only in a greatly reduced way, making it impossible to address in therapy what makes her anxious, sad, or angry in her daily life. She cannot explore why she has these feelings in situations that would trouble others much less. Nor can she work on how to better handle these conflictual situations, both internally and externally. After the end of psychotherapy, she will be just as helplessly at the mercy of these feelings if she reduces the medication or its effect wears off, so that she would remain dependent on them for life. Therefore, as early as possible in psychotherapy,

we should consider a gradual reduction of medication together with the patient and her psychiatrist. Step by step, the dampened feelings become perceptible, and a new, different way of dealing with them and their triggers can be found.

2. Likewise, feelings of joy, euphoria, happiness, love, friendship, and sexual desire are suppressed, because psychotropic drugs dampen affect both upwards and downwards. Loss of libido is mentioned as a side effect of many of these medications, as is weight gain. The latter is partly due to somatic causes, but is also partly related to the fact that the lack of joy and pleasure in life is compensated for by eating. In psychotherapy, patients cannot enjoy the changes they have achieved, cannot summon the courage to take new steps, and have more difficulty discovering what is dear to them in life and what would make them proud of themselves. Therefore, with regard to these feelings as well, a gradual reduction of psychotropic drugs is often very important.

Example

Fifty-four-year-old civil engineer Uwe came to me for treatment because of hypertension diagnosed as psychosomatic, after his blood pressure had risen further in response to anger and stress at work. In the first phase of therapy, when he was able to better allow himself to feel anger toward colleagues at work and to address conflicts, his blood pressure already decreased somewhat. In the second step, he addressed his marriage, which he found unsatisfying. When he came home at 6 p.m., his wife was asleep, only getting up around 10 p.m. when Uwe went to bed, to prepare for her teaching the next day. They hardly saw each other in the mornings either, as they got up and left the apartment at different times. In therapy, Uwe became aware that this living side by side made him angry and dissatisfied, so he began to address it with his wife and ask for more contact. Since she was not at all happy about this, she made an appointment for him with a psychiatrist, where she did most of the talking, describing his changes as sudden demands and aggression. He went along because she had threatened divorce if he refused. The psychiatrist, suspecting a manic reaction in view of the apparently sudden onset of aggression, prescribed Uwe amitriptyline, a common antidepressant—presumably because it also has a sedating, sleep-inducing effect—and additionally citalopram, another antidepressant. Since I was on vacation at the time, I only learned four weeks later that, due to the medication and his wife's threat, Uwe had abandoned all efforts to change anything in the marriage, which calmed the domestic situation but caused his blood pressure to rise again. All progress had been reversed, so I interpreted what had happened as resistance to the changes that had begun. After a couple's session with Uwe and his wife and a consultation with the psychiatrist, we were able to agree to gradually reduce and eventually discontinue the medication. With the help of a few more couple's sessions with me, the couple succeeded in communicating more openly, addressing conflicts in a constructive-aggressive manner, and reaching compromises on changes acceptable to both, so that his blood pressure improved again and they spent more time together. ◀

Conclusion

In many other cases, patients who had had to search for a long time for psychotherapy, or those who had not wanted to face their inner problems, came to me for treatment while on antidepressants or neuroleptics, sometimes in higher doses. A gradual reduction and, very often, eventual discontinuation of the medication made the dampened feelings accessible again and enabled them to learn to deal with them differently. Without these changes in medication, much would not have been workable or changeable in psychotherapy, so that the psychotropic drugs would have contributed to resistance.

2.1.9 Eating Disorders and Frame Resistances

▶ Unlike with addicts, we cannot expect people with eating disorders to abstain from their "addictive substance," food; on the contrary, they are supposed to learn how to eat healthily. In order to prevent the symptomatology of the eating disorder from becoming too strong a resistance, we must, on the one hand, set limiting boundaries, and on the other, keep the symptomatology in view.

In cases of binge eating disorder, a psychologically induced obesity, we should agree in the preliminary discussions on a body mass index (BMI) that must not be exceeded, for example, 45. If this limit is crossed, the patient must admit herself to a clinic to lose weight until she is below this value again. Similarly, in cases of anorexia, we should set a lower limit, for example, 15, and if this is undercut, the patient must go to a clinic until she gains enough weight to have a BMI above 15. For a patient who is 160 cm tall, the lower limit of 15 would be 38.5 kg, and the upper limit of 45 would be 115 kg. If a BMI of 15 is undercut, the patient enters a psychologically very restricted, sometimes euphoric state, where it is all about pure survival, and no engagement with inner conflicts is possible anymore. Ruge (2012) describes his time in Stalinist labor camps, where he and the other internees had to survive on 600–800 g of bread per day while doing heavy lumberjack work. All libido, all rebellion, all anger, but also suicides, disappeared among them, because everything was dominated by constant hunger and the struggle for survival. Only when they were given more food again did sexual and aggressive impulses reappear, as well as suicidal fantasies as a turning of anger against the self. From these extreme experiences, we can conclude how strongly an anorectic state kills all feelings internally, making it an insurmountable resistance to psychotherapy. The patient is also physically in mortal danger and must therefore be treated as an inpatient. Above a BMI of 45, there is no immediate danger to life, but in the longer term, life expectancy is massively reduced, as diseases such as type 2 diabetes mellitus, hypertension, and many other secondary illnesses damage and ultimately destroy the body. Psychologically, beyond 45, we often find a numbing of feelings and inner experience, as well as of thinking, so that therapeutic work becomes increasingly impossible. In the preliminary discussions, we should agree on regular weigh-ins, which are needed more frequently the closer the patient gets to the upper or lower limit, for example, once a quarter, a month, or a week. Since people with eating disorders are usually dishonest about their weight due to the massive body shame associated with the illness, we cannot rely on them weighing themselves at home and reporting the value to us. It is more sensible for them to be weighed by an employee at their general practitioner's office. Anorectic patients often hide heavy objects in their clothing to make the scale show a higher weight, so they should only be weighed in their underwear. Even then, they will often drink a lot of water beforehand to appear heavier, but we can only find this out in conversation. Overweight patients are interested in weighing less and therefore will not use such tricks. The result of the weighing is then brought to us by the patients as a certificate from their general practitioner, or the doctor transmits it to us via the telematics infrastructure. In this way, we have an overview of weight development and can interpret changes as progress in therapy or as resistance to it.

For all eating disorders, it is advisable to have patients keep food diaries. In bulimia, vomiting should also be recorded, or excessive exercise in the case of exercise bulimia. As Reich describes (2015, 2017, 2024), disordered eating behavior revolves around currently active conflicts, so we can read from it which feelings someone is currently swallowing or what someone finds sickening. If we were to give in to the patients' shame and not have them record and measure their eating, they would regulate their conflicts secretly at home through food instead of discussing them in therapy.

Example

With the obese Hannah, I had agreed on an upper limit of 125 kg. When she exceeded this, we interrupted the outpatient therapy and she admitted herself to a clinic with a ward for eating disorders. Upon admission, her suitcase was searched and various sweets for secret snacking were found and taken away. Through very regulated eating and nutritional counseling, her weight was reduced to 120 kg, so she was discharged and we could continue therapy. Two weeks later, she had a conflict with her mother, which led her to buy huge amounts of sweets, enough for several binge episodes. One binge had occurred, which we discussed in detail. At first, she tried to present it as if, in the evening after putting her children to bed, a flood of feelings—anger, sadness, and disappointment regarding her mother—had suddenly come up, so she had no choice but to eat several bars of chocolate and several boxes of pralines. I pointed out to her that the decision for the binge had been made much earlier, namely when she bought the sweets in the early afternoon. She was able to admit that she had already prepared herself for the evening and the binge at that point, even though she had her therapy session with me the next morning. It would have been better to feel the emotions, endure them, write them down, draw them, and then address them in the therapy session. Instead, she swallowed them down with the sweets and could only vaguely name them in therapy. In this way, binges become a resistance to insight and change, rather than a symptom to be treated, which I pointed out. With a heavy heart, Hannah decided to give away the remaining sweets at her children's school festival. Two weeks later, there was another binge, after she had again bought sweets in the afternoon, but this time without being able to name any external conflict. The evening with her husband had even been very pleasant. She felt happy, which she wanted to intensify on the one hand, but on the other hand, she felt a vague fear that the happiness could slip away. So she asked her normal-weight husband if he would like to eat sweets, which he affirmed, so she brought everything out. If he had declined, she would not have gotten anything for herself. Again, I pointed out that she had already decided on a binge when shopping in the afternoon. Instead of seeing how much happy and joyful feeling, how much eroticism she could tolerate, she pretended to fulfill her husband's wish. Instead of seducing him into sexuality, she seduced him into snacking together, so she ate away all her good feelings and ended up sitting there sluggishly with a full stomach and feelings of guilt. The joyful feelings were then hardly accessible in the next therapy session, so I addressed the resistance. Hannah became quite angry with me as a result. Some swear words came to her mind about me: "You don't understand me! You are an asshole without any empathy, a sadist, a slimy pickle, a sucked-out cheesecake, the afterbirth of a wild boar. You don't like me. I hate you." In this way, long-repressed aggressive feelings could be felt, expressed, and worked through within our therapeutic relationship, with the swear words being particularly interesting, as they referred to inedible foods. Unlike with sweets, I did not help her to avoid feeling emotions. Like a wild boar, I sniffed out what was buried and dug it up, and she, too, found a wild boar within herself that was very clever, procured sweets, and orchestrated binges. ◀

Conclusion
Despite—or precisely because—shame is a dominant affect in all eating disorders, we must closely observe and set limits on the symptomatology in psychotherapy if it is not to become a significant resistance to change and insight.

2.1.10 Esotericism, Religiosity, and Parallel Therapies

▶ Esotericism, religiosity, and therapies that play an important role in the patient's life alongside ongoing psychotherapy can stabilize her, provide support and comfort, and bring insights about herself and her relationships with others, but they can also become a resistance in psychotherapy if feelings, reassurance, and insights are sought primarily there instead of in therapy.

Esotericism derives from the ancient Greek "esoterikos," meaning belonging to the inner realm, understandable from within. Originally a philosophical doctrine, in modern times it represents a counter-movement against dogmatic religions, blind faith in science, and the disenchantment of the world by materialism. Today, it embodies a wealth of very diverse ideas and approaches intended to help understand one's own life and social processes. For this reason, it can be very beneficial to what Fonagy and Target (2015) have called mentalization, as it provides easily comprehensible insights into how we and others function psychologically. However, it becomes an obstacle to mentalization when the theories it espouses are overly one-sided and reduce everything that happens to a single cause. Some methods, such as family constellations according to Bert Hellinger, can also lead patients to significant destabilization or even decompensation, because, according to Haas (2005) or Reuter (2005), constellation work lacks conflict processing and a supportive therapeutic relationship. In approximately 20-minute scenes, the protagonist plays herself, while other group members, whom she does not know beforehand, take on the roles of her parents or siblings as "representatives." Depending on whom the protagonist happens to get as her scene partners, this often leads to very strong affective discharges, which are relieving for some participants, but disturbing for others, up to and including psychotic decompensations, as seen in some patients I have treated in the clinic. There are no prescribed interventions or rules for the leaders of such constellations, except those they know from Hellinger himself, such as the instruction to the protagonist: "A bow to your parents is finally due now!" For this reason, I advise my patients against family constellations according to Hellinger.

Example

In one session, Laura very courageously and self-critically explored her experiences in relationships with her partner, but also with other people, and came to the conclusion: "My partner is always very well liked and admired in groups, while I often feel uncomfortable there and would prefer to be alone with him. When I look in the mirror, I don't see a woman I love, someone I find beautiful and intelligent in her own way. That's why I probably have to manipulate and blame others again and again to get them to tell me what I can't acknowledge to myself in the mirror." I was somewhat startled by this degree of self-insight and wondered whether, at that point, I would have dared to offer her such a delicate interpretation of her experience, since she had previously reacted very irritated or hurt even to much more harmless interpretations. Often in therapy, it is two steps forward, then one step back. In the next session, she showed an esoteric variant of resistance. She had read in the spiritual book by Welwood (2014) something about how men and women are, which had revealed to her what all her relationship problems really consisted of. Men, she said, genetically lack any connectivity to their feelings, while women feel far too much and too intensely. Not only did she feel this way, but it was the same for all women everywhere in the world, which took the pressure off her and brought her peace. I was astonished that a patient for whom gender equality and the equal rights of women and men were otherwise so important would come up with such clichés, even though I could empathize with the relief it brought her. Instead of having to look into her own abysses, there is an all-encompassing explanation that applies to all people. She had photographed the most important pages of the book and sent them to her partner via her smartphone, which was also an enlightenment and reassurance for him. I said that I could understand the relief this theory brought, especially in light of the disturbing self-insights from the previous session, but that she was also putting a white lid over the abysses she had begun to look into. Besides, I am also a man. How did she want to continue working with me if I supposedly lack any connectivity to feelings? She angrily retorted that I hadn't noticed that she had been very unhappy and had cried after the previous session, while reading the book had calmed her down, which was actually what therapy was supposed to do. I realized that my shock from the previous session at the speed and depth of her self-insight was also a feeling the patient herself had, a sign that there had been too little resistance in the previous session and therefore too much in this one. If she had taken only one step forward instead of two in the last session, she might not have had to take one or only half a step back today. ◀

In addition to theistic religions shaped by belief in an almighty God, such as Christianity, with 2.1 billion followers worldwide, Islam with 1.3 billion, and Judaism with 13.5 million believers, there are also many people who belong to a religion in which there is no god, but rather one's own actions are central, such as Buddhism with 450 million followers. Karma is very much about thoughts, feelings, and actions, as well as the effects of deeds committed out of greed, hatred, or egocentrism, both for others and for oneself. Bad karma leads to punishment in the next life after reincarnation, whereas in theistic religions, hell or damnation is more likely to be threatened. Through religions, life gains meaning, moral boundaries, and values. They provide understanding for complicated human relationships and offer support, hope, and comfort. Just as the almighty God envelops and protects, so does the Jewish prayer shawl, the tallit, wrap the believer in prayer. The image of Jesus on the cross conveys the hope that one's own death and that of loved ones is not the end of everything, thus alleviating existential fears. Various aspects can become problematic for psychological development in therapy, above all, of course, guilt-laden prohibitions of sexual and aggressive impulses, which can greatly restrict life and the shaping of relationships, as well as prohibitions of desires for recognition, comfort, and affection from others, which are quickly interpreted as selfish and therefore forbidden.

Freud seems to have kept religious themes largely out of his analyses. "Freud counts religion among the untenable illusions. In any form and effect, he had no regard for it" (Stroeken, 1992, p. 31). For him, religious ideas were "illusions, fulfillments of the oldest, strongest, most urgent wishes of mankind; the secret of their strength is the strength of these wishes" (Freud, 1927, p. 352). Katharina Adler (2020), the great-granddaughter of Freud's patient Dora, whose real name was Ida Bauer, later Ida Adler, describes how Dora converted from Judaism to Christianity in 1905, together with her husband, in order to have their son, born in April 1905, baptized. Freud's case study (1905) contains no mention of her doubts about her faith or her fears of anti-Semitism, because they played no role there. I myself am an atheist and approach religions with interest and goodwill, without favoring or rejecting any. In this respect, I have so far been able to work well with patients of very different faiths by trying to understand what gives them support in their beliefs, but also when faith becomes a form of resistance. Therapists who are themselves religious should clarify internally for themselves whether and what influence their own faith has on therapy, on the one hand with patients of the same faith, and on the other hand with patients who are atheists or belong to another religion.

Example

A young Catholic patient confessed weekly that she had erotic fantasies about a colleague to whom she was not married, for which the priest imposed several rosary prayers as penance, thereby absolving her of the sin. In therapy, she was initially unwilling to talk even in the slightest about the erotic fantasies, because doing so would have required her to recall them, which she believed would be sinful. As a result, religious commandments became a form of resistance in therapy, which I addressed and which she was eventually able to reduce. Today, she is married to the colleague, has had children with him, and is able to enjoy a fulfilling, diverse sexuality with him that she can reconcile with her faith. A Buddhist patient was initially unwilling to deal with important, conflict-laden aspects of her femininity because she saw it as punishment for bad karma in a previous life that she was born into this world as a woman and not as a man. She believed that if she accumulated enough positive karma, she would surely be reborn as a man in her next life. Feelings of powerlessness, of having no influence over which gender we are born with, or whether we receive a healthy or sick, beautiful or unattractive body for our life's journey, were inaccessible to her, as were the sadness and anger over the fact that her parents had deeply wished for a boy and had essentially rejected her as a girl from the very first day of her life. Her faith led her to blame herself for this devaluation by her parents, which she internalized early on as a sense of inferiority. Her only hope was directed toward the next life. Therapeutic work was only possible because I addressed this resistance by, on the one hand, accepting her religion, but on the other hand, raising the question of whether she wanted to engage with aspects and conflicts of her current life and change something about them. With the idea that engaging with her own actions and thoughts could certainly accumulate positive karma, she eventually agreed and was able to find a very different relationship to her femininity and her body, and of course also to her parents. ◀

Parallel treatments can be just as enriching and supportive as esotericism and religiosity. Individual and group therapies can take place simultaneously. Psychotherapy is often combined with psychiatric treatment or couples and family therapy, as well as with visits to specialized therapy or self-help groups for patients with eating disorders, borderline personality disorder, anxiety, depression, PTSD, or addiction. In cases of professional reorientation, coaching may sometimes be appropriate. This can relieve psychotherapy of many aspects and details, allowing us more time for our main tasks: in psychodynamic therapies, working on the focus, and in behavioral therapies, implementing disorder-specific learning objectives. In psychotherapy, we could address resistances in the parallel setting, so that the patient dares to speak openly about her perspective in couples therapy or about why she finds it difficult to learn certain skills in skills training. However, at the beginning of therapy or parallel treatment, we should clarify exactly what is to happen where. Otherwise, the patient might talk in individual therapy about conflicts and problems with other members of her group therapy, and there about fears of what her individual therapist might ask or think about her. Or she might talk to her psychiatrist about her inner conflicts or behavioral exercises, but to her psychotherapist about how well the medication calms her and what side effects it has. In this way, resistances would arise everywhere and hinder or completely block change processes. Therefore, it is important to repeatedly ask what the patient is addressing and working on where, and to refer material from psychotherapy as resistance if it belongs elsewhere.

Example

Kai, whom I have already mentioned in connection with telephone contacts, had attempted suicide before our therapy, for which he was treated in a university psychiatric clinic. There, a two-year aftercare project for chronically suicidal patients was running, which gave him the opportunity to contact the clinic's psychologists around the clock if he could no longer control his suicidality, so that he could either be stabilized through a conversation or admitted to a ward. I had agreed to this arrangement to the extent that he was only allowed to call me from 9 a.m. to 9 p.m., and not in cases of acute suicidality. However, he also called the clinic during the day in situations when he was not suicidal at all, but the time until our next therapy session seemed too long to him. He managed to engage the mostly young, inexperienced psychologists in lengthy conversations in which they inquired about his life story and had him describe details of the sexual abuse by a neighbor or the aggressive assaults by his mother, so that he would leave the conversations distraught, full of fear, with flashbacks, or completely dissociated, sometimes not remembering how he even got home. In the next therapy sessions, we first had to repair the damage done and stabilize him. At the same time, I pointed out that he was using a parallel setting, which was actually supposed to help him, to discuss things that really belonged in psychotherapy with me, and as a result, he ultimately lost some of the stability and self-regulation we had painstakingly built up here. Thus, the parallel setting threatened to become a resistance instead of being supportive. He was able to express his anger that

I was not available to him for more than the agreed two therapy sessions per week, apart from possible emergency calls. He could go to the psychologists even when he was not suicidal at all and talk about topics that did not belong there. By expressing and working through his anger at our setting and my insistence on it, but also through the severe setbacks that the conversations with the crisis psychologists often caused, he was able to reduce his resistance and return to the agreed division of topics in the individual settings.

A different kind of problem developed with his psychiatrist. The psychiatrist took a lot of time for the patient because the patient is a doctor, and the psychiatrist saw him both as a patient and as a colleague. The psychiatrist increasingly shared details from his own private life, including erotic desires and disappointments. Before the board exam, the psychiatrist told him about his own exam, after which one of the examiners supposedly called his then chief physician to say that he had only ever seen one other candidate as stupid as him. He added that he would kill himself if he had to take a different, more difficult board exam than psychiatry, which was the case for the patient as a prospective internist. All these conversations, especially the last one, deeply unsettled the patient. Instead of continuing to feel the encouragement of his superiors and colleagues, who valued him both personally and professionally, and studying for the exam with confidence, he became anxious and long-overcome suicidal impulses returned. I had already questioned whether he should keep seeing this psychiatrist, who was apparently not helping him but rather undermining what we had achieved in therapy. I then urged him to stop seeing the psychiatrist, as I no longer considered the psychiatrist's behavior acceptable, and recommended taking professional ethical action against him. This was a great relief to the patient, because he now saw in me a father who forbade him to go to the neighbor who had sexually abused him as a child, and who considered legal action appropriate, instead of shrugging it off like his father had. If we did not take action in such cases, either because we could not imagine a colleague doing such things, or because we did not want to speak out against a colleague—since, as the saying goes, one crow does not peck out another's eye—then the parallel treatment would repeatedly undermine our psychotherapy. And I would have abandoned my patient instead of protecting him, just like his father, which might have finally destroyed his trust in helping people, made therapy with me and all future therapies impossible. ◄

Conclusion

Esotericism, religiosity, and parallel treatments are often very supportive and stabilizing for our patients. We should agree with them in detail which tasks, topics, and conflicts belong where, and address it during the course of therapy if resistances develop because patients do not adhere to this, but instead work on things in places where they do not belong. If possible, it is advisable to stay in regular contact with colleagues involved in parallel treatments in order to coordinate the work with the shared patient.

2.1.11 Trendy Diagnoses: ADHD, Hypersensitivity, and Autism

▶ Given the greater acceptance of mental illnesses and the accessibility of information about them—such as on the internet or social networks—patients are increasingly self-diagnosing, especially with autism, ADHD, or hypersensitivity. These can be important clues, as we may have overlooked something if we had not considered these diagnoses, such as milder forms of autism. However, such diagnoses often also serve as a form of resistance, as they are intended to be the sole and exclusive explanation for all problems and symptoms, so that the patient feels there is no need to look any further and instead needs medication rather than therapeutic conversations.

Haible-Baer and Kirsch (2024, pp. 159 ff.) state in a recent article on ADHD:

> "It is not uncommon for people to present in psychotherapeutic practices complaining of problems with their attention and/or impulsivity. Often, these individuals already have a suspected diagnosis 'in tow': they suspect they are suffering from attention deficit/hyperactivity disorder (ADHD). This may be because they previously took one of the available self-tests online (which, as screening tools, often have a high false positive rate) or because they are familiar with the symptoms from their family or social environment… We receive quite a few inquiries from people who simply have very high performance expectations of themselves. These individuals are often only impatient with themselves, for example, when they cannot study or work with concentration for eight to ten hours at a stretch."

In addition to the diagnostic criteria that must be met for ADHD, the article names various disorders that can lead to episodic symptoms of concentration difficulties and restlessness, such as depression, anxiety disorders, borderline personality disorder, or post-traumatic stress disorder, which should then be the focus of treatment. After all, the last letter in ADHD stands for syndrome, i.e., a collection of symptoms, of clinical signs from very different disorders.

Some patients who self-diagnose wish to be prescribed medication; some obtain methylphenidate prescriptions, often from non-psychiatric specialists. The concentration-enhancing and calming effect usually sets in relatively quickly, so that in psychotherapy it cannot be clarified what is actually disturbing the patient. As a result, she may become dependent on the medication for life. The supposed diagnosis and the medication then become a resistance against therapeutic understanding and change of the inner experience.

Example

Daniela, a patient of mine, had taken one of these self-tests online and was convinced she had ADHD. She believed this explained all her problems, both those with her parents—which she had just begun to address in therapy—and those with her two children, who were in treatment for psychological disorders, for which she felt very guilty. Now she knew that her impatience and inconsistency with her children were due to her ADHD, so she no longer needed to feel guilty. She understood ADHD as a congenital illness, unknown to her parents, so they could not deal with it and often disciplined her harshly and punished her strictly. In her anamnesis, she described herself as a quiet, well-behaved, and diligent child, as she was also perceived by other family members. Accordingly, I pointed out to her that there had been no signs of ADHD before the age of 12, so a main criterion for this diagnosis was not met. I suspected that she wanted to protect herself and her parents with her self-diagnosis, to avoid further dealing with the problems that had just become more apparent in our therapeutic process. Understandably, this interpretation of resistance initially made her very angry with me, but it paved the way for her to first be angry with me and engage with me, and later also with her parents and with herself as a mother. ◀

Similar to ADHD, hypersensitivity is merely a description of an experience of excessive permeability, of boundaries of the self that are too thin or fragile. It is often associated with anxiety, which sharpens our perception so that we can detect even the smallest, most hidden danger in the most inconspicuous corner. Borderline patients or those who have experienced trauma, for example, are often very sensitive and perceive things that remain hidden to others.

Autism is somewhat different: As a psychotherapist specializing in autistic disorders for 25 years, Wilczek (2015, pp. 120 f.) asks whether we are now dealing with a trendy diagnosis:

> "In recent years, there has been a clear increase in public and media interest in the phenomenon of autism, especially in the high-functioning forms. There are more and more television documentaries, but also feature films and series that play with catchy (clichéd) images of the perhaps quirky or sociopathic, but somehow brilliant Asperger's autistic. In addition, there are popular science articles, internet posts from a wide variety of sources and quality, as well as valuable specialist and first-person literature that bring the phenomenon of high-functioning autism to public awareness. So can the 'Asperger's syndrome' now be considered something of a fashion trend? … Not every peculiarity that appears 'autistic' on the outside actually has its roots in a corresponding pervasive developmental disorder! There are a multitude of clinical pictures that include aspects of autism, but arise from a different etiology and therefore must and can be treated differently."

False positive diagnoses can become a form of resistance by leading to patients not being treated, because some patients—and unfortunately also some therapists—consider autism to be unchangeable through psychotherapy. This is tragic, because in the case of a false positive diagnosis, there is no autism present and therapy would have been quite possible. If, after thorough assessment, the autism diagnosis is confirmed, psychotherapy should still be undertaken, because today we assume a very broad spectrum of autistic disorders (see, for example, Nissen, 2015), many of which are very treatable, for example through MBT, mentalization-based therapy. Fonagy (2003) and Fonagy et al. (2004)

describe in detail the early five phases of the development of mentalization. Due to the lack of mirroring and insufficient containing of the baby's feelings, in my experience, autistic individuals often reach only the third, teleological phase, in which they can perceive external actions of themselves and others, but have not developed representations of their own experience or that of others. Since they neither know what they need and want from others, nor what others feel and want towards them, they withdraw from the world into an autistic state. They sense themselves and others only through physical, motor actions. MBT can be very helpful in filling memory not only with numbers, but with representations of the feelings and experiences of oneself and others, as well as of relationships with them. As long as phases four and five of mentalization development have not been reached, autistic patients cannot tell us what they themselves and others are experiencing internally; in most cases, they do not even understand the question. They therefore cannot benefit from a classically conducted psychotherapy, which appears as resistance, but is actually related to the early disturbance of mental development. Until we have caught up with this development in therapy, we cannot conduct psychotherapy in the conventional sense, but afterwards we can.

Example

Twenty-three-year-old Antonia came to me with a long history of outpatient psychodynamic and behavioral treatments, none of which had helped her in the slightest, nor had several hospitalizations or various psychotropic medications. Antidepressants dampen strong feelings of sadness, neuroleptics more often strong anxiety, and incidentally also feelings of joy, love, and sexual desire. They could do nothing about the diffuse, wavering, incomprehensible emptiness inside her, because feelings that are not experienced cannot be dampened. Even an infusion treatment in a clinic with ketamine triggered nothing in her, fortunately also no hallucinations or dissociations. In her autistic world, she was unreachable for therapeutic interactions and substances of all kinds. Only through mentalization-based therapy did she gradually develop inner representations of herself, her wishes, intentions, feelings, and thoughts, and of the experiences of other people. This gave rise to relationships and the conflicts associated with them in her inner experience, which made psychodynamic therapy possible in the first place. The image of being awakened with a kiss, of bringing Sleeping Beauty to life, at whose autistic thorn hedge many others had previously failed, was, at the end of treatment, considered by the patient to be an apt metaphor for her development. ◀

Conclusion

ADHD or hypersensitivity, whether actually present or only suspected, and a false positive autism diagnosis can lead to massive resistance against psychotherapy. Truly existing autism makes therapy almost impossible as long as the patient has not developed basic mental functions.

2.2 Internal frame resistances

When the external framework is regulated and adhered to, the patient appears regularly and punctually for her sessions. Now the question is whether she also makes use of the protected space, and above all, whether she can stick to her task and role within the therapy sessions. In psychodynamic therapies, the fundamental rule and main task of the patient is free association. Any deviation from this is considered resistance, as are certain forms of silence or avoidance of separation. The main task of the therapist is evenly suspended attention. Violations of this are addressed under countertransference resistances.

2.2.1 Resistance to free association

▶ In psychodynamic therapies, the patient is not supposed to deliver an orderly weekly report or speak in an organized way about her symptoms. Nor is it helpful if she tailors her narratives to what the therapist apparently wants to hear, for example by orienting herself to the therapist's gaze, facial expression, nodding, or verbal reactions. That is why the fundamental rule of these therapies is free association, which is actually easy to learn, but is also repeatedly abandoned, because it sometimes leads to the core of a problem more quickly than expected, faster than a systematic, rational approach. Therefore, we consider abandoning free association as resistance.

Freud (1913, p. 469) suggests the following vivid instruction for free association, which we could give to our patients at the beginning of therapy:

> "One more thing before you begin. Your account should differ in one respect from an ordinary conversation. Whereas you would otherwise rightly try to keep the thread of coherence in your narrative and reject all distracting ideas and side thoughts so as not, as the saying goes, to go from one thing to another, here you should proceed differently. You will notice that during your account, various thoughts will come to you, which you would like to reject with certain critical objections. You will be tempted to say to yourself: this or that does not belong here, or it is completely unimportant, or it is nonsensical, so there is no need to mention it. Never give in to this criticism and say it anyway, precisely because you feel a reluctance to do so. The reason for this rule—actually the only one you are to follow—you will learn and come to understand later. So say everything that goes through your mind. Behave as, for example, a traveler sitting by the window in a railway carriage, describing to the person inside how the view changes before their eyes. And finally, never forget that you have promised complete honesty, and never pass over anything because, for some reason, you find it unpleasant to mention it."

Free, therefore, means for the patient not to intentionally or consciously exclude anything from being communicated. In psychotherapy, we do not conduct a normal conversation, as with a friend to whom we tell emotionally important topics, being careful not to change the subject too quickly and to respond to the other person's reactions. In psychodynamic therapy, the patient is to suspend conventional conversational rules. Instead, she should spontaneously and unfiltered share her thoughts, regardless of whether they seem important or unimportant, significant or trivial, rational or emotional, shameful or pleasant. Freud's train metaphor from the above quote is a beautiful image for this: The person looking out the window can tell the fellow traveler what she sees outside—a forest, a house, a cow. But as soon as it is named, what was seen is already gone. It cannot be held onto with the gaze, because something else appears, which again passes by as soon as it is mentioned. In the same way, we are not to look out the train window, but inward, and describe what passes by there—thoughts, feelings, inner images, memories, bodily sensations, and sensory impressions. We can list these six levels for the patient at the beginning, so she knows that impressions from all these areas are important and worth mentioning. Often it takes only two or three sessions for patients to understand and internalize this fundamental rule, but throughout the course of treatment, it repeatedly happens that they abandon the rule of free association. One reason may be that the patient comes to the session with a current experience that moves her deeply and wants to discuss it, which we of course address, returning to free association only after processing it. In this context, the multi-hour setting of two to six therapy sessions per week was introduced. Experience shows that with a frequency of three or more sessions per week, many patients are no longer able to fill the entire time with current topics, but instead, once these are told, move on to free association. Likewise, lying down on the couch is meant to support free association, because the patient is more relaxed, feels the difference from a normal everyday conversation more clearly, and because she cannot see the therapist's face, who sits behind the head of the couch. This makes her less likely to orient herself to what the therapist presumably wants to hear and what not. These are all beneficial changes to the setting. However, I have also had patients who lay on the couch five times a week and filled the entire time with current dramas instead of free associating. What helps best is to address the resistance to free association by asking what makes it so difficult to look into the inner train window and simply describe what appears and disappears there. Usually, patients can quickly share how hard it is to give up control over what they tell us, what comes up inside them, and what they then discuss with us. Some prefer to make notes before the session about what they want to address and in what order. One patient would mentally rehearse what she would say, what four possibilities I would then have to respond, how she could react to each of the four variants, and what comments she would then have to expect. In the end, she could tell me exactly that today we had taken turn 3B1C. Of course, this session brought her no gain in insight, but also did not evoke any unexpected images or feelings that could have unsettled or irritated her. Only by discussing her fears of the unknown in the course of the conversation was she gradually able to reduce her resistance to free association, which was due to a very high need for control. Sometimes, simply reminding the patient of free association is enough for her to give up her resistance to it, as in the following example.

Example

From Alexandra's treatment, I would like to present a brief excerpt. She had come to psychodynamically oriented therapy, among other reasons, because after having two daughters, she had a son, but could not accept and love him as deeply as the girls, which made her very sad and which she wanted to understand and change. In the eighth therapy session, the following dialogue unfolded between us:

- Alexandra first recounts, without any affect, a work-related event in which she was able to solve a practical problem quite well. Then she is silent for a minute, before slowly and drawn out saying: "Yes, that was that story. And otherwise, I've read a lot. I can't think of anything else to tell." She yawns.
- I perceive the scene as a resistance to free association and remind her of the basic rule: "Perhaps you remember the free association we discussed in the first therapy session, the request that you express here all thoughts, feelings, images, memories, bodily sensations, and sensory impressions without judging whether they are important or unimportant."
- Alexandra: "Oh yes, you probably mean the thing with the train window. Let's see. Outside the window I see the three trees. My son, Jan, he's just learning to speak. He would definitely say three legs, even though he means three trees. He often still mixes up the words." She laughs lovingly and amused.
- I notice that, for some time now, she has suddenly landed on her son, who was indeed a main reason for the therapy. At the mention of the third leg, I feel a bit of shame as I think of the penis, as if something about her son's gender is being expressed in this image. I suspect that the patient's shame is being mirrored in me. That's why I first cautiously ask about her son: "Jan suddenly appears here with us, the reason you actually came here in the first place."
- Alexandra: "Actually, I'm doing quite well with Jan at the moment. Only this gender thing, which is so embarrassing for me, which I don't want to have and yet do have, that doesn't go away. He's very attached to me. I'm also attached to him, but differently than to the girls, with whom I somehow have a stronger relationship, a different connection. The way Jan is learning to speak is totally sweet. He's learning lots of words right now and says little fish or little frog, diminutives, which he probably doesn't even know are diminutives. And he's always been able to communicate without language, to express what he wants. When he could walk, he would get himself what he wanted to drink, or the plate he wanted. Now he can express it with language."
- I am touched and reply: "You speak very lovingly of him, but say that something is missing."
- Alexandra: "I'm already on the verge of thinking about a fourth child. My partner totally freaks out when I even hint at it, because three children are already enough

for him. But I keep thinking about it. On the other hand, it's just a thought thing; when I'm with Jan, I'm very loving with him. He's really okay!"

- I suspect that the fourth child is supposed to be a girl, but I still ask: "What do you want the fourth child to be?"
- Alexandra groans at such naivety and blurts out: "A girl, of course! But there won't be a fourth child!"
- Me: "But the longing is there."
- Alexandra: "Yes, and how, I sat in front of the internet all night, reading terrible forums, the desire for a child doesn't stop." She cries and then continues: "I can't get rid of the topic! Even my grandmother always said she actually would have liked to have boys and only got 'slit violins' (girls). My mother was supposed to be called Karl and is now Karla, her sister was supposed to be Josef and is now Josefine, well, and I was supposed to be Alexander and am unfortunately only Alexandra. We all are missing something between our legs, yes, probably the third leg. Jan has it, even though I actually would have preferred a Jana."

Not every time do patients reach their core conflict with so few associations, here a phallic conflict, which they then pursue associatively, then pause and look at something, then associate again. I certainly chose this example for reasons of space, but also to illustrate how quickly resistance can be given up and the patient can reach the crucial point. It is important not to focus on the details of the previous work story or impatiently ask what she has to tell, or why she doesn't want to say anything today, but rather to remind her of free association and ask why she is avoiding it today. ◀

Therapy sessions today usually last 50 minutes. Some schedule double sessions because the patient only gets to the real, central conflicts after 45 minutes. They hope that by doubling the session time to 100 minutes, the patient will really get going from minute 45. But usually, the timing then shifts to minute 90 or 95, again so that the sensitive issues are only touched on, but not really discussed. It would be better to address the resistance that causes the patient to open up only at minute 45, or to name the resistance to free association as early as minute 5. If that succeeds, we can usually let free-floating association run its course until minute 25 or 30, accompanied by our evenly suspended attention. Then we should gradually switch to the synthetic mode and piece together what has come up and stood out during free association. Often, she will approach and then move away from the sensitive points several times. Where the most feelings are noticeable, that is where we now deepen and clarify in the second part of the session; perhaps we come to the so-called "confrontation," drawing attention to contradictions in the associations, perhaps even by minute 35 to an interpretation of internal connections or interpersonal conflicts. We should not interpret later, in order to give the patient enough time to let the interpretation take effect and to process it.

Conclusion

It is not easy for patients to repeatedly engage in free association, because it quickly brings them into dangerous waters, which is why they prefer to stay at the edge of the lake. For us, it is not an easy task to repeatedly draw attention to resistances against the basic rule, to understand the associated fears, and thus to get the associations flowing again. Nevertheless, I hope I have made it clear that it is worthwhile and greatly advances the therapy.

2.2.2 Silence and Chatter

▶ There are many types of silence: thoughtful, withdrawn, defiant, dissociated, waiting, controlling, hungry, anxious, relaxed, catching-one's-breath silence, and surely many other variants and numerous combinations thereof. Often, it is a form of resistance, because most things in therapy happen through language and dialogue. Sometimes, however, silence can be restorative and comforting, as the patient experiences that she does not have to say anything or perform, and yet is allowed to be here and is accepted.

Therapists should be able to clearly distinguish a particular form of silence from all others. Steele (2017) describes it as a physical, almost animalistic freezing in the face of extreme danger to life and limb. This occurs especially in traumatized patients who, triggered by seemingly insignificant cues to others—such as a movement by the other person, a barely perceptible smell, certain lighting conditions, or words—are reminded of childhood traumas. In these moments, they not only recall old images but feel completely like a child in the overwhelming situation, for example, with a father who, with a certain movement, initiates sexual abuse. They freeze in fear, unable to speak or move, sometimes barely able to breathe. In Chap. 3 I describe in Sect. 3.2.2 on dissociation such an example and a possible way of dealing with it. These forms of silence due to freezing also represent a resistance, because the patient cannot talk about what once deeply disturbed and internally disorganized her, even if she would like to. Neither interpretations nor sitting out the silence together are helpful here; instead, a supportive, trauma-therapeutic approach is needed, as described further below in the aforementioned section 3.2.2.

For all other forms of silence, it can be said that the periods of silence vary greatly from patient to patient, as well as across different phases of therapy. In the initial and final phases, there is often less silence than in the middle phase; at the beginning and in the middle of the session more often than at the end, since anything the patient brings up just before the end of the session does not have to be explored in depth. But therapists also differ greatly in how they deal with silence. Some therapists let their patient remain silent for 20 minutes without intervening, some even for the entire 50 minutes of a therapy session. I consider this ethically very problematic and also a waste of time, especially for the patient, since the therapist at least still receives her fee for the 50 minutes of silence. Neither party makes any progress in the process of insight and change. I ask about the reason for the silence after five minutes at the latest. Often, patients can then say something about it, such as that they are afraid to pursue a certain thought further because it would bring up many strong, terrible feelings. One patient said she would certainly burst into tears, but had to go straight to work after our therapy session from 8 to 9 a.m., where she faced a demanding day and did not want to show up with smeared makeup. I could understand that, and we considered that she should address this difficult topic in another session during the week, when she came to me at 6 p.m. and could go home afterwards. Since she was in analytic therapy, this was possible. In a one-hour setting, the patient would only have this one hour at 8 a.m. and would always have to go to work afterwards. In this case, it would make sense to reschedule the session to the evening as soon as possible, because otherwise it would never be possible to explore a topic emotionally in depth, and she would leave many things unspoken at the end of treatment.

Phobic patients often say three words and then look at the therapist in silence and expectation, wondering whether what they said was right or wrong, and whether they should continue thinking and speaking in this or that direction. Sometimes a nod or an approving "Mmh!" from the therapist is enough for them to say the next three words. Often, however, they remain silent until the therapist asks a question or gives a suggestion about what the patient could talk about next. But even that does not elicit more than three words from the patient, so that she and the therapist maneuver themselves into a tedious question-and-answer back-and-forth, or the patient falls silent when the therapist, exhausted or annoyed, gives up and stops asking. Therefore, it is important to address the resistance early on, to discuss the challenge of venturing into unknown, foggy, uncertain territory when the therapist does not specify every single step. We could ask what might happen if we did not nod every time, ask questions, or set the direction of the conversation. Patients can usually talk very well about their fears of where they might end up if they followed their own thoughts and feelings—namely, precisely to the feelings they most need to defend against, such as aggression, sadness, sexual desires, or love. Sometimes it also helps to look together at the painting "Wanderer above the Sea of Fog" by Caspar David Friedrich, in which the wanderer sees the mountain he would like to reach. The path through a deep valley, however, lies in the fog, in uncertainty. He does not know exactly what abysses, obstacles, or dangers await him, what icy slickness or wild animals he will encounter. We therapists do not know exactly either, but we have experience in mountaineering and will help at difficult points. Nevertheless, the patient must also dare to take some steps herself and take risks.

Other patients fill the sessions with stories that have little or no emotional content and often have little to do with the central core conflicts. Unlike those who remain silent, they fill three, four, or even five sessions a week with trivialities, so that increasing the session frequency does not help here either, in the hope that eventually they will get to the essential issues because they run out of things to chat about. Addressing the resistance could be done by asking whether the stories just told concern the things that emotionally preoccupy the patient and are related to the problems for which she came, or whether they are episodes that are not so upsetting and problematic. Many patients can then admit that they are actually moved by other feelings and fantasies, but these are delicate and they do not dare, or do not yet dare, to bring them up. The word "dare" could lead us to the word "trust," which often makes it possible to summon the courage to address truly sensitive matters with another person. Trust often increases when we carefully, kindly, but clearly address the resistance and accept that even more trust must develop before the patient can venture further. If enough trust is present, we could ask about the fear of what would happen if the patient spoke about the truly sensitive topics. Most often, they fear that talking about them could trigger too much pain, horror, disgust, shame, or guilt. The therapist accepts this as well, but tries to encourage the patient to take at least a few, cautious steps onto the dangerous terrain—only as many as the feelings remain bearable, and to stop for today when they become stronger and harder to tolerate. This approach is similar to systematic desensitization, in which the phobic patient approaches the spider only as far as the fear remains within a tolerable range, and each day a few centimeters further.

Example

Bea, for the umpteenth time, spoke hastily and without pause during a session, in a quiet, toneless, dry voice, with the topics changing but no feelings being perceptible. When I pointed out to her that I could not sense what emotions she associated with the various stories, she became thoughtful. A lot happened between our sessions that moved her deeply. But she put most of it away in a drawer when she entered the therapy room, because it did not seem so important, she thought I might not be interested, or she feared I might criticize her—for example, for not changing her bulimic rituals. At the same time, she found silence very uncomfortable, so she felt she had to say something—something that seemed to contain a problem, but not one so big that she might cry or become afraid. Since I knew from her life history that she had grown up very lonely and emotionally without resonance, and did not know how to share her feelings with anyone, but rather had learned that she was disturbing or bothering others with her emotional experience, I could understand why she preferred not to bring up truly significant topics here. I acknowledged that she had told me she put away moving things before the session. At the same time, I encouraged her to open the drawer a little from time to time, so that only as many feelings would come out as she could bear and share with me. If ever more were to pour out than she could tolerate, I would help her put them back in and close the drawer. With this image, I acknowledged her defense, but also pointed out the possibility of change. ◀

Conclusion

Without addressing resistance by chatting about trivial stories, we could spend many hours with our patients without understanding or changing anything.

2.2.3 Quando me sinto só: Separation Resistance

For thousands of years, people have grappled with death, through which we eventually lose loved ones forever or our own lives come to an end. At the center of many religions is the question of whether and how life continues after death, in an otherworldly, paradisiacal realm or in a next life after reincarnation. The truly gruesome image of the dead Jesus on the cross gives Christians hope, because they firmly believe that he rose again and continues to live with his divine father in heaven. Whether separations are final or whether we can endure them has profoundly influenced human thought and feeling for as far back as we can look. All the more astonishing, then, is how often topics like separation and death play little or no role in psychotherapy. Resistance to dealing with these sensitive topics comes not only from patients, but often also from therapists, who, before and after their vacations or at the foreseeable end of therapy, do not ask how the patient is coping with it.

Rank (1927) supplemented Freud's drive theory with various other basic human needs and fears. For him, life is a series of separations, starting with the "trauma of birth," a fundamental event for the child but also for the mother, followed by separation from the close bond with the mother, the adolescent's separation from parents during puberty, leaving one's hometown, later from one's own children, partner, until death as the final, ultimate separation. All these separations evoke very different feelings, which are reflected in the separations that occur during psychotherapy. The first separation already occurs after 7 sessions, when an application for therapy coverage is submitted to the patient's health insurance, which sometimes takes several weeks to be approved. All vacations of the therapist and the patient represent separations, with the patient's own vacations being self-initiated and therefore usually easier to bear. With every separation, the final parting at the end of psychotherapy resonates, after which there will be no reunion. This occurs because psychotherapy is a very close, very personal, yet professional relationship, because the therapist may find the patient likable, literally "suffers with" her (from the ancient Greek "pathos" = suffering, patient = the suffering one), but is only with her as long as she is being paid. Some patients find this relieving, as this knowledge allows them to express their feelings with less guilt, while others find it hurtful to be treated not out of friendship, but for money and compassion.

As a people with many seafarers, whose return is never certain, the Portuguese have captured many feelings of separation in Fado. In Mariza's "Quando me sinto só," for example, the lyrics say:

> "When I am lonely because you have left me, I am lonelier than a vagabond on his park bench. Then I feel pity for myself and, on the other hand, I hate the whole world because it separates us so. When I feel alone, my mouth tastes of Fado and I lament like someone who mourns the sorrow that weighs him down. My tired heart is like an old waterwheel, dying of

> thirst for water. So that it is not so obvious, I try not to scream. If someone asks, I lie, I do not want their pity. In a mad selfishness, I go so far as to wish that you could feel what I feel when I am lonely."

The song sounds sad on the one hand, but also forceful, in keeping with the Latin word "aggredī," to move toward something or someone, to approach, to advance, or to attack. Separation aggression is directed against the person from whom we feel abandoned, but it also gives us the momentum for a new beginning. In just a few words, the song contains everything our patients associate with small and large separations: feelings of loneliness, hatred, sadness, fear, and lack of energy, but also the ambivalence about whether to talk about their terrible feelings or to hide them, to lie in order not to elicit pity from others. Many patients, especially at the beginning of therapy, do not believe that shared sorrow is half sorrow, that grief is a processing emotion, as Freud (1917) already described in *Mourning and Melancholia.* At its core, he says: Those who mourn a separation do not become melancholic, that is, not depressed. Our patients fear that the therapist's compassion will double their own suffering or that they might burden the therapist too much. Therefore, as Mariza puts it, they lie, or they resist communicating any kind of separation feelings. The earlier we address and work through these resistances, the better we will manage the final farewell at the end of therapy. Not only grief and fear can then be consciously experienced, but also feelings of anger and powerlessness, without whose processing at the end of therapy there is a great danger that they could destroy everything that has been achieved, in order to make the separation more bearable: If I have achieved nothing in therapy, then it is not so bad that it is now ending. If, on the other hand, all feelings of separation have been consciously experienced and discussed, the patient can take with her an inner image of her therapist, which she will carry within herself for the rest of her life and which will stand by her internally in difficult, conflict-laden times, which she can consult in an inner dialogue, and which will also rejoice with her over beautiful and accomplished things. Worked-through separation aggression helps the patient, in the sense of "aggredī," to move forward and tackle her life after therapy. However, this working through is opposed by a resistance that is succinctly named in Mariza's song "Primavera" after describing the horror of a broken love: "Ninguém fale em primavera." No one should speak of spring, that so hard-to-imagine new beginning after a painful separation. Instead, the song ends with the words: "Quem me dera, quem nos dera, Ter morrido nesse dia," translated: "If only I had, if only we had died that day." Separation aggression can lead to murder or suicide, but also to depression, to the inner destruction of everything that has arisen with the other person, the internalized image of the object, as well as a part of the self associated with it. By working through separation resistance, we should prevent this. In the live version of the song at the Concerto em Lisboa, Mariza stops singing after twice pressing out the words "Ninguém fale" (no one speaks) very haltingly and drawn out, as if warning herself. Just as the audience encourages her to continue singing, we can also encourage our patients to keep talking, even when it is so difficult. At this point, Mariza brings a great deal of vitality and aggression into the previously rather sad song as she forces out "Primavera," thus beginning spring, the new start.

Early disturbed patients react very differently to whether the therapist goes on vacation for one, two, or more weeks. Many can somehow manage a few days. From the second week onward, the inner image, the object representation of the therapist, fades or disintegrates more and more. They experience it as if she has died, accompanied by existential fear and abandonment, to an extent that is hardly imaginable for us therapists unless we ourselves have lived through times of personality disturbance. Supportive elements can be helpful here to make it easier for the patient. Some want to take a photo of the therapist and her office with their smartphone to look at during the vacation and recall the relationship. Some want to take a small object from the practice, a shell, a stone, or another small item. Some want to be allowed to call in an emergency, or send an email to which the therapist responds only briefly with a smiley, but which lets the patient know that the therapist still exists. All of this can prevent the loss of the object representation and, with it, the trust built up in the therapeutic relationship so far. Otherwise, after our vacation, we would virtually have to start from scratch. That would not be resistance, but rather the result of mishandling the separation.

Example

Before my three-week summer vacation, Antonia said that the upcoming separation from me did not bother her or mean anything to her. At first, I did not consider this to be resistance, since she had a disorder from the autistic spectrum and I assumed that at this early stage of therapy, she would not yet have an internal image of me from which she would have to say goodbye. After my vacation, she told me about several evenings when she lay awake in bed and saw shadowy figures in a corner of the room, which made her stomach clench and her heart beat faster. Since she experienced it only physically, as a "physical agent," as Fonagy et al. (2004) would call it, I reflected to her that it was probably a feeling of anxiety that had set in. The shadow figure, which disappeared when she turned on the light, we associated with me. During my vacation, she was unable to conjure up an internal image of me in which, for example, my facial features would have been recognizable. The shadow figure was a first, still completely undifferentiated black spot, the early beginning of an internal representation of me. As lonely and lost as her autistic world felt, it was just as frightening that someone else should take on form and meaning in her and for her, especially since the shadow figure did nothing good or helpful yet, but instead appeared in her uncontrollably and disturbingly and haunted her. In this respect, the quick denial of the question of whether the upcoming vacation triggered anything in her was indeed a resistance. The figure I began to take on in her had already developed before the vacation, but she did not want to perceive it. ◀

Conclusion
Two weeks before and two weeks after a therapy interruption, we should pay attention to whether the patient addresses feelings of separation, such as anxiety, anger, sadness, but also joy about a period of autonomy. If she does not, this is a resistance against experiencing the separation, which we should name and work through.

3 Resistance Through Defense Mechanisms

> Every person possesses defense mechanisms, which are considered part of the ego functions. Psychologically healthy individuals or those with only mild neurotic disturbances have many and more mature defense mechanisms, whereas individuals with personality disorders and psychotic conditions tend to have fewer and more primitive defense mechanisms.

Defense mechanisms protect us from anxieties, and thus from internal or external dangers. They are activated to regulate conflicts. Conflicts exist between desires, needs, and drive impulses on the one hand, and closely related feelings of shame, guilt, fear, disgust, sadness, hurt, powerlessness, internal prohibitions, or ego ideals on the other. Defense mechanisms lead to unconscious compromises between both sides, so that wishes are partially and in a distorted way fulfilled, while feelings of shame or guilt do not become overwhelming. For this reason, they oppose processes of becoming aware, gaining insight, and making changes, and thus present themselves in therapy as resistances to therapeutic progress.

When people perceive their internal resources as insufficient to cope with a situation, a stress reaction occurs. The way of dealing with this is called coping. Lazarus (1991) distinguished three types of coping with stress: problem-focused, appraisal-focused, and emotion-focused coping, with defense mechanisms being found primarily in the latter. In emotion-focused coping, people attempt to reduce the emotional arousal that arises in an upsetting situation. Through coping research, an understanding of forms of defense has thus spread far beyond psychoanalysis, even if the latter is not always cited as the origin. For example, defense mechanisms are included in the "Defense Functioning Scale" in Appendix B of the DSM-IV-TR, the Diagnostic and Statistical Manual of the American

T. Abel, *Resistance in Psychotherapy*, https://doi.org/10.1007/978-3-662-72663-1_3

Psychiatric Association (APA). According to this, the clinician should list up to seven of the specific defense mechanisms or coping styles, starting with the most prominent, and then indicate the predominant level of defense shown by the individual.

Haan (1977) suggests that a person will cope if they can, defend if they must, and fragment if forced to do so. Seiffge-Krenke (2017) has compiled several long-term studies from therapy research that demonstrate how significantly defense can change during treatment.

3.1 Basic Conflicts, Defense Mechanisms, and Resistance

> Defense mechanisms represent attempts to find more or less functional or dysfunctional solutions to internal conflicts. Internally, unconscious wishes and needs, which are tempted by fantasies, thoughts, or external situations, come into conflict with antagonistic affects. Defense mechanisms are intended to find a compromise so that part of the wishes can be fulfilled in disguised form, while at the same time feelings of fear, shame, or guilt are kept within limits.

Whereas Freud focused primarily on drive conflicts, object relations psychology—which today represents the mainstream of psychoanalysis (see Abel, 2023)—has significantly expanded the range of conflicting wishes and basic needs

> "In particular, Freud's assumption that the psychic apparatus develops as a result of the frustration of childhood drives attributes the formation of psychic structures and functions to only one specific type of object relationship (namely, those in which the child's needs are frustrated). Object relations theories fundamentally differ from Freudian theory in the greater heterogeneity of relationship patterns considered relevant for the development of psychic structures. Object relations theories assume that the child's psyche is shaped by all early experiences with caregivers." (Fonagy & Target, 2015, p. 157)

Ermann (2012, pp. 66 ff.) formulates it similarly:

> "Pivotal for understanding the human being from this perspective is primary relatedness, i.e., the psychologically effective embeddedness of the self in the relationship with the human counterpart from the very beginning of life. Thus, with regard to life history and the etiology of psychological disorders, the early developmental stages and experiences move to the center of psychoanalytic consideration. This perspective led to a re-evaluation of the time before the Oedipus complex, i.e., the 3–4 pre-oedipal years of life, which concern fundamental questions of existence, security and basic trust, care and mirroring, and the development of basic abilities and skills. In comparison, the exploration of conflicts arising from sexual and aggressive drive impulses and the significance of the Oedipus complex in later childhood recede into the background. What becomes central now are the internalized relationship experiences, i.e., the conscious and unconscious representations a person has of themselves, their caregivers, and their relationships."

In the individual developmental phases of the self, certain wishes are at the forefront, which are opposed by antagonistic feelings, so that they are satisfied, over-fulfilled, denied, shamed, forbidden, or associated with fear. We distinguish the following four early phases:

1. Symbiotic or schizoid phase (up to the 6th month of life): On the one hand, it is about separation: the differentiation between baby and mother, between self and object, the process of detaching from the symbiosis with the mother. On the other hand, the baby has wishes for fusion, for remaining in or returning to a symbiotic union, for de-differentiation between self and object, between baby and mother, to be one with the other. These wishes are opposed by antagonistic feelings: the wishes for separation are met with existential fear of not surviving alone and unconnected, while the wishes for fusion are met with fear of losing any sense of identity in a very close symbiosis without boundaries between self and other.
2. Oral phase (6th to 12th month of life): Wishes for comfort, security, soothing, care, emotional nurturing, and being fed are opposed by antagonistic feelings of shame or guilt about being too greedy, too voracious, needing too much security, comfort, or attention, as well as disgust at one's own wishes and fear of devouring the other or destroying them through one's own needs.
3. Anal phase (2nd to 4th year of life): On the one hand, there are wishes for autonomy: independence, asserting one's own will, exercising power, control, and showing aggression; on the other hand, there are wishes for dependence: relinquishing power and control, following another's will, and submitting. Opposing these wishes are fears of autonomy, guilt about wanting to be independent, shame about feeling or showing aggressive feelings, shame about feeling dependent and powerless, and guilt about not being able to manage everything alone.
4. Phallic phase (5th to 7th year of life): This phase is dominated by wishes to be accepted in one's sexuality, to be admired for physical attractiveness and talents, to win in competition, to outdo others, to conquer an object and surpass another—who may be the parents (Oedipal), but also siblings. Opposing these wishes are feelings of shame about not being attractive, powerful, interesting, appealing, or smart enough to be accepted, shame about being an unwanted boy or girl, guilt about having entered into competition with others, having rivaled, excluded, or humiliated them, and fear of not being liked or accepted.

The wishes mentioned do not become irrelevant or meaningless after the end of each respective phase, but rather accompany us throughout our entire lives. However, they may temporarily recede into the background in favor of other wishes. If they are denied or only insufficiently satisfied, conflicts intensify in later phases. For example, if wishes for separation cannot be fulfilled because a mother keeps her child very close and prevents any attempt at detachment from the symbiosis, the child can only insufficiently distinguish between themselves and the object, and accordingly cannot distinguish between their own feelings and those of the other. The struggles for the fulfillment of autonomy wishes in the anal phase are made more difficult because the child cannot distinguish what is their own will and what is the mother's.

There are no perfect parents, but at best those who are "good enough," i.e., sufficiently good (Winnicott, 1996, p. 677). It is unavoidable to frustrate even a baby in an age-appropriate way, because not every wish can be fulfilled immediately. The child learns that it does not have unlimited control over its parents and its environment. However, the stronger the frustration in the individual phases, the more the affected wishes become associated with antagonistic feelings. If the wishes repeatedly encounter parental prohibitions, the child internalizes these prohibitions in its moral instance, the superego. It internally voices a prohibition whenever the relevant wishes are unconsciously tempted and threaten to become conscious, so that feelings of guilt arise. For example, unconscious wishes for autonomy may be stimulated—to assert one's own will, to make and stand by an independent decision, to assert oneself against another's will—which, however, are marked by the superego as something forbidden, leading to feelings of guilt for having wanted or even demanded something of one's own. In contrast, feelings of shame arise when wishes come into conflict with the ego ideal, an instance that contains all the internalized ideals of how we should be from the perspective of our family and society, or how we ourselves want to be. If, for example, the ego ideal includes the position that we should have no will of our own but always fulfill the will of the family and social community, we feel ashamed as soon as we want something different from the people around us. Anxiety becomes associated with our wishes when we have repeatedly experienced that something terrible happens as soon as we feel or express a certain wish. For example, if a defiant child experiences that his mother, in response to his demands or refusals, has a heart attack and seemingly almost dies, he will later in life react with fear to again triggering something terrible when he perceives expressions of his own will or wishes for autonomy within himself. Defense finds compromises between the wishes and the opposing feelings. In therapy, defense appears to us as resistance:

> "Defense mechanisms that are used for the purpose of resistance give the patient the opportunity to influence the pace of the therapeutic process and to adapt it to their tolerance limits." (König, 1997, p. 16)
>
> "If one assumes that patients, with the help of their resistance, have achieved the best possible conflict solutions for themselves and thus maintain their equilibrium, one will better do justice to the therapeutic task of creating the most favorable conditions for the reduction of these resistances." (Thomä & Kächele, 2006, p. 133)

We distinguish between primitive and mature defense mechanisms. In the following sections, the various defense mechanisms will be discussed in detail. In psychotherapy, they appear either one after the other, but sometimes also simultaneously, overlapping, complementing, and interwoven with each other. The therapist should be well acquainted with them in order to identify, differentiate, and address them in the therapeutic process.

Using an example, I would like to show how different defense mechanisms can occur in the same conflict in the same patient and become resistances:

Example

Sven grew up with a mother who suffered from severe depression, so that she often could not get up and take care of the children, was repeatedly admitted to a psychiatric clinic, and, moreover, although her drive was improved by antidepressants, she was emotionally restricted and not very empathetic. She could only sometimes adequately respond to his oral wishes for comfort, security, reassurance, or care. Often, however, she seemed powerless, annoyed, or overwhelmed as soon as he approached her, so that Sven internalized that his actually appropriate oral wishes were too much for others. He feared draining his mother, robbing her of her last life energy, almost destroying her, which explained to him why she lay immobile in bed for days or even had to be taken to the hospital. He internally linked oral wishes with fears and feelings of guilt about being too greedy and destructive. His wishes and the associated fears were gradually deposited in the unconscious in the face of guilt feelings. Sven would not have been able to consciously name this conflict. As an adult, he fell in love with Yvonne, an attractive and caring pediatric nurse. This romantic relationship unconsciously tempted his long-repressed oral wishes. At last, he too wanted to be cared for, nourished, comforted, and looked after. At the same time as these wishes, however, unconscious feelings of guilt arose—of being too greedy, too demanding, too shameless—as well as the fear of overwhelming or even destroying his new partner with his voracious wishes. The wishes on the one hand, and the feelings of guilt and fear on the other, constituted an oral conflict. Since both sides are equally strong, an unbearable conflict tension arises. To reduce it, Sven can employ various defense mechanisms:

1. Displacement: He can displace his oral wishes away from Yvonne, for example onto addictive substances. By drinking alcohol excessively, in the sense of poisoned mother's milk, he can fulfill some of his oral wishes. During consumption he feels calm, comforted, and secure. At the same time, he protects Yvonne from his wishes, which he experiences as too greedy, because he has displaced them from her onto the alcohol. Therefore, he does not have to feel guilty or anxious. Only because of the uncontrollable greed with which he "gulps down" the alcohol does he feel a little guilty, which can later lead to secret drinking.
2. Turning against the self: Due to the feelings of guilt and fear associated with oral wishes, Sven forbids himself to become aware of and fulfill his wishes. However, this triggers rage at disappointment, because it again seems impossible to finally satisfy long-unfulfilled oral wishes. He cannot direct this rage outward at his partner, because his disappointment would reveal to her how greedy, shameless, and insatiable his wishes actually are. Therefore, he turns his rage against himself,

resulting in depressive symptoms. This leads his partner to take care of him, to look after him, without him having to feel guilty—after all, he did not ask her to, but he is ill and cannot help it.

3. Altruistic surrender of wishes: Instead of admitting his own oral wishes, he projects them onto his partner, whom he then experiences as very needy and emotionally hungry, and self-sacrificingly takes care of her. When he has the impression that she enjoys the security, care, and comfort, he puts himself in her position in his imagination and secretly enjoys it from her perspective. It becomes difficult if the partner does not want to be cared for in this way or does not show enough gratitude, so that this attempt at defense comes to nothing. Then Sven might employ one of the other defense mechanisms or break up, because important wishes in the relationship seem unfulfillable. If Sven were a doctor or psychotherapist, he could project some of his oral wishes onto his patients and try to fulfill them in them. Since this usually remains unsatisfying in the long run, a helper syndrome or burnout could develop, predominantly with depressive symptoms, or he could displace the unfulfilled longings onto alcohol and drugs, which, given the increased rate of addiction disorders in helping professions, often seems to happen.

The defense mechanisms explain symptoms and irrational, otherwise difficult-to-understand behavior. Most people would expect that Sven might react with addiction or depression after a breakup, but not in a new romantic relationship. However, this becomes understandable through conflict and defense. But how do these defense mechanisms become resistances in the therapy that Sven begins in light of his symptoms?

1. Displacement: Sven hopes to receive from the therapist the long-awaited care and sense of security that he never dared to wish for with Yvonne. At the same time, however, this again gives rise to feelings of guilt and fears of being too greedy and destroying the therapist. Therefore, he once again displaces his oral wishes onto alcohol, so that after starting therapy, he consumes even more than before. The more comfortable and secure he feels in the deepening therapeutic relationship, the more he will need to drink. Instead of improving, his symptoms worsen. Any progress in therapy would mean understanding the function of the addiction, and thus also the strong oral wishes underlying it. Because these are associated with feelings of guilt and anxiety, they must not become conscious. They must continue to be displaced onto alcohol. This creates resistance to the change that therapy is actually intended to achieve. As an intervention, the following might be possible:

Sven: “After the last session, I felt relieved, but also somehow restless, jittery, anxious. I just couldn’t calm down. Suddenly, there were those two bottles of wine in my bag when I came out of the supermarket. At first, I only took a few sips. But Yvonne had to go to bed early, so I could drink the rest and make the bottles disappear.”

Therapist: "In the last session, you opened up, talked about various difficult topics, and were able to show some sadness, which is usually hard for you. Apparently, you felt relieved afterwards. But then it seems that an anxiety also came up that you couldn't bear. Can you tell me more about that?"

Sven: "I have no words for the anxiety. It was just a great, unpleasant restlessness. But I do remember thinking that you must be completely exhausted and drained in the evenings after work, having had patients like me all day. That's why I came here today with the intention not to cry today or in the next sessions."

Therapist: "Because you fear overwhelming and draining me with your feelings of sadness, you would rather not show them anymore, but numb them with wine. Yet you are actually here to open up emotionally and share your feelings. Can you tell me what you think would happen if you opened up more and more here and showed your feelings?"

Sven: "I think you might put up with it for a while, since it's your job, but then you'd think, now that's enough crying and I should just pull myself together. Maybe you'd end the therapy because I'm too much for you or because I just can't be helped."

The therapist decides to partially share the feelings the patient triggers in her in the countertransference: "I didn't find our last session exhausting. When you show yourself and open up emotionally, I can empathize with you. That makes it easier for me to understand you than when you are emotionally closed off or talk about topics that don't move you emotionally."

Sven: "I'm surprised that feelings are supposed to be important for understanding someone. I always thought people found me pleasant because I don't complain much, don't bother them with my feelings, but hold back or talk about practical things."

Therapist: "Then you basically never had the opportunity to relieve yourself emotionally or find comfort. That is very exhausting for you in the long run. In therapy, it is very important that feelings are allowed to be felt here, so that I can understand you and so that something can move and change within you. Maybe we can look together in each session at how far you can open up. If you start to feel afraid that you might burden me with your feelings, please tell me, so you are not left alone with it after the session. That way, we can regulate the pace of our work here together."

Resistance should always be addressed first before we use techniques typical of specific therapeutic approaches. If the patient gradually manages to reduce his resistance so that he can show more of his oral wishes, fears, and feelings of guilt, it becomes possible to address Sven's obvious transference of his overburdened, drained mother onto the therapist, which is present in the scene above. An interpretation of the transference that comes too early would at best lead to a rational insight, but would not reduce the resistance.

2. Turning against the self: Just as with his partner, Sven will also only rarely and cautiously risk becoming aware of his oral wishes with his therapist. Again, it makes him angry not to be able to fulfill his oral wishes here either, which he has had to forgo for so long. In order not to let the anger become visible, he turns it against himself, so that the depressive symptoms continue to worsen instead of improving through therapy. Under these circumstances, he could not arrive at therapeutic insights as long as he is not aware of the defense mechanism underlying this resistance.

Sven: "After the last therapy session, I felt very powerless, weighed down, exhausted, and depressed. I wondered whether therapy could really help me, because just talking doesn't change anything. That doesn't make my depression any better either."

Therapist: "It sounds like you were dissatisfied with what you got here in the last session."

Sven, startled, tries to cover up any impression of anger: "No, no! I wasn't dissatisfied with the session, but, if anything, with myself. I just wondered whether body therapy, hypnosis, or medication wouldn't help my depression better."

Therapist: "What do you imagine those would be like? How would those treatments help you?"

Sven: "Body therapy would definitely mean a nice massage, so my body would feel less heavy and tense. Hypnosis would mean finally switching off, being away, not brooding, and when I wake up, I feel much better. Medication would take away all my sad feelings."

Therapist: "You secretly wish for all of that from me here as well. That's why you're dissatisfied that I don't take away your oppressive, sad feelings and ruminations here."

Sven: "With you, I talk about what I'm thinking about, you ask a few questions. I try to answer the questions factually and briefly. That's all that's possible here."

Therapist: "I believe more is possible here. If you had the courage to show me more of your feelings, something could happen that is summed up in the saying: 'A burden shared is a burden halved.'"

Sven rolls his eyes in annoyance: "I've never understood that stupid saying. What comes out of it is actually double the burden, because I load someone else with my suffering, in addition to their own, and then I feel guilty for what I've burdened the other person with."

Therapist: "Now, through that hint of anger, I understand better how you imagine sharing feelings and why you want to avoid it at all costs. At the same time, with your thoughts about body therapy, hypnosis, and medication, you've expressed that you could only feel better if something changed in your feelings, if there were some way to get rid of the sadness and oppression. Let's carefully try together to see if sharing suffering can't actually work differently than you imagine. You could start by telling me, as you did today, about your dissatisfaction with a session, if you feel it. Then we can look at what you actually would have needed, what would have done you good, and why you couldn't express it."

It is important to the therapist that the patient understands and accepts what this process is about, and that he has the courage to engage in it. Resistances do not dissolve on their own, nor through a patient's self-realization. Therefore, the therapist must win the patient over to engage in the process, to stop directing aggression against himself, and instead to bring it more and more into the therapeutic process, but also to bring in the oral wishes that underlie it.

3. Altruistic surrender: If Sven resorts to this defense mechanism, the start of therapy will be particularly difficult. He will try to take care of the therapist so that his own oral wishes toward her do not become apparent, but so that he can secretly fulfill them by taking care of the therapist. At the beginning of the session, he will ask her how she is doing. If she inquires about the background of the question, he will empathetically explain how difficult her job must be, how tired she looks, how much she probably works, or whether she has very difficult patients. Even if these questions are repeated at the beginning of every session, Sven will not be able to fill the therapy time with them permanently. He will try to cheer her up, entertain her with interesting stories, or at least be as easy a patient as possible and not demand anything from her, in order to do her some good in this way. Thus, altruistic wish-delegation becomes a resistance against becoming aware of his own oral wishes and the associated feelings of guilt and anxiety. If the therapist does not recognize this and address it in conversation, Sven will terminate therapy at a very early stage.

Therapist: "Actually, you came here so that I could help you. But I notice that you seem more interested in taking care of me. Perhaps it is easier for you to worry about someone else's well-being than to be the focus of care yourself, because you fear that this might be unpleasant for the other person or quickly become too much."

Sven reacts with a face that is half startled and half disgusted: "When you said, 'to be the focus of care,' I felt an unpleasant sense of disgust. The image came to mind of a small, chubby child with snot running from its mouth and nose, drooling and crying because it wants something. That's just disgusting!"

Therapist: "You're afraid that I might perceive you like that child as soon as you show wishes here, and then turn away from you in disgust. That's why you do everything to not allow your own wishes. Instead, you prefer to focus on my needs."

Sven looks sad and recalls: "There were a number of people who were very close to me for a while, whom I constantly helped with emotional problems. Claudia was always pouring her heart out to me, but as soon as I tried to tell her about my problems with my boss, which were really weighing on me, she would raise her hands and say she couldn't take it, that I was burdening her with something else when she was already feeling so bad and had so much to bear. On the phone, she would often just hang up and block me if I started to talk about myself, as if I were dangerous, threatening, as if I could push her over the edge with her burden. Or Lilly or Judith, I told you similar things about them. Or my mother, whom I was always comforting and cheering up. But every time I just came to her, she looked at me so disgusted and overwhelmed, as if I was disturbing her. Once I heard her say to a social worker how exhausting and outrageous I was because I was always wanting something from her. I guess I'm just pathetic when I want something emotional from others."

Therapist: "This fear has probably kept you from sharing your feelings with others your whole life. It would be important for that to change so that you can feel better. Maybe we should look here at what you need when you feel the impulse to take care of me." ◀

Conclusion

In adults, certain wishes are unconsciously tempted by external situations, in interpersonal relationships, or by inner fantasies. At the same time, the antagonistic feelings of guilt, shame, or fear associated with these wishes are activated. This creates a conflict. The function of defense is to reduce the associated conflict tension to a bearable level. This usually happens through a compromise: the wishes become conscious only to a small extent and in a disguised form, so that not such strong feelings of guilt, shame, or fear have to arise. All people possess several defense mechanisms. The greater the number and variety of defense mechanisms, the better a person copes with the inevitable conflicts of life, the more diverse their relationships, but also the more varied and intertwined their resistances in the therapeutic process. The different ways in which this occurs in individuals will be described in the following sections.

3.2 Resistance Through Primitive Defense Mechanisms

▶ Primitive defense mechanisms are rather crude measures to protect the self from disintegration and to maintain relationships with other people.

People usually resort to them in times of greatest inner distress, either because as adults they find themselves in a life-threatening or traumatic situation, or because as children they grow up in emotional neglect or violence, so that they never really emerge from an inner state of emergency. For outsiders, these defense mechanisms are quite easy to recognize. For the therapist, however, it is often difficult to address them, because they are the last bastion before psychological breakdown. Usually, a solid working relationship is needed first, so that the therapist has become a self-object that helps the patient regulate the self, before she can reduce or relinquish the defense mechanisms.

3.2.1 Denial

In denial, a perception is deprived of its reality character when it is too threatening for a person. Something that exists is experienced as non-existent, something that has happened as if it had not happened, according to the motto: "It cannot be what must not be!" Denial plays a special role in severe somatic illnesses, eating and personality disorders, as well as in psychoses, in which reality is no longer perceived to a significant extent.

Denial in Severe Physical Illnesses

▶ In more severe physical illnesses, denial plays a major role.

For example, a patient with cancer may claim to herself and others that she is not ill or that her type of cancer is a harmless disease. Even when significant physical effects of the illness or its treatments are apparent, she will claim that she is doing very well and is physically completely fit. She "blanks out" her physical decline, because if she were to acknowledge it, she would have to feel and endure existential fear of death. In psycho-oncology, there is discussion about how much denial should be left to a patient so that she does not become too depressed or panicked, which would impair compliance with treatment measures, and where denial is too strong, so that the patient considers herself healthy and does not allow herself to be treated appropriately.

König (1997, p. 13) writes on this:

> "Denial of an illness or its severity can cause a patient not to follow medical instructions, but it can also prolong life, for example by avoiding stress, which could paralyze the immune system and thus increase the likelihood of a cancer recurrence. Even defense-distorted assessments, such as overestimating a chance of survival, can thus have a life-prolonging function; at the very least, they can improve a patient's quality of life by reducing anxiety and enabling hope."

The psychiatrist Elisabeth Kübler-Ross (2014) worked in the 1960s at the University of Chicago with dying patients, as well as with doctors and nursing staff. In doing so, she found that many of them avoided facing the reality of their patients' impending death. Therefore, she advocated for honesty in conversations with the dying. She asked directly about their feelings and thoughts and wanted to learn from them what kind of help they hoped for and how they wished to be treated. From this, she derived five stages of dying that people—often including their relatives—typically go through. These stages also apply to other losses, such as the loss of loved ones, a job, or even bodily functions due to the onset of a disability or chronic illness. There is no fixed order. Some stages may be skipped entirely:

1. Denial: A diagnosis is denied by considering it a misdiagnosis, or it is acknowledged but its severity or poor prognosis is denied. It is difficult to engage patients in conversation. They may partially refuse necessary treatment measures. Some purchase vitamin tablets promoted by healers in an attempt to treat a serious cancer. Some never move beyond this stage before their death. If it concerns relatives, such as parents of terminally ill children who deny their child's illness, they may refuse medically recommended treatments for their child. Physicians should try to build trust during this phase in order to engage with their patients and their families and to be perceived as supportive.
2. Anger: The question "Why me?" leads patients to experience strong feelings of envy and anger toward all those who are not afflicted and will continue to live, such as doctors, nurses, or relatives. Caregivers should not take this anger personally, but rather allow patients the opportunity to express these feelings.
3. Bargaining: When the futility of fighting becomes apparent, there is a regression to childlike states. Patients hope to strike a deal with God or fate, so that as a reward for certain actions or thoughts, they may survive or at least live longer. Sometimes, feelings of guilt play a role—for example, having caused lung cancer through years of smoking. The vow never to smoke again, provided one survives, would be such an attempt to bargain. For caregivers, it is important here to talk about these feelings of guilt. If, as in the example of smoking, patients have indeed contributed to the development of the illness through their lifestyle, they should be able to acknowledge, regret, and perhaps forgive themselves. If the guilt feelings are irrational—sometimes serving to ward off feelings of powerlessness and helplessness, such as believing that a fatal illness was caused by being too friendly or unfriendly to others, by violating religious rules, or similar—they need help in dispelling these feelings of guilt.
4. Depression: If fighting and bargaining are of no use, people are confronted with the despair over losses—those that have already occurred, such as a breast after surgery or irretrievably lost bodily functions, or those that are yet to come, such as the loss of life, loved ones, or cherished activities. Caregivers and relatives should support patients in this phase as they mourn these deeply painful losses, because grief is a processing emotion. If it cannot be felt and shared, depression often results, as Freud (1917) already described in *Mourning and Melancholia*. Mourning together with relatives can help recall shared experiences, express feelings of love and affection—perhaps more clearly than ever before or after a long time—and also to forgive hurtful or conflictual matters. Relatives can assure the dying that they will live on in them, which is often a source of comfort.
5. Acceptance: The struggle is over, the pain endured. The dying await their death. Problems of the outside world are unimportant. Relatives should, in this phase, primarily listen and show that they will accompany the patient until death.

Stages two through five demand a great deal from patients, caregivers, and relatives. Intense emotional upheavals must be endured and processed. In this respect, it is deeply understandable that some people from these three groups remain stuck in denial, lacking the courage and strength to face all that this defense mechanism keeps at bay. Physicians, psychotherapists, and nursing staff bear a special responsibility here. On the one hand, they need appropriate training to deal with the dying. On the other hand, Kübler-Ross (2014) considered it an important prerequisite that caregivers emotionally confront their own feelings and thoughts about their own death, in order to truly empathize with the emotional world of the dying and to be able to help them.

Example

Siegbert is suffering from metastatic liver cancer. After several rounds of chemotherapy and radiation, he is emaciated like a skeleton and has lost all his hair. When the doctor visits him in his hospital room, he cannot walk even a few steps without her support. Yet he says, "I'm feeling so well that I'll probably be discharged tomorrow, Saturday, after the ward round. I can easily imagine going back to work on Monday." The doctor, who knew he had only a few days left to live, did not contradict him so as not to discourage him. By maintaining denial of his condition, he was spared, until shortly before his death, from fear of dying and feelings of grief, depression, helplessness, and anger. At the same time, he was unable to say goodbye to his relatives who visited him over the weekend. As a result, some things remained unsaid and unresolved—things he might have wanted to share, give, or clarify with them had he acknowledged his impending death. Although his wife had been informed by the doctor about his approaching death, she did not dare to address it with her husband, fearing both his and her own emotions. On the aforementioned Monday, he died in her presence. ◀

In addition to dealing with one's own feelings about death and dying, it is worthwhile for physicians to read Eugen Drewermann's (1992) interpretation of the Grimm fairy tale "Godfather Death." The central, conflict laden motif in the tale is the young doctor who stands at the bedside of his patients and, unlike everyone else in the room, sees Death either at their heads or at their feet. In the former case, healing is possible with a certain herb; in the latter, the patient belongs to Death. For them, "no herb will help," as the tale says and as the saying has been adopted in popular parlance. The image of the doctor at the bedside vividly expresses what doctors often experience: Unlike everyone else in the room, they see whether the patient must die or can be helped. This perception is a heavy burden, as is the powerlessness of not being able to save someone. One way to cope is to deny death, to refuse to perceive it. The tale suggests another path: trying to outwit death, which the doctor pays for at a high price. Only if we can emotionally respect that death is our godfather—that is, our sponsor—will the burden of seeing him at the heads or feet of the sick be lessened. Through palliative medicine and the hospice movement, accompanying the dying has, in recent decades, increasingly become part of medical practice, because there, death is acknowledged rather than denied.

Denial in Psychoses

> Denial is one of the main defense mechanisms in all schizophrenic and affective psychoses. Both external reality is denied—ranging from the air temperature to other people and their concerns and functions—as well as internal reality, such as who the person is and what they are currently capable of.

Anna Freud (1936) regarded denial as a defense mechanism that frequently occurs in children and is quite normal there. Children deny being small, dependent, or inferior by pretending or fantasizing to be something grand and, in that moment, firmly believing it. Normally, however, they are also able to relinquish the denial:

> "Someone who was just a horse or an elephant, neighing or trumpeting on all fours, must be able, in the next moment, to sit relatively quietly and properly at the table. The lion tamer must be able to submit again to some nanny, the adventurer or pirate must accept being sent to bed, just when the most interesting things are beginning in the adult world. The adult's goodwill toward the child's denial mechanism ends the moment the transition between fantasy and reality is no longer smooth, immediate, and effortless, when the child wants to derive consequences for their real behavior from fantasy, or, to put it even more sharply: the moment the child's fantasy activity ceases to be play and becomes automatic or compulsive." (A. Freud, 1936, p. 87)

If denial appears in adults, it can lead to schizophrenic psychosis:

> "Under the conditions of the synthesized, unified adult ego organization, it disappears and only reappears where the relationship to reality is severely disturbed and reality testing is suspended. In psychotic delusion formation, for example, a piece of wood serves, just like such a protective object in childhood, to represent desired or lost objects." (A. Freud, 1936, pp. 91 f.)

For Mentzos (2009), denial is also typical of affective psychoses:

> "This is especially true for mania: The distinctly elevated (mainly cheerful, but occasionally also irritable) mood, the increased drive to move and talk, the loosening of associations resulting in flight of ideas, the striking disinhibition observed by others, the senseless purchases during shopping sprees, the reduced need for sleep, the tendency toward grandiosity, the uncritical over-optimism, the trivializing approach to problems, and the strong denial of both intrapsychic and external reality are, taken together, unmistakable characteristics of mania. The grandiosity can escalate to megalomania, and often the person becomes dangerous to themselves and others due to their impulsivity, disinhibition, and lack of judgment."

Example

Alesja came to Germany from Russia at the age of 20, at the beginning of the 1990s, as a resettler of German descent. She quickly learned to speak fluent German and got a one-room apartment in a high-rise on the outskirts of Berlin. She knew no one in

Germany, having left her mother and few relatives behind in Russia. As a result, she felt deeply abandoned and lost in her new apartment. She developed paranoid-hallucinatory schizophrenia. Like Margarita in Mikhail Bulgakov's book *The Master and Margarita*, she believed she possessed magical abilities. Barefoot and dressed only in a short shirt, she walked through the snowy streets of Berlin in severe cold, wanting to give love to people by making large, sweeping hand gestures and beaming at everyone she met. Eventually, she was picked up and brought to a locked psychiatric ward. She told me that she had not felt the cold of the snow on her feet. Her body, she said, was full of love and therefore completely warm. Since Margarita flew naked through the city on a broomstick, it was not offensive to Alesja to walk almost naked through Berlin. Even on the ward, she refused to wear more than a thin nightgown. She denied her existential loneliness, her vulnerability, the cold of winter, but also the unusualness of her appearance and the reactions of others to it. She did not understand that a fellow patient saw her as a young, slender, beautiful woman with long black hair and found her sexually attractive. When I brought this up, she called the fellow patient crazy, because she could not imagine that anyone could see something different in her than she herself did. However, she was not worried, because as Margarita she possessed magical abilities, so she had no doubt she could fend off any advances. After taking neuroleptics, the psychotic symptoms subsided relatively quickly. Alesja developed a post-psychotic depression with severe suicidality. The medication had lifted her denials. She felt cold again when not adequately dressed, was ashamed of what she had done during the psychosis because she could no longer deny the perceptions of others, and she gained access to existential feelings of loneliness, abandonment, grief, and panic about facing the future completely alone in a totally unfamiliar country, which was also being shaken by a wave of xenophobia at the time. I helped her to feel, endure, and share these feelings with me, so that she could mourn the loss of her mother and homeland and face her fear of the future. She was eventually discharged, began training as a nurse, found friends, a partner, and gradually made Germany her home. As far as I know, Alesja did not experience any further schizophrenic episodes, as she continued to receive medication and psychotherapy after her discharge from the clinic, until both the medication and therapy could be discontinued. ◀

Psychotic denials can also be resolved without medication, through psychotherapy alone. However, this requires much more time and a trusting, stable working relationship. In this respect, medication is a blessing, but only if, during the phase of post-psychotic depression that follows most psychotic episodes, there is someone who talks with the patient, has time and emotional space to share her feelings, and patiently helps her cope. Unfortunately, in recent decades, positions for psychologists in clinics have been increasingly cut, as have the time units officially allotted for conversations on psychiatric acute wards. If denials are lifted very quickly and patients lose the protection of this defense, they are suddenly exposed to mostly existential feelings with which they are often unable to cope on their own. If there is no one to support them, there is a risk that they may commit suicide, become severely depressed, or that the psychotic symptoms—that is, the denial—will return despite medication. Some patients secretly stop taking their medication in order to be able to deny again what they cannot bear.

Denial in Eating and Personality Disorders

▶ In eating disorders such as anorexia, bulimia, or binge eating disorder, massive denial can occur, especially when these disorders develop on the basis of a borderline personality disorder. This denial concerns, on the one hand, excessively high or low body weight, and on the other, the severe physical consequences of the illnesses.

Given their body image disturbances, patients deny that their body weight is too low, even though almost everyone in their environment gives them corresponding feedback. They insist that they are too fat and need to lose much more weight. Physical problems such as cessation of menstruation, weakness, or pain are either not perceived or attributed to other causes. This denial often cannot be overcome through therapeutic conversations for a long time, as patients first need to develop and establish other, more mature defense mechanisms in their lives before they can gradually reduce and relinquish denial. For this reason, for example, in transference-focused psychotherapy (Yeomans et al., 2017), a therapy agreement is used, which the patient must agree to before treatment begins. It stipulates that she must regularly be weighed in a general practitioner's office wearing only underwear—the more underweight she is, the more frequently this must occur. She then brings a stamped and signed certificate from the office once a month, weekly, or several times a week, stating her current body weight. Since patients may put stones or other heavy objects in their pockets or wear several sweaters on top of each other to conceal their true weight during weighing, it is important to find an arrangement where, for example, they are weighed almost unclothed by a medical assistant. Most psychotherapists cannot and do not want to do this in their own practice. However, the arrangement should be discussed with the relevant general practitioner's office.

Patients often request to receive the certificate in a sealed envelope so they do not have to see their weight. They also close their eyes while on the scale. In psychotherapy, the therapist can then ask about the feelings that would be triggered if she were to tell the patient what is written on the certificate. This can reveal initial fears, and perhaps also wishes, that trigger the denial. When these are contained, understood, and verbalized by the therapist, the patient feels somewhat relieved and can reduce the denial. She will then look at her weight herself and hand the therapist an open note. Nevertheless, she will not consider her weight to be too low, neither in herself nor in an anorexic friend. On the contrary, she will continue to try to lose weight. Therefore, the therapy agreement includes a minimum weight value, for example, at a BMI of 15.0 or in some cases 14.5.

If this value is undershot, psychotherapy is interrupted. The patient must undergo treatment in a clinic until the minimum weight is exceeded again and psychotherapy can be resumed. At the beginning of treatment, denial of one's own underweight can only be addressed by setting such a boundary, because the patient would be inaccessible to discussion. Some patients test whether the therapist is really serious and will interrupt psychotherapy if the minimum weight is undershot, and of course, whether they can return immediately once they exceed it. Most patients balance for a longer time just above the minimum weight without ever falling below it. For them, the therapist's concern is important, but also the knowledge that there is a boundary here that cannot be crossed despite internal denial. By perceiving the numbers and accepting the lower limit, denial is loosened. The weight, its fluctuations, the triggers for these, and the associated feelings can be discussed more and more in therapy, so that the underweight no longer needs to be denied, but can be seen as an indicator of emotional conflicts.

3.2.2 Dissociations

▶ Human experience is composed of perceptions from all our six sensory channels, thought processes, conscious and unconscious feelings, as well as impulses to act, all of which are complexly associated, i.e., connected and integrated. In dissociation, there are very different separations of these associations, leading to a disintegration and fragmentation of consciousness. Thought, action, perception, or emotional processes that actually belong together break down into largely separate, uncontrolled parts and individual phenomena.

As early as 1889, Pierre Janet coined the term dissociation as a consequence of traumatization, which is still considered one of the main causes today. In 1980, the diverse symptoms triggered by dissociations were included in the DSM (Diagnostic and Statistical Manual of Mental Disorders of the American Psychiatric Association), and in 1992 in the ICD10 of the World Health Organization. Dissociations occur in milder form in almost everyone at some point, for example, in the feeling of being beside oneself for a while after a car accident or a frightening experience. Outpatient psychiatric patients have pronounced dissociations in 15% of cases, and in inpatient settings even 30% of cases.

The very diverse forms of dissociation can be assigned to three main groups:

1. Derealization: There is a separation between the self and external reality, which is perceived as strange, unreal, distant, like a pseudo-world, disconnected from one's own experience, as if behind a dense fog, a thick pane of glass, like a nightmare or a dream that will hopefully end soon. Internally, there is a complete emotional emptiness, but sometimes also intense fear or a feeling of abandonment and being lost.

2. Depersonalization: The person feels alien in their own body, which does not seem to belong to them, which can sometimes move normally on the outside, sometimes becomes completely paralyzed (stupor) and can no longer be controlled, and sometimes is shaken by epilepsy-like seizures without loss of consciousness, by cramps or tremors. Usually, autoscopy occurs, in which one's own body is perceived from the outside, from the ceiling of the room or a position above the right shoulder, sometimes also from inside, from an empty abdominal cavity.
3. Dissociated self-parts: In all of us, self-parts from different developmental phases are stored. They arise in dyadic relationships with other people to whom we are emotionally connected in very different ways, for example, when we are happy about our mother's loving gesture or frightened by our father's anger. We internalize these experiences by storing imagos, inner images of ourselves and the other, the object, which are connected by the emotions experienced, as inner dyadic relationships, as dyads, in our emotional memory, partly consciously, partly unconsciously. The connections between these self-parts or these dyads can be more or less strongly separated from each other. In the extreme case of multiple personality, for example, a five-year-old self-part of a patient, who is anxiously connected to an angry father image, takes complete control of the psychic processes, without any access to other younger selves, to adolescent self-parts, or the adult inner person. The five-year-old does not remember the times of day when she was not in the foreground, nor do the other self-parts remember the time of the five-year-old. This leads to amnesia for large parts of the day or week. If the dissociation is not quite so pronounced, other self-parts and the adult self can still be sensed or intuited behind the five-year-old, but faintly and barely accessible. When younger selves are in the foreground, adequate, adult behavior in many situations is hardly possible. If object imagos, i.e., internalized images of other people, are in the foreground of action in this way, the patient's behavior appears as if possessed by a foreign spirit. When, in the case of identification with the aggressor, a perpetrator object controls the actions, the victim of traumatization can become the perpetrator and inflict on another person the same things they once had to endure as a child, such as violence or sexual abuse. The more strongly the connection to the victim self-part is severed, the less shame or guilt is experienced by the perpetrator part.

At the beginning of therapy, patients sometimes name dissociations because they have already become aware of them, but sometimes not, because they are part of normal, everyday life. In such cases, the therapist should address and clarify them when dissociative phenomena from everyday life are described or appear directly in the therapeutic contact. Their processing and gradual reduction should be a focus in the first part of treatment, as otherwise the patient can neither arrive in therapy nor develop a stable working relationship with the therapist. Often, dissociations then recede surprisingly quickly. Otherwise, they become an almost insurmountable resistance to insight and change.

Example

Lena is 23 and shortly after the start of the therapy session, she enters a state of derealization. Everything seems to her to be behind a thick glass wall, appears distant and strange. My voice reaches her as if from another world. Outwardly, she appears frozen, sits completely motionless, cannot speak, and cannot answer my questions, not even by nodding. I fetch her a glass of water and gently hold it to her hand so that she feels the coolness of the water and, with great effort, is able to grasp the glass and finally take a sip. Another option would have been to hold an open bottle of ammonia under her nose, place an ice pack in her hand, or something similar. In dialectical behavior therapy according to Linehan (2008), various such stimuli are included that can significantly improve severe derealizations, which the therapist cannot change with words alone. Already in the preliminary discussions of therapy and later in the initial phase, a list of stimuli is created with the patient that can help her out of these extreme states. She puts together an emergency kit and always has a capsule of ammonia, a bag of chili gummy bears, a spiky massage ball, a rubber band, or something else that triggers stronger sensations with her. She can either use these herself or discuss with close contacts to give them to her in such states. Often, these skills replace self-injurious behaviors, such as cutting or burning oneself, which in borderline patients or trauma survivors often served to escape tormenting derealizations. In the therapy session, we do not want the patient to cut herself; rather, our task is to show her other ways to come out of derealization.

When the patient is able to speak again, the "1, 2, 3, 4, 5" exercise might follow. In this, I ask Lena to first name one thing she sees, one thing she hears, and one thing she feels on her body, then two, three, four, and finally five. At first, it is still difficult for her to say or name something, but it becomes easier and easier. Without these and other techniques, which were originally discovered and found helpful by those affected and later further developed by behavioral therapy in DBT, we would not be able to make contact with a derealized patient; instead, Lena would, in the worst case, sit in front of me in a stuporous, frozen state for the entire session. This would prevent any therapeutic dialogue, any change, and would thus represent a massive resistance in treatment.

After Lena is able to speak again, the glass wall she experiences between herself and the world has become much thinner. I ask her if she remembers what triggered this state, what the trigger was. She recalls that she experienced my gaze when she arrived and during the greeting as serious, almost stern, which reminded her of her father's strict, angry face, which was often the harbinger of his beatings with his hand or with objects, something that recurred throughout many years of her childhood. She felt as if she were in a nightmare that had to end soon, later far away, as if behind glass, as if it were not really happening to her. During puberty, she began to inflict small cuts on her arms and legs, which at first helped her out of these derealization states. Later, she hardly felt more superficial cuts, just as she hardly felt her father's weaker blows, so she inflicted very deep cuts on herself, which left wide scars and often required emergency medical treatment. By learning these skills and becoming aware of triggers, she was soon able to forgo self-injury and intercept derealizations herself before they became too strong, and eventually, as therapy progressed, they disappeared entirely. It was also helpful that I commented on her perception, that I had seemed stern, by tuning in to myself and sharing that it was the last session of the day and I had felt somewhat exhausted and tense when she arrived, so I was probably a bit less open and friendly in my greeting than usual. This confirms the patient's perception that something was different, but also helps her understand that such a face does not always mean anger and impending violence. The improved perception of others further reduced derealizations. It becomes clear that much more is needed here than mere mirroring, interpretation, or explanation of what happened. At the onset of the described derealization, I had said to Lena: "You seem very far away today." Even if Lena had been able to answer me, that alone would not have significantly improved the derealization.

Lena had already experienced depersonalizations in the preliminary discussions. She no longer felt her body as belonging to herself, but instead slipped into a perceptual position high up at the ceiling of the room, from where she saw a young woman who was unfamiliar to her and who was not herself. I had the impression that she spoke about herself and her experiences of the past few days as if she were talking about a stranger. When I mirrored this to her, she was able to tell me about her position at the ceiling. The trigger here was a faint smell of disinfectant when she entered the practice room, which reminded her of the smell of alcohol, which with her father was often the harbinger of sexual abuse. As a child, she had viewed these abuse situations from above, from the ceiling, which greatly reduced, and sometimes even completely switched off, the pain, the terrible fear, and the disgust she suffered. Here, too, discussing the trigger, the alcohol-like smell, was important in order to better anticipate that she might experience a depersonalization. I explained to her that it might have been disinfectant that I had sprayed on my hands before the session. I offered to teach her the imagination of the inner observer (Reddemann, 2021). We explain that every person has a part within themselves that only observes, without feeling anything, like a kind of neutral chronicler. With this observer part, the patient consciously places herself in the position outside herself that she knows from depersonalizations. Lena sent the observer to the ceiling. I asked the observer about its perception: "What is the body doing?" The observer described how the body was sitting far forward on the chair, the feet tense on the floor, the arms cramped in front of the chest, and the face appeared pale and white. Then I asked the observer: "What are the feelings doing?" The observer was able to perceive a queasy feeling of fear, as well as shame. Third, I asked the observer about the thoughts, which the observer described as confused, chaotic, and fragmented. In later observer imagination exercises, I offered as support that Lena could try to imagine the feelings as colors and the thoughts as animals, which helped her to get an even more differentiated picture of her inner life.

At the end, I ask the observer to return to the body, thereby dissolving the artificially induced depersonalization. In this way, Lena learned to consciously and self-directedly induce a state similar to dissociation, thereby reducing her fears and at the same time gaining clarity about her condition. She and many others found this imagination technique very helpful, and it contributed to a rapid subsiding of the depersonalizations. Here, too, merely discussing and interpreting the depersonalization would not be sufficient to resolve it; rather, it would manifest as resistance in therapy, because the patient would, quite literally, always check out as soon as things became too emotional.

Finally, Lena also had dissociated self-parts that were not completely, but in some cases very extensively, separated from each other. Since there were still fragile connections between the five-year-old, the twelve-year-old, the adult, and other parts, this was not a case of multiple personality in the strict sense, but rather of more or less strongly dissociated parts, as is often seen in traumatized and borderline patients. I suggested to Lena that she record the therapy sessions with her smartphone and listen to them again later. She was often able to remember only small parts of the session, especially when younger selves were at the forefront. In the protected environment of her home, the adult self would then listen to the recording, so that what was experienced and spoken could be incorporated into the memory accessible to almost all parts. At the same time, this strengthened the connections, the associations between the different parts, thus counteracting dissociation. I also worked imaginatively with the younger selves by asking Lena to create images of the respective part. For example, the image appeared of Lena as a five-year-old girl, fearfully huddled in a corner of the hallway, her head resting on her bent knees, looking at the floor. Within the imagination, I helped Lena to care for the five-year-old self. A round, very loving, motherly woman appeared, who took the child by the hand and brought her home, where she received something warm to eat and drink, and could then sit on her lap and cuddle, so that she no longer felt anxious and powerless, but safe and held. After Lena had done this imagination with other, younger selves several times in therapy, she increasingly managed to care for younger selves imaginatively on her own, for example when she felt anxious or powerless at home or in interactions with other people. As a result, she no longer remained for hours in the dissociated position of the five-year-old child, but was able to involve other, more adult parts of her own self or internalized objects to calm herself. In therapy, the younger selves were then discussed in detail, for example, why the five-year-old had to hide fearfully and powerlessly in a corner. Lena was deeply moved by the film "Be a Winner" by Soleen Yusef, in which the director, who comes from the Kurdish part of Iraq, describes her escape to Germany at the age of 11. In touching scenes, the girl Mona, in conflictual and frightening situations in Germany, imagines herself back in her homeland, where her aunt Helim appears, smiles at her, and encourages her. Inner, imaginative dialogues with good, loving objects that give us support and comfort are depicted in this film as vividly and comprehensibly as rarely elsewhere. ◀

Conclusion

According to Luborsky (1984), psychodynamic therapies consist, in varying phases, of supportive and expressive approaches in different proportions. The imaginative care of younger selves is more of a supportive method. However, this transitions seamlessly into expressive work, as it helps to clarify and work through an internalized relationship dynamic, allowing us to better understand when certain fears arose and when they appear today. If the patient were to always feel dissociatively like the younger self, without access to observing or adult self-parts, a massive resistance would stand in the way of expressive processing, which she could not overcome despite her best intentions.

3.2.3 Introjection

> Ferenczi (1910) introduced the concept of introjection, which was further elaborated by Klein (1946) through the image of the good and bad mother's breast, from which the baby takes in the first contents from another person. This involves not only the intake of mother's milk. The child also internalizes the experiences of its parents and other significant caregivers, i.e., their feelings, their perceptions of other people and of the child itself, their images, and later also their words and thoughts.

Introjection serves, on the one hand, to help the baby cope with early separations from its mother, which it can endure longer the more it has taken in from her. In addition, introjection represents the first step in developing one's own personality from all that is taken in from outside. Introjection must be distinguished from internalization, in which something from outside is not only taken in but also processed and internally modified. Something introjected is a photographic memory of an experience or the absorbed, undigested emotional experience of another. Internalized objects, on the other hand, are processed images of other people and of their experiences and behaviors. Thus, the internalized representation of the mother often differs significantly between two siblings, both in the inner image of her appearance and in her way of relating. This section deals with the unprocessed form of intake, with introjection.

In fairy tales, introjections are illustrated, for example, by wolves who swallow Little Red Riding Hood, her grandmother, kids, or others, but do not tear or injure them with their teeth or digest them in their stomachs. They can be retrieved in unchanged, unprocessed form. The many generations of people who have passed on and slightly altered fairy tales here reflect a fundamental experience: that sometimes we take in others or something foreign without being able to digest or process it at all.

In treatment, we encounter introjections primarily in two areas:

1. In flashbacks, traumatized individuals often suddenly experience memories of the traumatic events, triggered by cues, sometimes very unspecific stimuli associated with the traumatic situation, such as the smell of a cigarette for a patient whose grandfather

always smoked in the basement before sexually abusing her. If she got off a bus and smelled cigarette smoke, she would suddenly see the abuse scene in every detail. She felt like a four-year-old girl, with all the fears, feelings of disgust and powerlessness, even the physical pain. In front of her, she saw the perpetrator introject, the grandfather, just as he had stood before her and looked at her back then. Outside of such flashbacks, she did not remember the abuse situation. Van der Kolk (2000) assumes that memories from traumatic situations are not stored in autobiographical memory like other experiences, but as non-symbolized, unprocessed memory traces in the trauma memory, which is more or less dissociated from the rest of memory in order to protect the everyday personality. Terrible life experiences, by definition, become traumatic events when they far exceed the affected person's coping and processing abilities, leaving them feeling helpless, defenseless, and powerless. What has been suffered can only be stored undigested, as far away from other memories as possible, and frozen. As a result, it is either not accessible at all in therapy or triggers such strong states of arousal that processing is not possible. Such flashbacks therefore represent a resistance to treatment. Only after stabilizing, supportive work with skills and imagination is trauma confrontation possible, allowing patients to look at the traumatic experiences in detail, feel all the feelings of disgust, anger, fear, and grief with the help of another who provides support and comfort, and gradually process what was suffered so that it is incorporated into autobiographical memory and becomes consciously accessible. Trauma confrontation in behavioral therapy settings is more likely to occur via EMDR, Eye Movement Desensitization and Reprocessing (see Bisson et al., 2007), and in psychodynamic settings via the observer or screen technique (Reddemann, 2021). Here, an additional trauma therapy qualification is required for the therapist.

2. People who were exposed to emotional abuse as children had to take in their parents' feelings, such as anger, fear, or sadness, at an early age without being able to process them, so that these remain within them as something undigested. Instead of the parents functioning as containers for their children's feelings, pre-digesting them and reflecting them back to the children, the children are parentified, i.e., made into parents and filled with the unprocessed conflicts of the parents. Often, they also tend to introject something from others as adults.

Example

Emilia, a bulimic patient who, even as a child, had to listen for hours to her mother's distress over her marriage to the manic-depressive father, her mother's emotional and sexual longings for other men, memories of her mother's unhappy childhood, and all her fears—and had to absorb all of this—was, even as an adult and during therapy, still used by her mother as a "garbage can" for all her feelings. Thus, she was the only one who knew about her mother's years-long sexual affair with another man, but had to promise not to tell anyone. Her father, too, would turn to her during phases of his illness with intense feelings of grief or hatred. It was enough for her to hint that she did not have the time or inner space to listen to him right then, or to ask if they could talk about it later, for him to angrily reject her, saying she was no longer his daughter. She got used to swallowing, wordlessly and without protest, whatever he conveyed to her. In a therapy session, she shamefully recounted a bulimic episode the previous evening, during which she vomited up the food she had hastily devoured. When nothing but liquid came up and she thought she had vomited everything, she still had a sensation in her gastrointestinal tract that there was something left she could not expel, but she could not say whether it was food or feelings. In my countertransference, I experienced strong feelings of anger, aversion, and disgust toward the patient, which I initially attributed to the fact that she had staged a bulimic episode the evening before a therapy session that had been prepared for all day, instead of waiting for the session the next day and discussing everything there—as if she had taken the easy way out, throwing up in her own toilet instead of here. However, the intensity of my feelings led me to suspect that she had deposited feelings in me as a garbage can, which I first wanted to understand and pre-digest before intervening in any way. She spoke about the time immediately before the bulimic episode. It turned out that she had had a long conversation with her mother, during which her mother had filled her with marital problems and new secrets. She could not feel or name any emotions about this, so, drawing on Fonagy and Target (2015), I mirrored the feelings to her in a marked way, which I had held and contained in myself for her for a while: "I could imagine that you felt a bit of anger and aversion when your mother once again used you as a garbage can for her feelings, maybe even a little disgust." The marking is done with words like "a bit" or "a little," so that we return the patient's feelings to her, toned down, in small bites from our container, while "maybe" indicates that we are offering a possibility, but that it could also be different, that we do not want to pin her down. Emilia could not immediately associate the vague feeling that remained after the bulimic episode with these mirrored feelings. Therefore, I moved on to the second stage of mirroring: "In me, you triggered such feelings of a bit of anger, aversion, and a little disgust when you told me about what happened." Very spontaneously and vehemently, she replied, "So you felt the same way with me as I often do with my mother when she tells me all her garbage." Very emotional memories of scenes surfaced, of anger and disgust toward her mother, but immediately also feelings of guilt, because she was not supposed to have these feelings, but was always supposed to be available for her mother. Only when the patient was increasingly able to vent her anger at always being used as a "garbage can" with me, and I helped her digest what had happened, did the vague feeling of pressure in her gastrointestinal tract disappear. As treatment progressed, I repeatedly made myself available as a garbage can, as a container for the patient's undigested feelings. I introjected them, processed them, and then returned them to the patient in digested form, which she could then take in and process further herself. In this way, something was made up for that the mother should have done with her as a baby and toddler, instead of reversing the roles and abusing the patient as a garbage can for her feelings. The more the patient was able to feel her anger, aversion, and disgust when her mother or someone else tried to fill her with their garbage, the more consciously she could decide whether and how much of it she wanted to take in, so that as therapy progressed, there was eventually nothing left that she unconsciously swallowed and tried to expel bulimically. ◀

Conclusion
In these treatments, an interpretation of introjection or the current conflict dynamic is often not sufficient. Especially with patients with structural ego impairments, an insurmountable resistance would arise if the treatment were not expanded by the technique of containing (Bion, 1962; Crepaldi, 2022). Possible difficulties on the part of the therapist in perceiving certain feelings within themselves, such as anger at or disgust toward the patient, make containing more difficult and are therefore described under countertransference resistances.

3.2.4 Projection

▶ In projection, what is internal is supposed to be external (König, 1997). The internal consists of object dyads, i.e., representations of relationships between a part of the self and an internal image of another person, an object representation. The self-part and the object are connected to each other by feelings. They can be projected onto other people, but also onto animals or objects. It does not matter whether the target of the projection notices or senses what is being projected onto it.

There are therefore two types of projections:

1. An internal object image, such as the image of the angry father, the rejecting mother, prohibitive conscience parts from the superego, but also ego ideals, are experienced in another person or in religious symbols, such as the cross. A patient had the experience that other people would look at him disparagingly, contemptuously, as if he were something bothersome, whenever he boarded a bus. Even if he pulled his hood far over his face and looked down, the other passengers could still recognize what a bad person he was and turn away in disgust, even if he entered through the very last door and stayed there. He projected his rejecting father onto the other passengers, from whom, it seemed, just as much aversion and contempt emanated as he had felt from his father when he came home and his father was sitting at the kitchen table. The early dyad was fully enacted: the childlike self-part, who feels ashamed, was experienced internally by the patient, the aggressive, rejecting father part in the others. The projection onto the bus passengers relieved the patient: the rejection was limited

to certain external situations, such as on the bus. Without projection, he would have felt his own self-rejection constantly inside, no matter where he was. In this way, the rejection was limited to a few situations and a few external objects, which he then tried to avoid. That is the gain from this defense. The other passengers were unaware of his projection. As treatment progressed, he noticed that they hardly noticed him at all, at most found him a little anxious, but quickly returned to their phones. In therapy, projections of this kind are what Freud called transference. The patient quickly experienced the therapist as contemptuous and rejecting, which only became clear to the therapist after some time, after he addressed small signs of shyness and concealment. In another defense mechanism, projective identification, the therapist is unconsciously manipulated to become identical with the projection, i.e., he feels like the rejecting father toward the patient. A projection, on the other hand, is conveyed much less clearly or not at all for a long time. Therefore, it was important for the therapist to pay very close attention to small signals and address them in order to clarify the projection. Otherwise, the patient would have hardly benefited from treatment with a therapist whom he experienced as rejecting and contemptuous.

2. Self-parts can also be projected. The same patient experienced a saleswoman at the bakery as being in love with him, even though she actually served him just as she did the customers before and after him. He was sure he perceived small signals, such as her winking at him, placing the bread a little more lovingly than for others, or having more warmth in her voice. He was unsettled and fascinated by her supposed courtship. He decided not to let anything show, but was surprised that she seemed to continue loving him. Further exploration revealed that he was projecting a child-like self-part onto the saleswoman, who had long tried to convey loving feelings to his mother, while the patient himself was in the role of the withdrawn mother, who was more frightened than touched by this, who could not do anything with her son's love and therefore did not respond to it. Self-parts are especially projected when they are associated with a lot of shame. The patient had experienced himself early on as an unlovable child, who only cautiously and inconspicuously expressed his affection for his mother, but still felt rejected by it. Weiss (1993) called this the role reversal test: the patient slips into the role of a parent and behaves toward the therapist, who is assigned the child role, as the parent once did toward the child. Here, too, it took some time before the therapist became aware of similar projections onto himself as onto the saleswoman. When he asked why the patient quickly withdrew his hand during greetings and crept into the office with his head down, the patient was able to say that he feared the therapist might be fond of him, similar to the saleswoman, which greatly unsettled him. Often it is such micro-scenes that make it possible to understand projections. Had the therapist focused only on what the patient addressed in the session, this projection would have become a massive resistance. Any understanding, any friendliness from the therapist would have led to further withdrawal and anxiety in the patient, perhaps even to termination of treatment.

Conclusion

Projections occur particularly intensely in schizophrenic patients. In some cases, they do not even need an external object in the sense of another person or thing, because they can project virtually into nothingness, for example by hearing a voice without seeing anything that is speaking. Paranoid patients project onto existing external objects, such as passengers on a bus or saleswomen, even if these show no external signs that even remotely correspond to the projection. To a lesser extent, however, projection is a very common defense mechanism that occurs in varying degrees in every person. Recognizing them in therapy helps us prevent them from becoming a resistance.

3.2.5 Projective Identification

> Projective identification is one of the interpersonal defense mechanisms that do not occur solely intrapsychically, but rather involve other people in stabilizing one's own psychological equilibrium, thereby altering and straining the relationships in question. Unwanted aspects of one's own experience are first projected onto others, who are then, in a second step, brought—usually through unconscious manipulations—to feel and act in ways that actually correspond to what was projected onto them.

Klein (1946) was the first to name this defense mechanism. Since then, the concept has evolved significantly. Here, it does not stop at projection, of which the other person is hardly or not at all aware; rather, the counterpart is unconsciously manipulated through interaction so that they internally identify with what has been projected. The patient does not merely experience the therapist as a rejecting, contemptuous father, as described in the previous section on projection; instead, the therapist actually feels these emotions toward the patient, and the earlier the patient's disturbance and the more impaired their personality structure, the stronger these feelings become.

Psychotic and borderline patients have internal images of other people, which we refer to as part-objects, since they experience them as only good, without any bad sides, or as only bad, without the slightest good. Accordingly, the intensity of what they trigger in therapists can be considerable. When, in the acute psychiatric clinic where I worked for 10 years, a borderline patient triggered highly aggressive and contemptuous feelings in everyone on the team, accompanied by the idea that we would prefer to throw her out, we were alarmed and thought of suicidality. Often, she had projected an internal bad part-object onto the team members and unconsciously manipulated them into identifying with it, so that we felt and thought similarly to her—that we did not want her, could not tolerate her, that she would be better off away from us. In conversation, it often became apparent that the patient had come to us seeking support and care, but felt just as rejected and cast out by us as by her family and many other people, and was therefore indeed contemplating suicide.

> "In borderline patients, projective identifications are particularly effective. If they transfer a bad object, they generate rejecting feelings in the therapist through the interactional component of projective identification, feelings that correspond to those of a bad object and can lead the therapist to quickly become convinced that they 'cannot work' with the patient. Other borderline patients, who transfer a good object onto the therapist, seduce the therapist through the interactional component of projective identification into making an overoptimistic prognosis, offering them dysfunctional therapy options, and engaging in dysfunctional efforts on their behalf. When making treatment indications, it is important to be aware of the high effectiveness of projective identifications in borderline patients. If a realistic assessment of therapeutic possibilities is lacking, inappropriate decisions are made. These may concern whether to take the patient into treatment at all. Some therapists overload themselves with borderline patients, which can impair the quality of their work. If borderline patients initially transfer a bad object, the chances for a therapeutic working relationship are low. This applies to the patient's motivation to engage in a working relationship, but also to the therapist's motivation to work with the patient. Some patients evoke aversive feelings in the therapist through projective identification that exceed a realistic level. The therapist then considers them untreatable and advises against psychotherapy, even though they might have a chance of improvement with another therapist who would have triggered a different transference in them." (König, 2004, pp. 148 f.)

Thus, projective identification can become a resistance originating from both sides and can even influence fundamental considerations regarding the initiation and indication of treatment.

While Clarkin, Yeomans, and Kernberg (2008) consider projective identification to be a rather early, primitive form of defense that occurs primarily in personality-disordered individuals, I share König's position (1993, 1995, 1997, 2004) that it is also found in neurotic and psychologically healthy individuals.

König (1993, pp. 21 f.) distinguishes four forms of projective identification, which are not limited to the analytic treatment setting:

> "- Projective identification of the transference type aims to make transference real, in order to achieve a feeling of security [...] or, more broadly, of familiarity [...]—a sense of familiarity that evokes a feeling of safety.
>
> - Projective identification of the conflict-relief type aims to turn an internal conflict into an interpersonal one, which relieves the patient's inner world.
> - Projective identification of the communicative type aims to ensure that patient and analyst feel the same, thereby enabling better understanding.
> - Accordingly, one can also assume a projective identification of the demarcation type. People with fears of fusion elicit unempathic behavior in the other person by projectively identifying them with an unempathic mother or father object. This reinforces their fantasy that the other is completely different and not similar, which reduces their fears of fusion. An analyst should keep this in mind when difficulties arise in empathizing with the patient."

Example

Silvy cancels her therapy session on Thursday because she has an appointment at the employment office. Later, she calls again to ask if she can still come, which the therapist affirms, and whether it would be all right with him if she now came after all, which he also affirms. When she arrives a few minutes late for the session, she asks if he would have preferred to have the time off, since therapists are always so overworked. The therapist feels a bit annoyed and irritated, but does not immediately find a suitable intervention to bring these still vague feelings into the conversation. Therefore, he denies the question, remarking that it is her appointment and he is glad she came. The patient then falls silent. The therapist asks what is on her mind, to which she shrugs her shoulders and says, "No idea!" After some pondering, she adds that it must be interesting for the therapist if she says something. The therapist tries with a few questions to find out why she believes that, why she can only talk about something that interests him and not about what moves her, why it was important to her to keep the appointment today after all, what she actually did at the employment office. Most of the time, she responds with the shoulder-shrugging "No idea!" The therapist feels increasingly irritated and at the same time like a strict examiner, whose examinee's unwillingness and ignorance is increasingly annoying. He says to her, "I am more and more falling into the role of an examiner who asks you one question after another and gets no real answer." Silvy says triumphantly, "I know that very well from my life, starting with my father, many people were like that with me. My father sometimes took me for a walk on Sundays, which always made me very happy. Finally, he had time for me. Then we would go into churches, which he was interested in architecturally. Suddenly, he would ask me about a picture, a piece of furniture, or something else, what it was. If I didn't know, he was very disappointed in me and remained withdrawn for the rest of the time. Even at 8, I tried to read up on what everything was in a church, so I would have answers to his questions. But again and again, we quickly reached the point where I didn't know something and had to say: No idea!" The therapist reflects the palpable fear of not immediately knowing the right answer to a question, but also the anger contained in the somewhat flippant Berlin dialect expression: "No idea!" She vehemently confirms both feelings and is able to explore them further in the conversation, so that a lot of anger toward her father and other men who were similar examiners came to light. Had the therapist remained in the role of the annoyed examiner, the projective identification with a scrutinizing father object would have created a serious resistance in the therapy. ◀

Conclusion

Projective identifications can endanger treatments by preventing them from taking place at all, leading to incorrect treatment indications, or preventing empathy. However, if it is possible to utilize their communicative and conflict-relieving aspects, they can improve understanding and significantly accelerate treatment.

3.2.6 Identification with the Aggressor

> When children are sexually abused, exposed to physical or emotional violence, or severely neglected by parents or other caregivers on whom they depend and from whom they expect protection, they are subjected to existential feelings of fear, powerlessness, and helplessness. They internalize the image of the attacker as a perpetrator introject and adopt his perspective, so that they no longer experience themselves as defenseless and powerless, but as powerful and in control of the situation.

This identification with the aggressor is, alongside the dissociation described above, often the only defense mechanism left to victims of traumatic violence that cannot be coped with using existing ego functions, allowing for psychological survival.

In a milder form, this defense mechanism can occur in all people. Anna Freud (1936, pp. 109 f.) describes a vivid example:

> "August Aichhorn reports from his practice as an educational counselor about the case of an elementary school student who was referred to him for making faces. The teacher complains that the boy cannot accept reprimands and admonitions in a normal way. On such occasions, he makes faces... The teacher's statements are easily confirmed; the grimacing is repeated during the counseling session. At the same time, the three-way conversation brings clarification of the situation. Careful observation of the two shows that the boy's grimaces are nothing more than a distorted reflection of the angry teacher's facial expressions. The boy, who is supposed to withstand the teacher's reprimand, copes with his fear through involuntary imitation of the angry person. He takes on the teacher's anger himself and follows the teacher's words with the teacher's own, unrecognized expressive movements. Here, grimacing thus serves to align or identify with the feared object in the external world."

Ferenczi (1933) dealt extensively with the sexual traumatization of children. In doing so, he took up the seduction theory that shaped Freud's early publications, but from which Freud later distanced himself out of shock at the extent of sexual violence inflicted on children. Ferenczi believed that children, out of fear of the uninhibited and deranged adults to whom they are exposed, identify with them in order to regain control over the incomprehensible, unbearable situation. The image of the perpetrator is internalized, the event is experienced from his perspective, so that the terrible thing that is happening seems right. The child sees everything through the eyes of the perpetrator and identifies with his feelings of power and hatred.

This defense mechanism became known under the term "Stockholm Syndrome," which goes back to a hostage situation at Norrmalmstorg in Stockholm in 1973. During a bank robbery, four hostages were held for over 131 hours. The Stockholm police psychologist Nils Bejerot coined the term to describe the unusual and disturbing affection the hostages showed toward their captors. The hostage-taker, the incestuous father, the sadistic mother, but also the concentration camp commandant or the torturer in a dictatorship—people may carry such figures within them for a lifetime and give them a place in their lives. Gruen (2000) aptly called this in the title of his book *The Stranger Within Us* and sees it as a betrayal of the self.

Identification with the aggressor can manifest in life after the trauma in two ways:

1. In the active mode, the traumatized person never wants to be a victim again and, at the latest from adolescence, behaves only like the perpetrator; in adults, this can occur immediately after surviving the trauma. The sexually abused boy abuses his younger siblings or later his own children. Torture victims become torturers. Children left alone for days become similarly neglectful parents. Men tend to take this path more often.
2. In the passive mode, the victim of, for example, childhood sexual abuse remains in the victim position and, as an adult, becomes a prostitute. She feels she is good for nothing else and believes that what is done to her body every day is right. To alleviate pain, disgust, and fear, she experiences her body from the outside, from the perspective of her clients, and identifies with their feelings of power and arousal. It is estimated that 90% of prostitutes were once sexually abused girls. In a similar way, children who were aggressively abused may, as adults, seek out partnerships in which they experience severe violence. As mentioned above, in Germany every 3 minutes a girl or woman suffers domestic violence at the hands of close relatives. It is apparent that women tend to be more inclined toward this mode.

In these ways, transgenerational traumatization occurs, i.e., the transmission of psychological trauma from generation to generation.

In psychotherapy, resistance in the active mode arises from the fact that patients are still very strongly identified with the perpetrators. Even if they are being treated in prison or have already served their sentence, they cannot see anything wrong in their actions. To do so, they would have to give up their identification with the aggressor, which would make them aware of the terrible things they have done to others and what was done to them by someone who was actually a beloved parent, whom they trusted and from whom they expected protection. In group therapy, in the presence of other perpetrators, this is often easier for them, for example in prison or in outpatient facilities such as "Kind im Zentrum" in Berlin. Hirsch (2018) works with mixed groups in which perpetrators and victims of sexual abuse meet. In the presence of other perpetrators or victims, they feel more exposed, making it easier for them to relinquish identification with the perpetrator, to painfully confront their guilt, but also the horror they themselves suffered, which often leads to deep depression with intense suicidal impulses. In individual therapy, it is much harder for them to give up identification with the aggressor, because they suspect that the person sitting across from them has not accumulated guilt in a similar way, and they would be mortified with shame if they admitted their actions. It is therefore especially important here to repeatedly address this resistance in order to gradually reduce it together, so that shame, guilt, and one's own suffering can become consciously bearable in manageable doses.

For female patients in the passive mode, the starting point is the therapist's witnessing, as Benjamin (2019, 2020) calls it. The parent who looks away, who neither helped the abused or sexually abused child nor told them that what happened to them was not right, conveys to the child that all of it is perfectly acceptable. The child has little choice but to identify with the perpetrator in order to somehow cope with their disturbing feelings. The therapist is often the first witness to acknowledge that something terrible happened back then, something that should never be done to a human being. Nevertheless, even after this, the first steps toward dealing with the feelings left by the trauma are very unsettling and therefore met with resistance. Imaginative work with perpetrator introjects according to Reddemann (2021) is helpful, in which internalized perpetrator parts are depicted in guided daydreams as images, opening up an inner dialogue with them and helping to gradually relinquish identification with the aggressors.

Example

As a child, Viktoria suffered years of sexual abuse by her father. Feeling that she was good for nothing else anyway, she turned to prostitution. During the violent acts of clients and pimps, she sometimes dissociated, seeing everything as a neutral observer from the ceiling, but most often she identified with the perpetrators and tried to perceive the humiliation of her body from their position of power. After a particularly violent experience, she was so badly injured that she needed to be hospitalized. The psychologist who called in the surgery team became the first witness to emotionally acknowledge that everything that had happened to her was cruel violence. Viktoria initially reacted with surprise, but also with relief, when she could not help but accept the psychologist's words herself. The more she was able to acknowledge them internally, the more sadness and anger about all she had suffered became tangible for her. After leaving the hospital, she secretly left her hometown to escape the tight network of pimps and started a new life and psychotherapy with me in Berlin. In a phase of mourning, she was gradually able to reduce her identification with the aggressor. She met a kind young man who respected her boundaries and had a very loving family. This completely new world was so confusing and unsettling for her because she had never known relationships that were not exploitative and abusive. Again and again, the identification with the aggressor resurfaced, as she tried to get her partner to have violent sex with her, or wanted to leave him and return to prostitution. In this way, the repeatedly flaring identification with the perpetrator became a resistance to further development in therapy; without repeatedly working through it, she would likely have dropped out of therapy and returned to her old environment. ◀

3.2.7 Splitting, Primitive Idealization, and Devaluation

▶ Parts of the self, internal representations of objects, and feelings between the two are radically split into those that are absolutely only good, and those that are only evil or bad.

König (1997, p. 95) describes the process very vividly:

> "The ego of the person concerned also cannot bear to confront the fact that he himself, but also people in the outside world and people he remembers, can have both good and bad qualities. Since he experiences himself and other people in an immature, archaic way, qualities that are experienced as good or as bad (evil) are so strongly pronounced that they cannot coexist. The bad or evil in himself and in others must, so to speak, be placed in a reserve of 'bad or evil self' or in a reserve of 'bad or evil object' in order not to contaminate the good. Then the bad or evil can also be fought more easily without endangering the good. The 'good' is also locked away in a reserve for its protection. It is said that the self and the objects are split, namely into 'good' and 'bad' or 'evil'. This process is called splitting."

Klein (1957, p. 305) locates splitting as a primary defense mechanism very early in childhood:

> "Let us return to that process of splitting, which I understand as a prerequisite for a relative stability of the small infant; during the first months of his life, he usually keeps the good object far away from the bad one. In this way, he can preserve it on a fundamental level—which also means that the ego gains greater security."

Through what Klein (1957) called the depressive position, good and bad are brought together. The toddler, for example, who has forcefully pulled on his mother's necklace and visibly caused her pain, is shocked, sad, and remorseful about what he has done to his mother, which gave the position its name. He develops feelings of guilt, which later arise even at the impulse to want to pull hard on his mother's necklace again. He remembers having hurt her before by doing so. Gradually, the child internalizes that some things he does make other people happy, while others cause them pain; that he thinks good and bad things, feels and acts both well and badly, that he has good and bad sides, just as others do. His own self-parts and internal objects now become ambivalently invested: they are both good and bad at the same time. Mature feelings of guilt can be experienced. Sometimes, these already prevent him in advance from acting on a wish or impulse that could hurt others, or lead him afterwards to apologize.

If a child does not reach the depressive position, according to Clarkin, Yeomans, and Kernberg (2008, p. 5), a borderline personality organization develops:

> "If development proceeds normally, there is a gradual integration of these extremely good and bad self- and object representations over the first years of life, resulting in more complex and realistic internal representations of the self and others, and the recognition that people are a mixture of good and bad attributes and have the capacity to be gratifying at

> some moments and frustrating at others [...]. Children who develop borderline personality disorder lack this process of integration. Instead, the separation between idealized and persecutory aspects of highly affect-laden experiences becomes a stable, albeit pathological, intrapsychic structure."

If a child has already reached the depressive position, traumatic experiences can cause a regression back to splitting. Adults, too, after traumatic experiences such as war, abandon the depressive position and once again experience themselves and others as good or evil, friend or foe, perpetrator or victim. The term position expresses that this is not a phase that, once passed through, never returns, but rather something fragile that can be acquired, lost, and regained. Perpetrators, such as in cases of sexual abuse, have not reached the depressive position, so they feel no guilt toward the abused child, but at most a fear of punishment, of being caught and prosecuted.

Splitting is often accompanied by a primitive, absolutely unlimited idealization of the only good part-object or only good part of the self, because they do not have the slightest flaw or blemish, or by a primitive, complete devaluation of the bad part-object or part of the self, which are only black and bad and have not a single white spot, nothing good about them.

In the Grimm fairy tale "Hans My Hedgehog," the main character is physically split into two parts: Hans has the legs of a little boy, but his upper body is covered with spines, like a hedgehog. A princess whom he embraces suffers lifelong wounds that never heal. He is either a dear boy without fault or blame, or a bad, spiky hedgehog who injures and crosses boundaries (see also Röhr, 1996).

Example

Even when describing her current difficulties and problematic relationships in her professional, personal, and erotic life, the therapist struggled to form a picture of the other people involved or to even remotely understand their behavior. They were portrayed as either only loving, only good, completely free of any faults or negative sides, or, on the contrary, as entirely evil and dangerous. Taking the patient's history was actually quite feasible, as the patient could state exactly when she started school or what occupations her parents had and when. While she described her mother only in positive terms, attributing only good character traits to her, she was unable, despite repeated questioning by the therapist, to name even the slightest weakness, any fault, or any inappropriate behavior, whereas with her father she mentioned only hateful, destructive, and devious personality traits. All siblings, relatives, teachers, and other significant figures were either good or evil, but never a mix of both. With current significant others, the patient's perception often shifted, sometimes seemingly without cause: if a friend was just recently good and lovable, a single word or gesture could suffice for the patient to perceive her as completely malicious. Just as quickly, the patient could see herself, from one moment to the next, not as purely good but only as bad and corrupt, a burden and nuisance to everyone else. Because the therapist found it nearly impossible to empathize with or recognize the patient's view of life, significant others, and herself, she considered a transference-focused therapy according to Yeomans, Clarkin, and Kernberg (2017) to be indicated. Since we can only form a very vague idea of what the patient experiences outside, in this form of therapy for borderline patients, we focus on what happens in the transference, i.e., in the direct relationship between patient and therapist. For a long time, the patient experienced the therapist as only good, and herself at times also as only good, but sometimes suddenly shifting to feeling only bad, hateful, and evil. These shifts in perception were addressed, so that the patient gradually became very aware of her splitting, including the associated idealization of the good and devaluation of the bad self or object. One day, when the patient sat down in her chair on a hot summer day and opened a bottle of cola, a large amount of liquid sprayed onto the leather chair. The therapist reacted somewhat annoyed and asked the patient to go to the bathroom to wipe the splashes off the chair with a cloth and paper towel. She indignantly refused, as she saw herself as a purely good being who just wanted something to drink in the heat. She found the therapist to be unreasonably mean and heartless and accused her of professional failure: "My general practitioner also has chairs that can withstand things, and she cleans them afterwards if someone was incontinent or if blood was spilled. How is it my fault that you don't set up your practice properly? And I certainly don't see why I should wipe away a few spots—I'm the patient here and I didn't do it on purpose." The therapist wiped up the cola herself to prevent permanent damage to her furniture, but then worked through the incident intensively. It became clear that the patient had switched roles and taken on her father's perspective, who always claimed to be completely good and that only others did something wrong and were to blame for any problem, never himself, while the therapist embodied the bad, uncomprehending self that doesn't know what's going on, can't anticipate things, does everything wrong, and then even demands something from the good ones. After some time, the patient was able to admit that she actually knew that cola can be under a lot of pressure in great heat and can spray out when the bottle is opened, but that she hadn't thought of it at that moment because she was so thirsty for the invigorating drink and the therapist's care. She began to develop the first signs of guilt, at first barely noticeable, then very intense and tormenting, more than the situation warranted, and finally somewhere in between. She was sad and contrite for having caused damage to the therapist and her furniture, and relieved that the therapist accepted her apology and forgave her for what had happened. She realized that she could do something wrong even when she experienced herself as good and lovable, so that, gradually, over a longer process involving several such incidents, the depressive position and ambivalent representations of self and objects as simultaneously good and bad began to develop. ◀

3.3 Resistance through Mature Defense Mechanisms

> The emergence of more mature defense mechanisms depends on a degree of self-organization in which, on the one hand, the id and the ego are sufficiently and clearly separated from each other—that is, unconscious and conscious experience—and, on the other hand, the depressive position described in the previous section has been achieved.

If this depressive position must be relinquished again in the course of life, for example due to war trauma, already acquired ego functions are lost, as are more mature defense mechanisms. Ego organization reverts to primitive defense mechanisms in order to survive in a world experienced as threatening and full of mistrust, where there are only friends and enemies.

This section will describe the more mature defense mechanisms and the types of resistance they can lead to in psychotherapy.

3.3.1 Displacement

> Needs, wishes, fantasies, or impulses that are associated with anxiety, shame, or guilt are shifted from the person to whom they are actually directed onto another person or an object, where they can be satisfied with less or no anxiety, shame, or guilt.

Some people learn as babies that their oral wishes for comfort, soothing, or care are not answered directly, either because the parents do not understand them or because it is too much for the parents, so that any kind of crying leads to being nursed and fed, even if the baby is crying out of fear or sadness and not out of hunger. They internalize that these wishes are too much for their parents. All of them later displace these needs onto food, nicotine, alcohol, or drugs. These are supposed to quiet their crying, just as the too quickly and too often given breast milk used to take away their fears, soothe, comfort, stimulate, encourage, and energize them. This poisoned breast milk gives them everything they no longer dare to expect from people in direct interaction. When these needs are displaced onto other people, it is not those to whom they actually belong, but, for example, prostitutes. There, they are fulfilled through orally tinged sexuality, or more often directly through conversation. A patient who was a high-class prostitute at the beginning of her treatment reported that many of her clients would talk about themselves for 50 minutes and sometimes even cry with her before they remembered why they had officially come to her. By paying, the feeling of guilt for having satisfied forbidden needs not with an object but with another person is compensated. It is even more problematic when adults do not direct their oral wishes for care and comfort to their adult attachment figures, but instead displace them onto their children, who then have to fulfill them, which constitutes emotional abuse. We call this parentification, from the Latin "parentes" (parents) and "facere" (to make). Here, children are made into parents for their own parents.

Feelings of anger and desires for power can be displaced away from real people onto computer games, where they are acted out virtually, disguised as an avatar who shoots, tortures, or subjugates other beings. Here, too, displacement onto people is possible, for example, anger at an unjust, unappreciative boss, which is taken home and displaced onto the partner or even the children, who are then yelled at, humiliated, or beaten.

In phobias, there is a displacement of the underlying anxiety onto objectively relatively minor external dangers. In claustrophobia, the anxiety is triggered by the closing door of an elevator or bus. The patient fears that in the confined space, which she cannot leave for a while, she might suffocate or at least faint and be at the mercy of others. Usually, this is the fear of dependency, of psychological powerlessness in the sense of being at someone's mercy, of not being able to escape, which arises in a significant interpersonal relationship, such as a new romantic relationship, with family members, or with powerful superiors, and is displaced onto the bus or elevator. The patient can avoid these, whereas she often cannot so easily avoid the relationships she actually fears. Agoraphobia, on the other hand, is often the displacement of fears of autonomy, which the patient desires in interpersonal relationships, onto agoras, that is, large open spaces. She fears that something terrible could happen to her, the larger the space, the freer the surroundings, or the more people are present. She avoids these dangers, but in doing so also avoids autonomy, because she can often only leave the house and go somewhere accompanied by another person. In all phobias, we find such displacements. In psychotherapy, they become a form of resistance, because the patient, on the one hand, wants to get rid of her tormenting, constricting phobia, but on the other hand, the re-displacement onto the actual sources of anxiety is even more unsettling, at least as long as she has not understood why, for example, dependency or autonomy frighten her so much. Only when she begins to understand the irrational and often biographically rooted aspects of these overwhelming fears can she gradually undo the displacement.

▶ In treatment, we must pay attention to every kind of displacement, address it, understand it, and help patients to redirect the fulfillment of their needs back to the people to whom they actually belong, or at least to people who can fulfill them appropriately.

Example

In addiction clinics, the consumption of alcohol and drugs can largely be prevented through regulations, so that oral wishes can no longer be displaced onto the actual addictive substances and instead seek a new target. This may be increased consumption of nicotine or food, but this is often not enough. Therefore, the wishes are often and intensely directed at the therapists and staff, and sometimes at fellow patients. When I started working at age 24, after studying psychology, in a rehabilitation clinic that really should have been called a "re-displacement clinic," I briefly doubted whether the mostly middle-aged men would take me seriously at all. However, their wishes for comfort, soothing, and care were so strong that I felt them immediately and, together with the other staff and fellow patients in the groups, tried to fulfill them. In the evenings, I felt drained and empty, sometimes going to bed as early as 6 p.m. A psychoanalytic supervisor explained to me at the time the defense mechanism of displacement in my patients, which helped me to become more consciously aware of what was happening beneath the surface in direct contact with them. This allowed me to fulfill some of their oral wishes, and to name others. Some very early childhood needs, such as being held and carried back and forth by a good, loving mother as a toddler, could not be fulfilled in their original form. The patients could only mourn the fact that some wishes were never fulfilled in their early childhood and can never again be fulfilled in a childlike way. Through mourning, people can emotionally say goodbye to these early wishes and then no longer need to displace them. Resistance wants to maintain the displacement. It is directed against feeling the deep grief over something that can never be fully replaced or made right. If it is not addressed and the grief is avoided, the patient will, as soon as possible, again displace the wishes she has not let go of onto objects or other people. Among sober alcoholics, it sometimes happens that they speak to us in a very dry, very sober manner, but do not direct their oral wishes for comfort and security at us. They then internally maintain the displacement onto alcohol. A patient who spoke about herself in a very brittle and barely perceptible way during therapy sessions dreamed the night after of a large beer mug with a beautiful foamy head, which she drank in one go. Wishes she did not dare to fulfill with me remained displaced onto the beer. Only by addressing this displacement resistance onto the beer did she gradually give up the displacement and direct the underlying needs at me, and as described above, also let go of and mourn some of them, because she is no longer a baby and I cannot lay her at a liter-sized breast. Incidentally, after the supervision mentioned, my severe fatigue disappeared almost overnight, because I had gained an understanding of displacement, resistance, and containing, of everything that was happening beneath the surface between the patients and me, so that since then I have been enthusiastic about psychoanalysis and have pursued training and further education in this field. ◀

In outpatient therapy, depending on whether there is a dependency or an abuse, the framework of the treatment should be clarified, as I described above regarding framework resistance for addicts and people with eating disorders. Without such regulations, these patients would not give up their displacement and would keep the corresponding feelings and needs out of the therapy.

When anger is displaced onto children or the partner, resulting in psychological or physical violence, drastic measures are often necessary, such as involving child protective services, a temporary removal of the violent person from the home, or even involving law enforcement authorities. In my experience, a no-contact order with the victims is easier to implement than some might think, because only people who at least have some sense of guilt toward the victims come to us for therapy—perhaps even seeking therapy because they repeatedly lose control over their anger. Many perpetrators lack any sense of guilt, so they would not come to us at all.

Conclusion
Displacements must in any case be discussed and understood so that they can be relinquished. Often, a temporary displacement of sensitive, forbidden wishes into the therapy is useful, where they can be partially fulfilled by the therapist and partially worked through, before being displaced outward again onto real reference persons of the patients, who can then satisfy them. Treatment agreements that are reviewed are necessary in cases of addiction, eating disorders, and more severe abuse, because otherwise these will always be preferred over working through them in therapy, and the displacement onto addictive substances becomes an insurmountable resistance to giving up the displacement.

3.3.2 Altruistic Surrender

▶ Personal wishes, such as for security, being cared for, or comfort, which a person associates with shame, fear, or guilt, cannot be experienced by the individual themselves. Instead, they perceive these wishes very sensitively in others who are able to express them more openly, such as the sick or otherwise needy. When they help these people, they sense that the others feel relieved, supported, cared for, secure, and grateful. They identify with the person they have helped and experience, in a diminished form, the fulfillment of those oral wishes. Thus, through altruistic help, one's own internally forbidden needs are fulfilled in the other, and their satisfaction is enjoyed through identification with the other person.

As long as this can only happen through others, one's own wishes ultimately remain unfulfilled, so they must be repeatedly perceived and satisfied in others.

Anna Freud (1936) considered altruistic surrender to be a socially valuable defense mechanism, which occurs especially in helping professions. König (1997) points out that not every act of helping is a defense mechanism, but that there is also a primary wish to help others. However, in people with altruistic delegation, it is noticeable that they themselves cannot accept the help they give to others. In helping professions, this can, in the worst case, lead to burnout syndrome, a pronounced depressive state of exhaustion with severe sleep disturbances. It is similar to the fairy tale "The Star Talers" by the Brothers Grimm. It tells of a little girl whose parents have both died, leaving her with only a piece of bread. She gives it to a man sitting by the roadside complaining of hunger. She does not, for example, divide the bread in half so that she could also satisfy her own needs, but gives away everything she has. Afterwards, she gives needy children pieces of her clothing one by one, and finally, after giving away her last shirt, she stands completely naked and alone in a dark, cold forest. The darkness vividly expresses the depressive mood, the exhaustion, and the danger of freezing, but also the loneliness. No one is there to help. Fortunately, the stars then fall from the sky in the form of golden coins. These could represent the hospital salary of the doctor or social worker, or the insurance payments of the outpatient psychotherapist, which are enough for a while to fulfill some needs, but cannot protect against burnout in the long run. It would be better if the star talers symbolized the proverbial penny that drops, that is, an insight that comes to the altruistic person. We should help them achieve this realization in therapy.

Example

Patients in whom this defense mechanism dominates usually come to us for treatment only very late, for example, when they have already given everything, literally their last shirt, and are in the dark forest, in burnout. Due to the enormous exhaustion, depression, and sleep disturbances, there is a brief window of very high distress that prompts them to seek help. Only if we give them an appointment quickly and, ideally, already in the initial consultation interpret and discuss the resistance that is palpable there due to altruistic wish-delegation, is there a small chance of engaging them in therapy. The fairy tale "The Star Talers" is a vivid depiction of these patients' experience. A psychologist to whom I mentioned the fairy tale partially remembered it, especially with great matter-of-factness that the little girl gave away all the bread. When I told her how puzzled I was that it seemed completely natural to her that the little girl gave the adult man not just a piece but all the bread, and that I suspected there would be no other option for her either, she became thoughtful and wanted to know what I thought the other options for the little girl might be. She spoke in a tone as if I were talking about completely unknown and distant galaxies, subtly implying that I was a bit crazy to even consider such far-fetched ideas as giving away only part of the bread or even asking the man for help. I reflected these impressions back to her, so we could discuss other perspectives and I could interpret her great difficulties in even coming to see me. She confirmed that she had only come because others had urged her to finally make an appointment with a colleague. Using the image of the bread and being sent, we were able to talk, even in the first session, about the impossibility of even perceiving, let alone fulfilling, her own wishes for support. An interpretation of the resistance through altruistic wish-delegation helped her at least rationally accept starting a very low-threshold therapy of one session every three weeks. Appointments were always hard to find because she had to take care of her elderly, sick mother, her mentally ill sister who lived with her, her depressed partner, and of course her own patients, leaving little time for our sessions. When, in the initial consultations and first therapy sessions, we uncovered the altruistic wish-delegation emotionally as well, she was gradually able to let go of it and engage in therapy. At the end of each session, she felt a great deal of pity for me, imagining how hard it must be for me to spend even half a day with people like her. She gave me flowers, wanted to add sweets, and even a few star talers in the form of extra fees, to express and alleviate her enormous feelings of guilt toward me. Some star talers, like flowers, we might accept to make it easier for the patient to cautiously reveal wishes for comfort and care with us. I declined chocolate and money, however, with the remark that I would like to know which feelings of guilt she was trying to pay off with them. ◀

Conclusion
Without very quickly addressing and working through the altruistic surrender and the resulting resistance to help from a therapist as an external, unfamiliar person, we are likely to lose these patients sooner rather than later. However, if the resistance is identified and worked through early, these patients can have previously unimaginable experiences of comfort and care with us and can profoundly change themselves and their entire lives.

3.3.3 Turning Against the Self

▶ People can direct very different feelings and impulses toward themselves instead of toward other people. Narcissistic personalities, for example, direct their libido toward themselves because it seems too dangerous to them to direct it toward others, who might not reciprocate or could disappoint them. Most often, however, this defense mechanism is used to mark the turning of aggression away from others and toward the self. This happens either out of feelings of guilt associated with aggressive impulses, or in order to spare important attachment figures and not lose their love.

> "There are defense mechanisms that protect a person's ego from affects and moods it cannot tolerate, and defense mechanisms that prevent impulses from arising in the ego with which it, as a mediator between the inner and outer world, cannot deal in a socially appropriate way. These include defense mechanisms that keep the interpersonal field free from disturbances.
>
> The prototype of a defense mechanism that keeps the interpersonal field free of aggression is the turning of aggression against the self. Aggressive impulses are directed against the self and thus do not strike the object to which they were originally directed." (König, 1997, p. 32)

Turning aggression against the self is a main cause of depression, where it manifests as self-accusation, sometimes as self-hatred, as an impulse toward self-destruction, or at least as a pathogenic feeling of guilt—believing one does everything wrong, is fundamentally flawed. The lack of drive in depression arises because aggression cannot be directed outward, into the world and toward other people, but instead remains turned against the self. Aggression comes from the Latin word "aggredī," which can be translated as "to move toward something or someone, to approach something or others." Depressed individuals lack the courage and strength for this, so they remain in a strong withdrawal from all relationships for a long time, often also from the professional world. As long as this defense mechanism is maintained, it functions as resistance to therapeutic change, even if we work very intensively on the pathological cognitions. As soon as we have refuted one rumination, the patients move on to the next. That is why it is important to address the resistance—when and why the patient directs her aggression against herself. The frequent, recurring nightmares of depressed individuals are helpful here, in which they are always attacked, injured, or almost killed by others, by dark figures, in the same way, making the turning against the self very apparent. If the patient notes when she had these dreams, we can consider in therapy whom she was angry with the day before, and work on the turning of aggression against herself.

Example

A vivid case from Anna Freud (1936, pp. 51 f.) will serve as an example:

> "I choose as an example the case of a young social worker. She is a middle child among many siblings. Her childhood is filled with intense penis envy toward her older and younger brother and with jealousy, which is constantly renewed by the mother's repeated pregnancies. Envy and jealousy eventually combine into a strong hostility toward the mother. But since her attachment to her mother is no less than her hatred of her, after an initial period of unrestrained wildness and naughtiness, she begins an intense defensive struggle against these negative feelings. She is afraid of losing her mother's love, which she cannot do without, by expressing her own feelings of hatred. She fears her mother's punishments; and she harshly criticizes herself for her own forbidden desires for revenge. … The girl's ego … turns the hatred, which until then was directed exclusively at the outside world, against herself. The child torments herself with self-punishing accusations and feelings of inferiority, spends her childhood and youth, and even into adulthood, doing everything to disadvantage and harm herself, and constantly puts her own needs behind those of others. From the outside, since the adoption of this defense technique, she appears to have become masochistic." ◀

3.3.4 Undoing

▶ With this defense mechanism, people try to undo something they almost did—had they followed inner thoughts, feelings, or impulses they consider forbidden—by means of a ritual of penance or magic.

This plays a role in all obsessive thoughts and compulsive actions, which is why it is very important to ask exactly what the patient thinks would happen if she did not perform her compulsion long or often enough. In the case of a checking compulsion, for example, the patient initially had to check three times, later ten times, eventually twenty times, whether she had really turned off the stove, or whether she had forgotten, so that gas would escape and the house would explode. It turned out that she disliked living in the apartment because the neighbors were too loud or unfriendly, because the apartment was too small, and the building was dingy. Secretly, she had aggressive fantasies of destroying everything she hated. She feared being inattentive for a moment, so that these aggressive impulses would lead her to make a mistake and she would accidentally not turn off the stove. Therefore, she tried, through compulsive actions, to prevent her secret aggressive feelings from coming out and to undo the actions fantasized within them. Freud (1916) described in the "*Introductory Lectures on Psychoanalysis*" the slip of a ceremonial speaker who invited those present to burp to the boss's health instead of toasting. This unintentionally expressed an aggressive feeling toward the boss. Compulsions are magical rituals intended to prevent such slips, or rituals of penance if, despite all vigilance, they do occur.

At the beginning of psychotherapy, compulsions often intensify because the patient's forbidden impulses begin to become more conscious, simply by talking about what must be prevented or undone. Behavioral changes are often not possible for the patient. To prevent compulsions from becoming a resistance to therapeutic progress, we must work together to understand why the impulses are forbidden and help the patient find socially acceptable ways to express them. The patient with the checking compulsion described as an example could internally acknowledge that her anger at the neighbors or the house itself is justified, and then look for more appropriate ways to express her feelings than blowing up the house.

Example

Sandra came to therapy with the compulsion to check for 20 minutes whether she had really locked her apartment door. When I asked her in the initial interview about her life otherwise, she said: "Three months ago, I finally closed the door on my boyfriend, even though I love him very much. But he is married and not willing to leave his wife for me." When I asked her about her phrasing with the door, she was confused. She remembered having sleepwalked a few weeks earlier and opening her apartment door at night. She woke up in the morning and was shocked to see the door wide open. From a bruise on her thigh and a slightly moved table on the way to the apartment door, which she must have bumped into, she realized that she herself had opened the door in her sleep. This made her aware of her wish to open the door to her lover again, which she had symbolically closed to him, but also the meaning of the magical ritual with which she wanted to absolutely prevent the realization of this wish every day anew, ever since she learned five months ago that he was married, and even more so since their breakup three months ago. This realization alone led to a slight reduction in the compulsive symptoms. But it was also important to mourn internally the unfulfillability of her wish and to consider to whom else she could open her door.

Unmarried men caused Sandra great anxiety, which is not surprising in a patient who only knows doors that are either wide open or completely closed, that is, who does not have a flexible ability to set boundaries, where there are also half- or quarter-closed doors. The desire for closeness from unattached men was initially very threatening for her. Only after we worked through what was frightening about her wishes to open the door did the compulsion disappear completely. ◀

3.3.5 Rationalization and Intellectualization

▶ The term rationalization comes from the Latin word "ratio," meaning calculation, consideration, or reason. As a defense mechanism, it refers to the process in which only the rational motives are acknowledged and mentioned, while these serve to cloak the irrational, unreasonable needs, wishes, longings, feelings, and impulses with something logically comprehensible. Intellectualization goes a step further: through abstraction, generalization, and universalization, contact with concrete, sensually experienced reality and the baser motives of one's own experience and the behavior of others is lost. All emotional aspects are explained with rational reasons or highly abstract theories, thereby freeing them from any feelings of guilt, shame, disgust, or fear that would arise if the irrational, passionate aspects became apparent.

König (1995, p. 38) provides a vivid description of how these defense mechanisms can become forms of resistance:

> "Even the fruitless, more or less intellectualizing reflection on a situation or a relationship usually serves to maintain the status quo. DAVANLOO uses the term 'rumination' here, that is, chewing the cud. The term is, of course, not entirely accurate, because in animals, chewing the cud is part of a digestive process, whereas in ruminating patients, this is precisely not the case. Especially among those in psychological and educational professions, endless conversations about relationships often take up a great deal of space, without anything actually changing. There is interpersonal 'brooding.' Here, brooding is not thinking, but a mental going in circles."

Of course, there are always important, rational considerations for explaining one's own or others' behavior. Without mental theories about our own experiences and those of others, we would not get far in the world. Some people read psychology textbooks or study psychology in order to finally understand why those around them often behave so unexpectedly. Rationalization and intellectualization become forms of resistance when, in therapeutic conversation, they obscure the emotional, irrational aspects of wishing and experiencing. If we do not detect any affective involvement from the patient while speaking, we should address it, because without feelings, there can be no insight and no change. At such moments, I like to say: “What you are saying is very logical, but not psycho-logical.” Usually, the patient then understands quite well that the rational and intellectual explanations of her actions are not sufficient for me, and she can share what makes it so difficult for her to access her feelings.

In a time full of brutal, highly technological wars and unscrupulous, profit-driven environmental destruction, I cannot avoid glancing out the window of my consulting room and would like to let König (2004, pp. 79 f.) have his say on the topic of rationalization:

> “Drives and relational wishes are not only altered by the use of defense mechanisms, but also justified by them. For example, in the enforcement of law and order, a sadistic component is often denied or justified by rationalizing reference to higher goals. A war may be started to gain power and prestige, or for material advantage. The reasons given for warwill be different. This has a long tradition in the Western world, and probably everywhere; think of the Crusades, the violent Christianization of the New World with its mineral resources and other riches, or wars over oil. Values are not only shaped by personality structure; they can also serve to mask self-serving motives with altruistic, rationalizing reasons. It often happens that the share of such altruistic motives is emphasized and the share of self-serving motives is trivialized.”

Example

A case vignette from Riemann (1961, pp. 112 f.) is intended to illustrate the above:

> “A patient recounts a dream in analysis and then continues: ‘Does it even make sense to assign meaning to dreams? After all, everything is always relative, you can read anything into them or out of them—who’s to say I’ve found the right association? Maybe I’ve already changed the dream while telling it or don’t even remember it exactly anymore? Doesn’t that make everything questionable? Dreams are just illusions anyway, dealing with them is unscientific. Freud and Jung even had completely different views on dreams and interpreted them differently. So obviously, there is nothing binding or reliable. And the associations! What am I supposed to come up with… that leads into the uncontrollable… you completely lose yourself in the unknown… besides, nothing comes to mind for me anyway…’ The attempt to secure himself, here through skillful rationalization placed in front of the experience from which he is shielding himself, is clearly recognizable; his fear of the ‘uncontrollable’ becomes evident—it was not at all about scientifically discussing dreams, he was simply supposed to let himself go with his associations. Some may think here that the patient’s doubts about dreams were entirely justified—but they would overlook the fact that the patient was only using them to evade; moreover, his doubts were by no means limited to dreams—he was afraid of everything he considered ‘uncertain’ and tried to avoid it. Many compulsive individuals, for similar motives of securing themselves, get stuck in preparations for something, as a joke aptly illustrates: A man arrives in heaven, sees two doors labeled ‘Gate to the Kingdom of Heaven’ and ‘Gate to Lectures about the Kingdom of Heaven’—and he goes through the second door.” ◀

3.3.6 Isolation from Affect and from Context

▶ In isolation, something that actually belongs together is internally separated and kept apart. On the one hand, thoughts can be isolated from unbearable feelings that they would normally trigger. On the other hand, connections are dissolved in order to isolate things from each other that might otherwise come into conflict.

As early as Anna Freud (1936, p. 43) noted, isolation and undoing are particularly common in obsessive individuals:

> "On the other hand, we hear that the obsessive-compulsive ego uses the defense technique of isolation in symptom formation. It thus only tears apart the meaningful connections and keeps the drive impulses in consciousness. Accordingly, the resistance of the obsessive-compulsive patient is also different. This patient does not remain silent; even in resistance, he speaks, but he tears apart the connections between his associations, isolating idea and affect while speaking."

König (1997, p. 55) explains:

> "Patients who habitually isolate themselves strongly from affect often know a lot about themselves in terms of content, because more could become conscious through the isolation from affect than in people who isolate less from affect. They speak freely about content that one would expect to be difficult to share, because it should evoke intense feelings of anxiety, guilt, or shame."

Example

In contrast to repression, on the one hand, mental content and, on the other, even strong feelings are quite consciously accessible, but are so separated from each other as if they had nothing to do with one another. For example, the patient can describe in great detail the words or actions by which her supervisor mistreated her, and clench her fists while doing so. When asked about it, she says she has been irritable all day without knowing why. But it has nothing to do with her boss. If the therapist were to say, "If I were in your place, I would certainly have become a little angry with the boss," the patient would look at her in irritation, as if she were not quite right in the head, to associate inappropriate feelings of anger with such a normal work event. Here, too, the rule applies: it is better to address the resistance than to connect the isolated content and affects, for example by saying: "You emphasize that there can be no connection at all between an event you are talking about and a feeling for which you know no cause. Why can't you even consider whether there might be a connection?" The patient would probably reply: "I would be mortified if I were angry about such a normal action by my supervisor. I can already hear my father's voice in my ear, saying that a normal person doesn't get angry about such things." If she did not isolate her anger from the event, she would be an abnormal person, an inhuman one. If the patient is gradually able to reduce her isolation from affect, we must help her to socialize the anger now associated with the event, because something long defended against does not at first appear in a civilized, socially acceptable form, but rather too intense and destructive, which unsettles others and endangers relationships, so that the patient soon resorts again to isolating from affect. Ideally, the isolated feelings would first emerge within the therapeutic relationship and there be accepted and civilized by the two of us or in the therapy group. ◀

Isolation from context is very similar, except that here, connections between events and experiences that are obvious to others are kept apart, as if the patient were unable to put two and two together.

Example

This can be well illustrated by an example from König (1997, p. 40):

> "A patient indignantly reports to her analyst that she found letters from another woman in her husband's secretary desk in their shared living and work room. Later, the analyst asks why she searched her husband's desk. He initially suspects that the patient did so because of a specific suspicion. But the patient replies, 'I was looking everywhere for my train ticket.' It then emerged that it was a ticket the patient had bought to visit a friend she had met during her vacation. The patient denied the commonality between her husband's infidelity and her own, and thus gained the advantage of being able to be more indignant toward her husband than she would have been able to if she had kept the commonality in mind." ◀

3.3.7 Affectualization, Sexualization, and Reaction Formation

▶ There are two variants of affectualization: In the first, in the sense of dramatization, a great deal of emotion is outwardly displayed where internally there is little or no feeling. In the second form, one emotion, such as aggression, is transformed into another, equally strong emotion, such as sadness.

Crying appears more acceptable in interpersonal interactions than angrily shouting. It prompts the other person to take our hand with care and ask what is troubling us, whereas the open expression of anger leads the other to distance themselves and retreat behind a protective shield to withstand the attacks. For this reason, women more often transform their aggression into apparent sadness. Men, on the other hand, tend to convert their sadness into overtly displayed anger, so as not to appear weak, dependent, or needy like a little boy. In all genders, sexualization can lead to shame-laden oral longings for care and cuddling being replaced by intense sexual advances or sexuality without tenderness and foreplay. In "vanilla sex," the opposite occurs: pressing, drive sexual impulses are replaced by cute, childlike cuddling, where intercourse is not the focus at all.

Reaction formations are special cases of affectualizations, because in them a feeling is transformed precisely into its opposite:

> "In reaction formation, feelings can be suppressed by opposite feelings. Thus, aggressive tendencies can be suppressed by generating feelings of particular sympathy or strong compassion toward the person who could provoke aggression. … One can observe that people who feel aggression, the expression of which would be incompatible with their professional role—for example, members of the helping professions, but also salespeople or flight attendants—deal with people who provoke their anger in an exaggeratedly polite manner. … In reaction formation, this takes place in the unconscious. Only the friendly feelings are conscious. The opposite also exists: feelings of love can be overlaid by feelings of hatred when the feelings of love seem dangerous." (König, 1997, pp. 28 f.)

Even the Greek fabulist Aesop expressed this in the story of the very hungry fox, who repeatedly jumps in vain for grapes, but then turns away from the object of his desire in disgust, saying: "They are not ripe yet; and I do not want to pick them sour." This is the sour grapes effect in reactance theory.

In psychotherapy, as therapists we are initially pleased when the patient shows feelings, since treatment without emotional involvement leads to no change at all. For this reason, some affectualization is initially taken at face value, without questioning whether the displayed sadness or anger is actually appropriate to the situation described. This can then become a resistance, because the feelings warded off by affectualization, laden with shame, cannot be shown openly and honestly even in therapy.

König (1997) describes various relations between content and affect: In the isolation from affect, there is a great deal of content, many thoughts and brooding, without any affect. In the first variant of affectualization, on the other hand, we are dealing with a lot of affect and little content.

> "Some people habitually affectualize. That is, the intensity of their expression regularly exceeds the intensity of their feelings. This is found in people with hysterical structures, but also, developmentally, in many adolescents. … One can find that the feelings are described as moderate or slight, but are expressed intensely. … Among psychoanalytic therapists, there is probably consensus that a cathartic release of affect without insight is of little use; insight without affect is also of little use. That the isolation from affect can hinder psychotherapy is hardly disputed by any therapist. It is different, however, when it comes to evaluating patient statements that contain a lot of affect and allow little insight. When patients repeatedly express their anger in aggressive statements without asking themselves why they are so angry and whether it would be desirable for them to continue to be so angry in the future, most therapists address this behavior as a resistance to change. But there are also therapists who already see something therapeutically effective in such expressions of affect and therefore reinforce a behavior that repeatedly brings the patient into social difficulties. Such an approach is, of course, inappropriate." (König, 1997, pp. 55 f.)

Example

Laura enthusiastically recounts a bodywork session she treated herself to between two of our therapy sessions. The body therapist pressed on various points of her body and triggered a great deal of sadness. He found her shoulders and jaw to be hardened and tense. Crying, she says: "The bodywork helps me much more than our therapy here. There I can just feel. Here you always ask me why I am crying, and I have to think, which is often very exhausting." The crying did not seem to fit the content of what was said, so I questioned the affect. Laura was able to share that she had cried out of anger, because she often found me very exhausting with my questioning. Anxiously, she turned on the couch so she could see me, to know how I would react to her feelings of anger. She found it difficult to show anger directly, because her mother would scold, punish, and sometimes hit her when she yelled at her or slammed doors, while leaving her alone when she lay crying on her bed. This led us to discuss the conflict between aggression and fear, which had been concealed by the affectualization. Had I left her to cry on the couch undisturbed, the conflict would have remained hidden by the affectualization resistance. ◀

3.3.8 Identification

▶ In identification, people adopt aspects of the character, behavior, experiences, and ways of interacting with others, animals, objects, or themselves from important attachment figures.

For example, children imitate the table manners with which their parents eat, that they often leave the house unkempt, or that they behave helpfully or selfishly. Characteristics or behavioral patterns of other people are internalized and, in a somewhat modified form, become parts of one's own self, which is composed of many different identifications with various people. Identification is the most common and simplest way to learn. We first identify with our parents, later with other children in kindergarten or school, with adults such as teachers, which makes it easier for us to detach from our parents. There are lasting identifications that remain throughout life and shape our character, but also temporary identifications, for example when we watch a movie and leave the cinema imitating cowboy movements (cf. König, 1997, p. 25) or go to a Taylor Swift concert wearing a Swiftie shirt.

In counter-identifications, we internalize the opposite of another person's characteristics or behaviors. In contrast to a father who often greeted his child in a bad mood, a part of the adolescent's self develops that always greets others very warmly and overly friendly.

Identification differs from primitive introjection, which is an almost unmodulated absorption of an attachment figure as an internal object, in that what is internalized is, first, changed and modified, and second, does not become an internal object but rather a part of the self. The TV documentary "The Wagner-Brothers" is about two brothers who grew up in Berlin and are now very successful basketball players in the NBA in the USA. Moritz, the older of the two, recounts that his father, a psychotherapist from Berlin, enjoys playing handball in his free time. He wanted to do something similar, but not the same, and therefore chose basketball. He could just as well have identified with his father's profession and studied psychology, but instead picked out a particular aspect of his father that impressed him and internally modified it. His younger brother Franz, on the other hand, identified very strongly with his role model Moritz and, like him, became a basketball player. A part of his identity, his professional self, closely resembles the internalized image of his brother with whom he identified.

König (1997, p. 26) makes an important distinction:

> "As-if personalities do not identify with other people, but with the expectations of others. They 'are as they are wanted to be.' … In hysterical personalities, identification with the expectations of others is often difficult to distinguish from an actor-like role play. The person behaves according to expectations in order to be liked or accepted, which often leads them to 'play' different roles in different relationships that are contradictory in content."

In this respect, there is much to be said for replacing the term hysterical with histrionic, which derives from the Latin noun "histrio" for actor. Conversely, only those who can identify very quickly and flexibly with the most diverse expectations of roles become good actors.

As long as a patient identifies with positive aspects of her therapist and thereby perhaps develops new, more appropriate, friendlier behaviors, this is of course very beneficial for therapy. Likewise, as psychotherapists, we identify with aspects of our experiential learning leaders or supervisors. We behave in our therapies very similarly, but never identically, to them. This defense mechanism only becomes a resistance when the patient clings to identifications with negative, developmentally inhibiting aspects of important attachment figures or to exaggerated counter-identifications.

Example

Uwe did not like his mother's sometimes irascible, rough manner, who would quickly become loud and irrational and slam doors. Therefore, he developed a counter-identification, spoke very softly, was never even remotely angry or aggressive, and always tried to close the old, heavy wooden door of my practice quietly, which was impossible. In his relationships, he allowed himself to be taken advantage of because he could not demand anything or set boundaries, which partly persisted even after we had worked through his feelings of guilt about aggressive impulses. It was only when it became clear that the counter-identification—not wanting to be like his mother under any circumstances—also represented a resistance, that he was able to speak louder and more assertively, occasionally show constructive aggression, and slam my practice door with a little bang instead of fiddling with it for minutes. In addition to addressing his resistance to giving up the counter-identification, it was important for him to realize that even when he speaks more clearly, sets boundaries, or expresses justified anger, he is not completely identical with the rejected character trait of his mother, because he had also received much from her that had to do only with her, not with him. ◀

Conclusion
Therefore, we should always question whether an affect is appropriate in its intensity and whether it is a feeling that matches the described event.

3.3.9 Idealization

▶ "In an idealization, the person or object being idealized is attributed with qualities and behaviors that correspond to the ideal notions of the person making the attribution. These ideal notions are related to how the individual would like to be themselves, or how the objects they interact with should be. Idealizations prevent the recognition of reality." (König, 1997, p. 81)

In our ego ideal, we have internalized how other people and we ourselves should ideally be. More mature idealizations lead to perceiving real aspects as more ideal than they actually are. The other person or one's own self is perceived as more beautiful, smarter, friendlier, more powerful, younger, or more mature than is actually the case. In infatuation, a psychological state of exception, there is a strong idealization of the desired person. Typically, after four to six months, the idealization diminishes, leading to disappointment, the lifting of the illusion, and de-idealization. The question then is whether enough lovable qualities remain in the once-adored person to develop a mature and deep love, in which we love the other person not only despite their flaws and shortcomings, but perhaps even because of them.

Some people find it difficult to scale back their idealizations because they would then have to confront the shortcomings of the beloved being, would be less able to avoid conflicts, but also because their own self-esteem had been elevated by being loved by such an ideal person. By ignoring the negative sides of the object, unpleasant surprises are inevitable at some point—surprises that would not have occurred with a more realistic image of the object, one that includes faults and deficiencies.

In the film "Match Point" by Woody Allen from 2005, tennis coach Chris Wilton, who comes from very humble circumstances in Ireland, which he is ashamed of, enters the family of the wealthy industrialist Tom Howett, whose daughter Chloe he marries. There are mutual idealizations among all involved, but the relationship between Chris and Chloe remains passionless and indifferent, no matter how beautiful and perfect everything appears. Intense sexual desire, as well as ultimately murderous aggression, remain displaced into a secret affair Chris has with the unsuccessful actress Nola Rice. None of this is allowed to intrude into the idealized world of the Howetts. At the end of the film, Chris stares absently out the window while the others celebrate the birth of his son. Even Scotland Yard has not discovered, up to the very end, what had to remain outside, who killed Nola Rice, and what is really troubling Chris internally. We will have a similar experience in psychotherapy if we do not question idealizations. They then become a form of resistance, because the patient does not feel emotions such as anger, forbidden drive wishes, or sadness that would arise if she perceived the person she is thinking about more realistically. König (1997, p. 82 ff.) emphasizes:

> "Idealization often prevents the awareness of aggressive feelings and impulses. For example, a patient may idealize a therapist in order not to have to attack him. ... Idealization can also make one passive. For instance, a therapist may be attributed with the ability to heal his patients without them having to participate in the therapy. ... Experiences in the relationship with an idealized therapist are difficult to apply outside the therapeutic dyad. They remain tied to the special relationship with the therapist, or they lead to negative experiences because they do not fit into everyday life."

Even though working with a patient who idealizes us is more pleasant than with one who is annoyed with us or feels misunderstood by us, it is worthwhile to question the patient's idealization. Otherwise, much would remain in the dark, thereby blocking further development in the sense of an idealization resistance.

Example

Nora at times idealized her lovers, but also superiors and friends, in an almost rapturous way. Time and again, however, she experienced bitter disappointments when others did something she had not expected at all. She developed relationship anxieties because she simply did not understand people. In group therapy, she very soon idealized me as well and was unsettled by any group member who felt misunderstood by me or someone else, or even became angry. She asked anxiously how one could dwell on such trifles, talk about such banalities, instead of being happy to be dealing with such a wonderful person. Only gradually was she able to reduce her resistance to de-idealization and—initially with much fear—risk being angry, envious, or jealous. To her surprise, she found that this did not destroy her relationships with me, the other group members, or her significant others outside of therapy, but actually deepened and enriched them. ◀

3.3.10 Conversion, Somatization, and Psychosomatics

▶ In some mental disorders, physical symptoms are at the forefront, for which there are either no or no sufficient organic medical causes. Patients seek psychotherapy in order to work on the psychological aspects of their physical complaints. At the same time, however, these complaints are sometimes easier to bear than the underlying conflicts that give rise to them as a form of reinforced defense. Therefore, somatic symptoms are often also a form of resistance: they are maintained in order to avoid having to understand what they are meant to conceal.

There are four groups of disorders in which psychological issues and physical symptoms intermingle, all of which share the characteristic that patients are not imagining their somatic complaints, but actually experience them as painful:

1. In somatization, physical symptoms are present, but no organic cause can be found despite thorough medical examinations. These can include abdominal pain, nausea, diarrhea, chest pain, pain during urination, limb pain, or numbness in the extremities, accompanied by sweating, palpitations, fatigue, or dizziness.
2. In conversion disorders, the physical symptoms also have no organic causes, but they have a symbolic meaning. For example, a painful stabbing sensation in the heart region can represent a "stab in the heart," that is, disappointment, hurt, or lovesickness. The term comes from the Latin "conversio," meaning turning around, specifically the transformation of psychological impulses into physical reactions.
3. In contrast, psychosomatic disorders involve a diagnosis of an organic disease, but this does not sufficiently explain the severity and fluctuations of the symptoms. These include the seven psychosomatic illnesses described by Franz Alexander (1950, 1951): 1. Ulcus ventriculi (gastric ulcer) and Ulcus duodeni (duodenal ulcer), 2. bronchial asthma, 3. rheumatoid arthritis, 4. neurodermatitis, 5. essential hypertension, 6. hyperthyroidism (overactive thyroid), and 7. ulcerative colitis and Crohn's disease (chronic inflammatory bowel diseases). These "holy seven" were later supplemented by migraine.
4. In somatopsychic disorders, there is an often severe or chronic underlying organic disease, during the processing of which psychological problems may arise, as described by Kübler-Ross (2014) in her five stages of coping with illness. Details on this can be found above in Sect. 3.2.1 on denial in severe physical illnesses, so I will not go into further detail on this group here.

Through the defense mechanism of conversion, expressive illnesses arise because the physical symptoms express something about the underlying conflict, as mentioned above with the stabbing heart pain. Alexander (1950, 1951) and later Thure von Uexküll (1963) referred to psychosomatic disorders as "Bereitstellungskrankheiten" (provisioning diseases). For example, when people feel fear or aggression, blood pressure and heart rate are physiologically increased in everyone. The brain and extremities are well supplied with blood to prepare the body for flight or fight. If a person neither flees nor fights, nor even expresses their fear or anger in words, blood pressure remains permanently elevated because what was prepared is not discharged. Therefore, people with inhibited aggressiveness sometimes have high blood pressure, known as essential hypertension. Some also experience shoulder or neck pain, as the arm muscles are tensed in preparation for fighting. This tension remains if the aggression is not released physically or verbally.

Example

Uwe, about whom I have already written in Sect. 2.1.8 and Chap. 7, suffered from essential hypertension and neck pain because, due to feelings of guilt, he had to suppress aggressive impulses and expressions of his own will. When he felt anger or rage, his body physiologically prepared by increasing blood pressure and tensing the shoulder and arm muscles, but Uwe was unable to express or release these feelings. As a result, the feelings literally got stuck inside him, and he suffered from chronic high blood pressure and shoulder pain. In the therapy group, he was nice and friendly, but would often turn bright red in the face. When other group members asked him if he was angry, he denied it. He would say it was just very warm in the room and that he suffered from hypertension. Even in situations where others could imagine feeling anger, he did not feel it, or if he did, he did not express it. Given his feelings of guilt, it was easier to talk about his high blood pressure. For a while, this served as a form of resistance, until we were able to talk about the forces motivating his psychosomatic defense—namely, his feelings of guilt whenever he sensed aggression. When he observed that other group members were not punished for showing their anger, his feelings of guilt diminished further. He began to make notes on small slips of paper, which, as it turned out, were about the speaking times of other group members. One day, he tapped his note and read aloud who had spoken for how many minutes in recent group sessions. From this, he concluded that he had had much less speaking time than everyone else and therefore was entitled to more. By tapping the paper with his pen, he physically discharged some of his anger about being shortchanged, as he did with his firmer and more forceful voice. Increasingly, he was able to express feelings of anger and rage, which gradually improved his blood pressure. ◀

3.3.11 Regression and Progression

▶ The word regression comes from the Latin "regressus," meaning setback or reversion. As a defense mechanism, the term describes a return to an earlier psychological developmental level that had actually already been overcome. Progression, on the other hand, comes from the Latin "progressio," meaning advancement. As a defensive process, it refers to a hasty leap forward in development when the current level becomes unbearable.

An extreme and at the same time touching example of regression is the wounded soldier who calls for his mother. In his distress, he slips back into the experience of a small child, hoping that his mother will make everything right if only she would finally take care of him. In the Grimm fairy tale "Hansel and Gretel," Hansel demonstrates progression: Abandoned by their parents in the forest, he does not complain and lament like his sister Gretel, but suddenly seems to become an adult. Like their father once did, he takes the frightened Gretel by the hand and seeks a way for both of them through the dark forest, through the depression of abandonment. Parentified children, who have to care for their sick parents from an early age, remain for life in a fragile, prematurely adult state of progression.

König (1997, p. 88) refers to these defense mechanisms as a flight backward or forward:

> "Personalities who, in fleeing from conflicts of earlier developmental stages, have experienced a kind of emergency maturity, feel insecure at the developmental stage they have reached. The foundation of sufficiently mastered previous developmental phases is lacking, while characteristics of the achieved developmental stages are excessively emphasized."

In behavioral therapies, progression is the goal, for example through cognitive restructuring, problem-solving techniques, stress immunization, or self-management methods. Regression would be considered a form of resistance here. Likewise, an overly rapid progression in the sense of emergency maturation due to too short stays in clinics or restriction to outpatient short-term therapy is only seemingly effective, because patients quickly relapse into earlier, already overcome states, contributing to the revolving door effect in psychiatry, where patients are discharged quickly but just as quickly readmitted.

In systemic therapies, the entire family system takes a developmental step forward, toward more mature patterns of interaction. However, the family must be accompanied over a longer period to prevent a relapse into old habits.

In psychodynamic therapies, the initial focus is on utilizing regressive processes, returning to earlier developmental levels, in order to then launch into progression with less pathological conflict resolution. Too much regression to too early stages or too rapid progression constitutes resistance—a flight from the currently active conflict, either backward or forward.

Example

In the case of a phobic patient who, out of fear, does not dare to take steps toward autonomy and thus remains unhappily stuck in dependent relationships, we would likely focus treatment on an anal conflict between autonomy and fear. However, if in therapy she does not address her fears of autonomy and the aggression required for it, but instead extensively talks about her wishes to be held, stroked, and warmed by her boyfriend in a spooning position, and to be cooked for after cuddling, we would suspect a regression to an oral level. If this does not happen just once on a cold, exhausting day, but is repeated often, it would be considered resistance: She then flees into earlier wishes for oral nurturing and pampering, for warmth and security with her mother, instead of confronting her fears of leaving her mother's arms and venturing into the not entirely safe world full of other, still unfamiliar people. If we did not address this regressive resistance, the patient would remain in cuddle mode until the end of treatment, perhaps even in a figurative sense with us, where she cries and seeks comfort. Her fears of autonomy and separation would remain unprocessed, so that in the end we would be sending a little chick out into the world that would then have to cope on its own. Unfortunately, some therapies end in such malignant regression because this type of resistance was not addressed. A progression resistance in this patient would be if she did not address her autonomy conflict, but instead fled forward into a phallic self-esteem conflict. She might then focus extensively on her beauty, whether she is attractive to men or not, too fat or too thin, whether she appears clever and nice to others, whether she likes herself as she is, or furrows her brow when she looks in the mirror, as her father once did. Cinderella was also able to leave her parental home for a short time with borrowed clothes and win the prince for herself. However, she only truly gained her autonomy after blood had been shed, after she had aggressively confronted her stepmother and stepsisters and thus freed herself from her dependency. If we were to spend a long time in therapy focusing on the patient's progressively advanced self-esteem conflict, this would be resistance against facing the fears of autonomy, aggression, power, and control. Perhaps the patient would look at herself in the mirror with a little more affection at the end of therapy, but even Cinderella did not escape her parental home just by wearing a beautiful dress. The unresolved autonomy conflict would continue to accompany the patient on her path, and therapy would have changed little. As an intervention to address regressive or progressive resistance, I would suggest the following: "It seems to me that you prefer to focus on the topic of care and security or the topic of self-esteem rather than on the fears that actually brought you to treatment with me, perhaps because that would be more unsettling." In the summary at the end of therapy, patients often mention such interventions, which initially irritated or annoyed them, but then set a great deal of development in motion. ◀

3.3.12 Repression, Forgetting, and Sublimation

▶ We repress emotionally significant content, while we forget experiences that do not evoke any feelings in us. Both are associated with very different forms of resistance. Sublimation expresses explosive, forbidden, or conflict-laden experiences in a culturally acceptable and valuable way, as art, but also in the form of a profession. It helps us lift the fog of resistance, but can also obscure or distort certain things.

The term repression is controversial, firstly because it simply states that some content is somehow removed from consciousness, without describing in detail how, as is the case with other defense mechanisms. Secondly, Sigmund Freud repeatedly alternated between the terms defense and repression, so that repression was sometimes understood as defense as a whole. His daughter Anna Freud (1936, p. 50) classified it as follows: "Repression is downgraded in its significance to a 'special case of defense'." For her, repression and sublimation are defense mechanisms that develop very late, because both presuppose a mature conscience, a superego. It is the superego that decides, in the case of repression, what must be permanently removed from consciousness and what can be retrieved from the unconscious.

König (1997, pp. 18 f.) compares this to the theater stage:

> "What we experience and think does not remain continuously in consciousness. Our consciousness could be compared to a stage, where actors repeatedly enter and exit. In principle, any actor can return; they remain, as it were, in the wings and wait for their cue. … Repression now intervenes in the process of forgetting and remembering. It excludes actors who evoked unpleasant feelings when they were on stage from reappearing."

Forgetting is something different from repression: Physiologically, experiences are first stored in short-term memory. With the help of the limbic system, our emotional center in the brain, it is checked whether the current experience triggers positive or negative feelings in us. If not, it is irretrievably deleted, i.e., it is forgotten. The hippocampus and the corpora mamillaria are parts of the limbic system. Because they are particularly severely damaged by Alzheimer's and Korsakoff's disease, in these cases no feelings are triggered, no matter what is contained in short-term memory. That is why forgetting plays such a major role in these diseases. Beyond all illnesses, however, forgetting is important for all of us, so that we do not suffocate under a mass of useless memory content. If patients can no longer remember the last therapy session, they may have forgotten its content because it did not evoke any feelings in them. The resistance in this case would be that we talked about emotionally unimportant topics and did not address the absence of affect.

With repression resistance, it is different: When I told a patient who could not remember the previous session that she had talked about a dream and cried during it, everything came back to her. She said, startled, that a lot of feelings had come up, perhaps too many. The inability to remember here is therefore a repression resistance. Repressing because of too many feelings and forgetting because of none at all are thus two fundamentally different phenomena for us, which we should distinguish clearly.

Sublimation, finally, is the most culturally valuable form of defense. Longings, wishes, basic needs and impulses, as well as the prohibitions and feelings of guilt, shame, fear, envy, jealousy, or disgust that oppose them, are expressed in a socially and societally acceptable form as a compromise. These can be pictures, poems, novels, sculptures, or other works of art that partly express, partly conceal, or transform the current prevailing situation of the creative person. Lasting sublimations can become part of one's character, in the form of relationship patterns or a profession that truly becomes a calling. The clever comedian Hape Kerkeling, for example, had a depressive mother who died by suicide when he was seven. The film "Der Junge muss an die frische Luft" ("The Boy Needs Fresh Air") depicts his life, including how he tried to cheer up both himself and his sad mother with comedy, in order to process his empathy for her suffering and his fear for her and for himself through humor. In his first TV show "Kerkelings Kinderstube," which he produced at age 20, he played all the family members, including the preschool child Hannilein, who comments on the adults' actions while holding a toy. A sublimating, performative humor that helped him cope with his mother's depression and suicide became a part of his character and significantly shaped his later career. Edvard Munch expressed a moment of deepest despair during a walk along the Oslofjord, the emotionally charged landscape of his youth, in his painting "The Scream" in 1893. The elongated oval of the mouth and the orange-red of the sky express his anxiety in a very moving way, while violet and dark blue convey his melancholy. He was able to express and process much from his turbulent life in his paintings.

In psychotherapy, sublimation helps us to understand the patient's experience together, when she brings us pictures, but also when she talks about films or music that have moved her. We can treat patients' works of art like dreams, which are also a kind of sublimation, since, like an inner film, they depict a current experience in all its contradictions. In dreams, there is the manifest content, which allows us insights, but also the inaccessible, latent part, into which some things have been repressed because they were too explosive to express. It is similar with pictures or poetry: the patient expresses much of herself in them, but also hides some things. This is where resistance through sublimation lies. When we work with her, we should not only clarify what she reveals to us, but also point out the places where something remains hidden, and understand why. Another variant of resistance is when the patient overwhelms us with so many sublimations that we do not get the chance to understand the symbolism within them. We must also address this resistance and find out what might become apparent if we had more time for individual points.

Example

As an example, the song by Ziganka, a patient about whom I had already written something in "Gypsy Girl: The Foreign Citizen as a Mass Phenomenon" (Abel, 2011a). Even in her traumatic childhood, she was able to rescue herself from great depths through sublimation via music and later became a songwriter as an adult. The song illustrated for us at the time her oral wishes for drinking and devouring, her longings for incorporation and fusion, which she did not fulfill directly, but through sexualization. The resistance concerns the poor heart, because it remains unclear whether it is freezing out of fear or because it does not dare to reveal what is truly desired.

"Charm: A shiver runs down my back, beads of sweat on your skin, hands wander, they discover down, warmth, goosebumps, lips kiss, fingers explore. Slowly everything starts to spin. Sighing, longing to the point of madness, Only the most tender remains silent. I am so hot, Only my poor heart is freezing.

Words whisper, wither away In the death of the night, It is a grasping and a pulling, The incorporation with all its might. I want to drink and devour you. When you break me apart. Longing, sighing to the point of madness, Only the most tender remains silent. I am so hot, Only my poor heart is freezing." ◀

4 Transference Resistances

> Important wishes, needs, but also the conflicting feelings of anxiety, shame, disgust, or guilt often manifest in therapy within the transference, in the relationship between the patient and the therapist.

What is transferred are the internal images of people with whom the patient has had conflicted relationships in her life, in which she was unable to fulfill central needs, or only partially, because the other person responded with shame or rejection, or in which she was not allowed to express feelings such as love or aggression because they were met with prohibition. In the therapist, personality traits of parents, siblings, teachers, friends, partners, supervisors, and even of her own children can be relived. This can help make unconscious conflicts accessible to consciousness. However, it can also become a form of resistance, as the patient may develop the feeling that, even here with her therapist, she is not allowed to name, let alone experience or express, important feelings or needs. From the patient's perspective, we are then no longer experienced as mildly positive, friendly companions, but as critical, prohibitive, or shaming in relation to important feelings and impulses—even if we ourselves do not perceive ourselves that way. Therefore, it is important to recognize and address such transferences early on, so that conflicts are brought to consciousness instead of blocking the therapeutic relationship.

According to Thomä and Kächele (2006), transference resistance can be subdivided as follows:

1. resistance to becoming aware of the transference at all,
2. resistance through clinging to transferences, such as transference love or negative transferences that the patient does not relinquish in order to ward off something more threatening, because they serve to satisfy childish needs or because they represent something painful but familiar, and

T. Abel, *Resistance in Psychotherapy*, https://doi.org/10.1007/978-3-662-72663-1_4

3. resistance to the resolution of the transference, because we do not support our patients in transferring what they have learned into their real-life relationships, these relationships do not change, and the patients therefore remain dependent on the transference in therapy.

These three forms of transference resistance will be illustrated in the following sections, based on Abel (2013), using dreams of Yvonne, a patient of mine.

4.1 Resistance to Becoming Aware of Transference

▶ Even in the selection of the therapist, various resistances play a role, through which the patient seeks to keep conflict-laden experiences out of the therapeutic relationship. For example, she may have conflicts with men in her life—her father, partners, or bosses—but chooses a woman of her own age, on the one hand to be understood and to identify with, but on the other hand also to avoid having to face the difficult conflicts with men in the relationship with a therapist. Not infrequently, in addition to gender, images or texts on the therapist's website are important for the selection, perhaps her voice on the answering machine, recommendations from others with similar illnesses in online forums, or impressions from the initial consultation. We should inquire why the patient has come specifically to us and wants to undergo therapy with us.

König (1995, p. 18) wrote on this: "The wish to relieve an inner conflict by converting it into an interpersonal one (in the relationship with the therapist) often comes into conflict with the wish to keep the relationship with the therapist as free of conflict as possible." If a patient would like to go to a particular therapist, but that therapist does not have an opening for one or two years, she comes to us out of necessity because we currently have availability. We should find out what draws the patient to the desired therapist. If an important conflict could be reflected in the transference there, we should encourage the patient to accept the waiting period, perhaps with the help of acute treatment with us to address current issues. However, if the desired therapist rather represents an avoidance of inner conflicts, as in the example of the patient with problems with men who seeks out a female therapist to avoid her conflicts, we could consider whether, as a male therapist, we might actually be more suitable to trigger the negative transferences. Coming to us out of necessity could then conceal the patient's fear of having to relive the same discord with us as with other men. In any case, we should ensure that there is a sufficient degree of mutual sympathy on both sides. Otherwise, the prognosis for the treatment is very poor. For example, a patient reported that her previous therapy had not helped her at all. The therapist, though conveniently located near her home and with a quick opening, was not sympathetic to her and often fell asleep. Both initially benefited: the patient did not have to search further and had no additional travel to sessions, and the therapist could quickly fill an open slot. Since sympathy derives from pathos, suffering, meaning compassion or empathy, falling asleep expresses the opposite—indifference and boredom. Neither was sympathetic to the other. Such a setting is doomed to fail from the outset.

Patients with personality disorders, such as those with borderline personality disorder, have fewer resistances to becoming aware of transferences. Put simply, they can transfer anything onto anyone. Regardless of our gender, through projective identifications and their intense affects, they quickly make us into the bad father, the good grandmother, or the envious brother, depending on what is currently at issue. At the beginning, they only choose us if they can transfer only a good object onto us. Here, the question is rather how much of the roles attributed to us we can tolerate, about which more can be read in Chap. 9 on countertransference resistances.

Example

In the third session of her therapy, Yvonne recounted the following dream: "I am on a train. The conductor closes the strange doors, which are completely airtight. Then the train goes underwater. You can look outside. I feel completely safe on this train." When I asked her for associations, she said that dreams in which subways or elevators travel underwater occurred often and were a horror for her, because the doors would always burst open and the water would flood inside and drown everything. In this dream, however, she felt safe because, for the first time in such a dream, the doors remained closed and she could calmly watch everything passing by outside. The first thing that came to mind about the train was her train ride to get here, then that in the first session of the analysis I had explained free association using Freud's train metaphor (1913). In the instruction, I had said the patient should imagine we were sitting on a train, she was looking outside and describing to me, as a fellow passenger inside the train, what was passing by the window, without being able to fix it with her eyes. The conductor thus represented me as her travel companion. The dream shows that the patient feels safe in the therapeutic space. She believes that on our journey she will not go under, not drown in the floods, not be overwhelmed by them. This speaks for a secure working relationship with me. At the same time, however, she also hopes to be able to look at the sea, which represents the world of feelings, without actually coming into direct contact with it, as if to say: "Wash me, but don't get me wet!" The hermetically sealed doors thus also symbolize a resistance through isolation from affect. In her dream, she dreams of me as a functionary, a travel companion to whom she tells what she sees passing by outside the window, as I had offered myself in the explanation of free association. The conductor had no further personal characteristics for her. She said he is neither good nor bad, but appears only in his function, as someone who collects money, closes and opens doors, and controls events to ensure a smooth ride. She perceived me only in my function as a therapist, not as a person. This neutral depiction in the dream is surprising, because the patient had developed transferences onto me and a colleague from the very beginning. Originally, I was only supposed to conduct the initial interview with her. She was then to be referred to a colleague in psychoanalytic training at an institute, who would take the anamnesis. However, she feared that a female therapist could quickly become as domineering and rivalrous as her mother. She hoped to avoid a negative mother transference with me. I knew the colleague from several supervisions as a gentle and very caring therapist, with whom patients often quickly developed wishes for security and being cared for. With Yvonne, who did perceive the colleague as friendly and giving, this activated resistances against a positive oral transference of her grandmother, who had been very loving to her in childhood, but whom she saw only rarely and who died early, so that many longings for care remained unfulfilled. If these were now to become conscious in the transference, it would be associated with strong sadness and anger at the mother, who was not very giving orally, which the patient preferred not to encounter again in therapy. In this respect, resistance against a positive grandmother transference also led her to me as a man. She even accepted a longer waiting period. But even with me, transference resistances appeared. Yvonne was very preoccupied with her appearance. Her 40th birthday was approaching, which was repeatedly associated by her mother with the melancholy that at 40 a woman is faded and ugly, no longer desirable to men. Since I am blind, she hoped I would not be able to perceive her impending ugliness, so she would feel less shame and anxiety. In addition, the patient lived in a small town 80 km from Berlin, but deliberately undertook a 30-minute train ride to reach me. Using the image of the train in the dream, she was able to express that she hoped all the guilt- and shame-laden material she would tell me would remain far away from her home in Berlin, a large and corrupt city. In her small town, she had experienced some erotic excesses, in a district on the other side of the river. She developed a bridge phobia, so that she could no longer cross the river and thus could not be tempted to do something blameworthy. We also discussed this, using the train image and the theme of distance. At the end of therapy, she said in retrospect that her heart had opened in the third session—a beautiful image for what happens when resistances to becoming aware of transferences can be relinquished. Without working through these resistances, the heart would likely have remained closed. Yvonne subsequently developed various transferences, which will be presented in the next section. ◄

4.2 Resistance Through Clinging to a Transference

▶ When transferences have become conscious, patients often continue to hold on to this type of relationship with the therapist for an extended period, even when it has actually already been thoroughly worked through and all its aspects and associated feelings have been clarified.

In the case of a positive transference, such as that of a good, caring object, the patient may hold on to it in order to finally feel lovingly secure and cared for without guilt, as she was far too rarely able to experience as a child. The therapist can fulfill these wishes for a time, as a kind of compensatory development. If the patient clings to it for too long, it becomes a resistance against becoming aware of another, perhaps negative, transference—such as that of a bad, devaluing part of father or mother, associated with feelings of fear or anger that she does not want to impose on the therapist, whom she is currently experiencing as loving. But patients can also persistently hold on to negative transferences. Even if they experience the therapist for a long time as annoying, devaluing, or overly critical, these feelings are still easier to bear and more familiar than allowing a positive transference in which shame-laden wishes for care, recognition, or autonomy could become conscious.

Example

The repressed transference onto me became apparent to Yvonne soon after working through the dream with the conductor from the third session, in the 13th session, in another dream: "I am lying in my room at home in bed, just as I do here on the couch. You are sitting behind the head of the bed, just as you sit here. I am telling you something important, which is very difficult for me. After a while, you say, annoyed, that you are going out briefly to get cigarettes, and you disappear." Regarding the fact that she is at home in the dream, has essentially brought me into her room, and is lying in her bed, the patient notes that she is opening up very intimately here. Her father always used to say he was going out for cigarettes when he came home from work, put down his briefcase, and then disappeared to the pub or to a lover. He would then be gone all evening, leaving the patient alone with her mother. She always experiences it with me as a kind of dismissal when I stand up at the end of the session and open the door. Much like her father's disappearance, she experiences our parting here as if I have had enough of her. The neutral conductor has now quite clearly become an annoyed, abandoning father who is uninterested in the patient. However, details suggest that behind the overtly negative transference, wishes are concealed—that is, the patient is using a negative transference so that other, shame-laden wishes do not become conscious. Thus, the negative transference becomes a resistance against becoming aware of other transferences. One detail is that the patient brings me from my practice into her home. She wishes for a private, not a professional, relationship with me, because such a relationship does not end when a therapeutic task is completed. My disappearance at the end of the dream embodies the fear of relationships, the fear that one day she will ultimately be abandoned, which essentially makes it pointless to engage in relationships at all. That is why it is so difficult for her to tell me the important things and to engage more deeply in the relationship. Another detail became apparent when I asked about the phrase "in my room." The patient lived with her partner and daughter in an apartment where she did not have her own room.

However, as a child, she did have her own room. So, the dream also contains childish wishes, because I am brought into her childhood room. There I sit, as a good father could have sat, listening to her before she fell asleep or telling her fairy tales. Finally, a further inquiry revealed that she was naked in her bed, but covered. This now also contains hidden erotic wishes. My leaving is reminiscent of the common cliché of the lover who, after a night together, supposedly goes out for cigarettes and does not return. Thus, the erotic desire is countered by the fear of not being attractive enough to keep my interest permanently. All these conflicts are only hinted at very cautiously, almost disappearing behind the very overt negative father transference, which thus becomes a resistance against perceiving these wishes—especially if we were tempted to remain with this negative transference and overlook what lies behind it.

After working through this transference resistance, Yvonne brought the following dream to the 31st session: "The two of us are sitting naked in front of a blazing fireplace. You are holding me in your arms. Later, you cover me with a white blanket. It is a beautiful, warm feeling." The dream contains all the wishes she cannot fulfill with her partner, because he quickly sees her as a "whore" whenever she expresses sexual desires. The patient apparently projects her punitive superego onto her partner. Before her bridge phobia, she sometimes secretly crossed the river and had clandestine erotic adventures in the other, disreputable part of town, after which she felt dirty and guilty, like a whore. The phobia prevented her from having to feel this way, but also from fulfilling erotic wishes. The white color of the blanket I spread over her erotic desires thus symbolizes the wish to experience sexuality as innocent and pure, and to enjoy it free of guilt. In this dream, the patient fulfills the wish that I accept and embrace her erotic desire as something good, instead of judging, devaluing, or abandoning her as in the previous dream. Again, she dreams of us dyadically, as a couple. In contrast to the conductor and the cigarette-getter, I am now the lover who stays and accepts her femininity. In this way, she fulfills wishes that remained unfulfilled with her father and her partner. However, even here, a very overt erotic transference is presented, which conceals something else. In the dream with the house from which the patient looks out onto a beach (Sect. 1.5), the theme of warmth plays a role. In this dream, the word warm also appears, namely at the end. The blazing fireplace made the patient think of blazing passion, a fire that burns. The fireplace here thus symbolizes the sexual act, repressed from the manifest dream content. But with a warm feeling and being held in the arms, the patient associates security, leaning on someone, relaxing—thus, oral wishes. The overtly presented erotic transference is a transference resistance, because it conceals here guilt-laden oral wishes for care, which are only betrayed in the details.

I cannot describe the entire further process here, but perhaps just hint that the initially still repressed oral transference appeared in further dreams, in which the patient moved in with me at home, felt secure and cared for, but in which it was also subtly suggested that she was being confined—thus, conflicts between autonomy and dependence. Through the ongoing working through of resistance and transference, much changed for the patient. Before my summer vacation, after 120 hours, Yvonne summarized that her phobias, intense jealousy, and fears of abandonment had disappeared, as had the feeling of choking on food and the nightly nightmares. She had "rediscovered love for other people." ◀

Conclusion
A transference is initially repressed by directing resistance against its becoming conscious; then the transference itself becomes a resistance against the awareness of other, underlying transferences and the wishes and fears associated with them. By working through resistance and transference, one gradually, at a pace appropriate for the patient, reaches ever deeper conflicts. Symptoms no longer need to be used to relieve conflict and dissolve.

4.3 Resistance to the Resolution of Transference

▶ In the transference relationships with the therapist, the patient repeats painful or inadequate experiences from her life history. Sometimes, transferences do not resolve, or there is no transfer of what has been learned into real-life relationships outside of therapy.

By making transferences conscious and working through them, the patient understands, for example, that she cannot fulfill oral longings for care with us out of shame, for fear of being too greedy or gluttonous, or that she does not express impulses for autonomy with us due to feelings of guilt about asserting her own will. She learns that oral wishes and expressions of will are not bad or forbidden, so she can express and partially fulfill them with us. The positive new experiences that have become possible with us must be transferred in parallel to her real-life relationships, so that she can find and enjoy care and security there, or also assert her will and represent her autonomy. If the real-life relationships in the patient's everyday life outside our consulting room do not change, she will forever be dependent on finding comfort and security with us or on expressing her will. For some, it is enough for a while to know that they can come to us to cry once to five times a week, so they do not develop a relationship outside where this is also possible. Sometimes, however, it is also due to the therapists, because they do not sufficiently promote the transfer of insight into real-life relationships, following the motto: "She has understood it now, she no longer feels shame about oral wishes, no more guilt about expressing her will. So she can interact with people outside in a completely different way."

Greenson (1982, p. 184) wrote on this:

> "The purpose of working through is to make insight effective, that is, to bring about significant and lasting changes in the patient. By making insight the focal point, we can distinguish between resistances that prevent insight and resistances that make it impossible for insight to bring about change."

Often, a misunderstood abstinence can lead us to not sufficiently support our patients in making their therapeutically gained insights effective, by leaving them alone with the transfer into reality.

Example

Yvonne dreamed in this context: "I complain to my partner that he is not at all proud of me for being pregnant and giving birth to our baby so uncomplainingly and without any fuss. He reacts grumpily and says that's just normal." In working through this dream, the patient was able to share that she had wished I would be proud of our therapeutic baby, of what we have achieved together here. For example, in the previous session, I could have said that I was proud that she dared to present her work at a larger trade fair, which she did not have to do and which had previously made her very anxious. Thanks to the affirming experiences with me, however, she had found the courage to do so and received a lot of positive feedback, perhaps even new clients. But by now, she had already given up hope that we would celebrate successes out there together. We should take such remarks very seriously, because leaving old patterns behind takes a lot of effort and courage. Here, in the previous session, I left my patient alone through an overly abstinent, reserved reaction, instead of acknowledging her new step. ◀

Conclusion

If such processes go unrecognized, we ultimately prevent insights from the therapeutic process from becoming effective in our patients' lives. They are then unable to relinquish the positively transformed transference toward us, because they only dare to fulfill their wishes here, or they remain stuck in a negative transference because we do not acknowledge whatever they achieve and change outside. They then spend many years in therapy, gain insights, but nothing changes in their lives.

5 Guilt and Shame: Superego and Ego-Ideal Resistance

> There are resistances that are caused by a very strict, prohibitive superego, as well as those that are related to an inflated, never attainable ego ideal.

The conscience instance of our patients, their superego, is often noticeably stricter, more prohibitive, or more devaluing than in other people. It then forbids any kind of positive change, joy, pride, or personal will. As soon as the patient achieves a small improvement, the superego intervenes and forbids it. The superego primarily triggers feelings of guilt. The ego ideal contains the image of how we would like to be in order to be recognized and perhaps even admired by ourselves and others. If the patient's self-image is very far from the ego ideal, she experiences shame and feelings of inferiority. For many patients, the ego ideal is so inflated that it would be unattainable even with the greatest effort. It then belittles every change as small, insignificant, and ridiculous, so that the patient eventually gives up all efforts to change. The ego ideal also belittles the therapist as a simple-minded, undemanding being if she is pleased or acknowledges a small change in the patient. In this way, every change is nipped in the bud.

The ego ideal of obsessive patients, for example, demands perfection from them. If a change still shows a small mistake or flaw, it does not count for the ego ideal, but is devalued in a shaming way. For instance, a patient for whom grades like 1.2 were, of course, unbearably bad marks, could not even be happy about a 1.0, because she suspected she had placed a comma incorrectly, only the superficial teacher had not noticed it or, even worse, had given her a 1.0 anyway. She will then no longer trust this teacher's grades.

On superego resistance, Freud wrote (1923, p. 278):

> "There are people who behave quite peculiarly in analytic work. When you give them hope and show satisfaction with the progress of the treatment, they seem dissatisfied and their condition regularly worsens. At first, this is thought to be defiance and an effort to prove

T. Abel, *Resistance in Psychotherapy*, https://doi.org/10.1007/978-3-662-72663-1_5

> their superiority to the doctor. Later, one arrives at a deeper and fairer understanding. One becomes convinced not only that these people cannot tolerate praise and recognition, but that they react to the progress of the cure in a contrary way. Every partial solution that should, and does in others, result in improvement or temporary suspension of symptoms, causes in them a momentary intensification of their suffering; they worsen during treatment instead of improving."

He suspects behind this an unconscious feeling of guilt, "which finds its satisfaction in being ill and does not want to forgo the punishment of suffering" (Freud, 1923, p. 279).

Feelings of guilt—not being allowed to be this way or to be at all, not being allowed to feel good or alive—are something I encounter again and again in patients. It is as if they are not allowed to feel well. Everything they work out in their therapy, they must undo again out of a deep sense of guilt. Hirsch (2002) has contributed greatly to an improved understanding of feelings of guilt, drawing also on Niederland's studies of survivor guilt among victims of Nazi terror, who felt guilty for having survived a concentration camp while others were killed there. He distinguishes four forms of guilt feelings:

1. Basic guilt feeling: This is a feeling of guilt due to the mere existence of the child, for example in the case of unwanted or rape-conceived children, or because of their very being, especially their gender, such as when a boy was supposed to have been a girl because a sexually traumatized mother hates males.
2. Guilt feelings from vitality: Expansive drives, the desire to be successful, to be alive, or to surpass others, are experienced as guilt-inducing because they cannot be accepted by the family environment.
3. Separation guilt: Here, the child's striving for autonomy at all ages is associated with feelings of guilt, since separation represents a threat to the parental objects.
4. Traumatic guilt feeling: Severe experiences of violence and loss leave an introject in the self that causes feelings of guilt. Sexually abused children are told early on by perpetrators, but also by other relatives, that they are to blame for the abuse because they are so pretty, because they supposedly wanted it themselves. Aggressively abused children are made to believe that their misbehavior justifiably triggered the beatings and abuse. These feelings of guilt act as a resistance, preventing the patient from acknowledging her trauma, which is important at the beginning of therapy.

I have written in more detail elsewhere about different feelings of guilt in the context of migration (Abel, 2011a).

If these feelings of guilt go unrecognized, they act as powerful forces opposing therapeutic change.

Example

I would like to present as an example a dream from Yvonne in the 24th session: "I enter an old building. In the hallway hang five pictures depicting Mary, Justitia, Jesus,

Venus as she rises from the shell, and Medusa. Upstairs, the therapy session with you takes place. You tell me to pick out new clothes from a wardrobe, but they are all too romantic for me, with fur and such. I tell you that these would have suited me in the past, whereupon you are not disappointed, but end the session. Downstairs is a large car that actually belongs to me, but I do not get in, preferring to walk."

At the sight of Medusa, she thought of the other part of her hometown, which she does not visit because she used to live there, had many affairs, and cheated on her husband. Medusa is also the name of a brothel in a side street near my practice. This association already indicated that the patient was coming into contact with erotic wishes in analysis, as did the image of the wardrobe full of romantic clothes. By saying that these clothes would have suited her in the past, the patient in the dream was referring to what she called her "depraved, extravagant time" in the other part of the city. My suggestion that she pick out new clothes was connected to previous sessions in which the patient had the impression that I responded kindly and empathetically when she cautiously spoke of erotic wishes, and encouraged her to explore this further. What remained outside, in the hallway, were important superego aspects: Mary as the pure, innocent, asexual woman and embodiment of the patient's ego ideal; Justitia, who weighs and judges; and Jesus, with whom the patient associates guilt, suffering, and punishment, both embodying the superego. The dream illustrated to me that I had focused too much on the content behind the resistance. The resistance, which here appeared in the form of idealizing but also judging and prohibitive superego aspects, prevented the patient from allowing herself romantic new clothes or using the fancy car. Only by working through and understanding these resistances could further development take place. Further focusing on the content behind the resistance would have led to the patient continuing to have to reject the offered clothes and cars in the future. ◀

The Familiar: Id Resistance

6

> In Chap. 1 it was already mentioned in the context of compliance that, according to the WHO, only 50% of patients in the entire medical system follow the agreements made with their doctors, while the other half do not. This concerns not only the intake of medication but especially changes in lifestyle, such as healthier eating, more exercise, or abstaining from tobacco, alcohol, and other addictive substances. Here, but also in our relationship with ourselves and in our relationships with others, we cling to the familiar and habitual for a long time, even when it has long been clear to us that some aspects of it are not good for us or for others.

Freud attributed this to the conservative nature of the drive, to the stickiness, inertia, and sluggishness of the libido. Instead of giving up the satisfaction of erotic wishes through remembering and reality testing, the patient seeks their repetition. From the perspective of contemporary psychoanalysis, whose main current is object relations psychology (Abel, 2023), we could expand the concept of libido to include a multitude of other human wishes, needs, longings, and impulses that are repeatedly fulfilled in the same way or remain unsatisfied, even when we are already well aware of the emotional backgrounds.

Almost all fairy tales deal with this theme, because the protagonists, despite initial insights, try the same thing twice, four times, sometimes even six times unsuccessfully, before finally, on the third, fifth, or seventh attempt, the usual path is abandoned and a new pattern is tried. In the Grimm fairy tale "The Iron Stove," for example, the princess stands twice at the bed of her beloved, whom she has rescued from a forest and an iron stove and whom she then seeks, for which she has crossed a glass mountain, three swords, and a great body of water, without him awakening or hearing her. Only on the third evening, after his servants had told him of the princess's words, did he forgo his

T. Abel, *Resistance in Psychotherapy*, https://doi.org/10.1007/978-3-662-72663-1_6

usual sleeping potion, heard her, and married her. If one takes the rescue in the fairy tale and the princess's long and dangerous journey as a metaphor for a person's long development, for example in therapy, then something old and familiar, the sleeping potion, can prevent the new from reaching him, making it impossible for him to accept it. The task of the servants then falls to us as therapists: We must tell the prince within the patient that a part of her has come a long way and has changed greatly, but another part still numbs itself every evening and does not allow any of the achievements to reach her. Only then can all that has developed be recognized and become part of the new life. Even then, in the fairy tale, a dangerous stretch of the journey still awaits the two, a piece of integration, before they sit as king and queen in the castle. Without the help of the servants, however, the prince would have slept deeply through the third night as well. Because the princess had only three nuts with her, which allowed her access to his bedchamber, there would have been no fourth opportunity for her to be heard and accepted by him. Our patients, too, do not have an infinite number of repetitions of the old and familiar. If they do not at some point recognize and accept the development they have undergone, they will continue to numb themselves and everything will remain as it was.

With resistances due to defense mechanisms, the issue was more about not destabilizing a laboriously achieved inner, psychological equilibrium by introducing something new; here, it is about giving up something old. For all addicts, it is easier and more familiar to satisfy oral wishes through the addictive substance than to find ways to express their needs for care and security in relationships. In patients with borderline personality disorder, I have often observed that they still resort to self-injurious or sadistic behavior even when they have already found other ways to encounter themselves, to calm themselves, to regulate closeness, or to resolve dissociations. In my experience, it is not always fear or shame that prevents patients from finding new forms of satisfaction for affects and drive impulses, but sometimes also a certain convenience, a preference for solving things in the old, familiar way.

Example

The following dream from Yvonne serves as an example: "My ex-husband picks me up. He wants to go on vacation with me and my daughter, which I have absolutely no desire to do. Nevertheless, I reluctantly go along. I don't like it at the vacation spot. There are old people sitting around, it's dingy and it smells. I run away. I get into a fancy black car that belongs to me and drive off. I feel good and centered and can drive wherever I want. There is also a baby in the car, a boy who is only a few months old, whom no one knows about yet. It is my baby, whom I love very, very much and have to look at constantly with joy. Eventually, I am even able to tell others that I have a baby. They are happy for me. Then my ex-husband is at the door again and wants to go on vacation with me and my daughter. Reluctantly, I go with him again."

The rhythm of the dream is interesting: at the end, the same thing happens as at the beginning. As in the film "Groundhog Day" by Harold Ramis, the same thing happens every morning, as if time had been turned back, as if nothing had happened in between, as if there had been no development. The film is a vivid example of an id resistance. No matter what attempts and changes are tried, everything remains the same. The same is true in the patient's dream. After reluctantly joining her husband at the beginning, she is able to free herself from the old in the middle of the dream. She gains autonomy in the form of the fancy black car. The baby embodies the therapeutic child, as the treatment had only been underway for a few months at that time. It points to something new that has developed within the patient and has come to new life, to a newly discovered part of the self that she loves and enjoys. But suddenly it is as in the film, when the radio alarm clock rings again at six in the morning and Phil Connors realizes that February 2nd is starting all over again. Again, the ex-husband is at the door and again the patient reluctantly gets into his car. The baby and the fancy black car have disappeared, as if they had never existed. This dream illustrates people's tendency to return again and again to the old, familiar patterns and conflicts, even when they are unsatisfying. There are no pursuers in the dream, no superego influences forcing the patient to start over. Id resistances have a different dynamic. They are connected to the stickiness of the drives, as Freud put it, or simply to our tendency to remain with the old and familiar. ◀

Resistances Arising from Illness-related Gains

7

> A "morbid gain," or secondary gain, refers to the objective or subjective advantages that a patient or her environment derives from her illness. Recovery through medication or psychotherapeutic treatment calls this gain into question, which is why it can lead to noncompliance with treatment measures or resistance to improvement of the illness.

We distinguish several forms of illness-related gains:

1. Primary gain is the benefit the patient herself derives from her illness. The symptom represents a compromise solution in a conflict between desires and impulses on the one hand, and antagonistic feelings such as fear, shame, or guilt on the other. The symptoms reduce internal tension. This is the gain the patient herself draws from her symptoms. In the case of a delusion, evil is projected outside the patient. If she hallucinates voices, such as neighbors in the hallway or in their apartments constantly talking about her, about what she is doing or thinking, then she is no longer completely lonely and abandoned in her one-room apartment in an anonymous high-rise in the suburbs. If the hallucinations were to suddenly disappear due to a neuroleptic or psychotherapy, she would feel that no one is interested in her, no one notices her, she has no contacts, and would therefore feel completely abandoned and suffer existential fears of an objectless void. With every illness, we should be aware of the primary gain in order to anticipate what the patient will face if she partially or completely gives up her symptoms, even if the symptoms seem threatening to us from the outside, such as hallucinated voices of malicious neighbors.
2. Secondary gain is the external benefit that patients derive from their illness, on the one hand within their relationships, such as being allowed to stay in bed, being cared for or spared by others. For example, an agoraphobic patient, due to her fear of

T. Abel, *Resistance in Psychotherapy*, https://doi.org/10.1007/978-3-662-72663-1_7

crowds, could not use public transportation such as buses or subways, so her partner drove her everywhere by car. On the other hand, this also involves occupational or financial gain for the patients, such as being on sick leave or receiving a disability pension. With an average of 48 days, mental illnesses lead to the longest periods of work absence due to illness. The proportion of people applying for a disability pension due to these illnesses in Germany has risen from 18.6% to 41.7% over the past 25 years. If an application for a disability pension is pending, in which psychological symptoms play an important role, the patient has no interest in getting better, because the pension insurance would then reject the application. As a result, secondary gain becomes an insurmountable resistance to any change. Psychotherapy therefore only makes sense once a final decision has been made on the application. In the case of a temporary pension, for example for two years, we should pay attention to whether changes that have already been achieved and lived out begin to regress in the second year, in order not to jeopardize the extension of pension payments.

3. Tertiary gain refers to advantages for the patient's environment. Relatives who care for bedridden depressives, provide legal or personal support for people with schizophrenia, or accompany those with phobias, feel needed, useful, and that they have a special function or competence without which the person they support could not live, or not live as well. It boosts their self-esteem, gives them power, and sometimes even gives their life meaning. Changes in the patient often mean that she needs her relatives less or in a different way, which can be very confusing and unsettling for them, so that they consciously or unconsciously do something to push back the patient's positive developments. After a patient in inpatient addiction therapy cautiously raised a few questions about their marriage with his wife during the first visiting weekend in order to initiate some changes, she placed his favorite types of alcohol in the spots where he used to hide them before his admission, from where they had both removed them together before he entered the clinic, just before the second weekend leave. From her perspective, before anything changed, it would be better for everything to stay the same. She preferred a husband who was dependent not only on alcohol, but also on her. For this reason, systemic therapy works not only on changes in the index patient—the one who first comes to the practice—but on the entire family system. Likewise, child therapists regularly hold discussions with parents to involve them in their child's developmental process, which is sometimes the much more difficult part of the work. In individual or inpatient settings, we should keep in mind how the relatives are coping with what is new and different in our patient, and perhaps consider family meetings to avoid jeopardizing the success of therapy.
4. Quaternary gain refers to ideological or societal attitudes about what is considered mentally ill, what is not, and how the community deals with it. For example, during German reunification in 1989, two very different perspectives collided: In the authoritarian, dictatorial regime of the GDR, compliant, submissive people were highly desired, so those with phobias, inhibited aggression, or mild depression attracted little attention, while people with desires for autonomy and openly expressed aggression

quickly ran into trouble. In his book *Der Gefühlsstau*, the psychiatrist and psychotherapist Maaz, who worked in the GDR (1990), described the interactions between state repression in the GDR system and the psychological state of the population. In contrast, Maaz (2012) describes in his book "*Die narzisstische Gesellschaft*" the effects of Western, democratic, free societies that place self-actualization as the highest goal on what we consider healthy and ill. There would be much more to say about this. Here, perhaps just a brief look beyond our country's borders to Afghanistan. The manifold suffering of women there, who are only allowed to leave the house veiled and accompanied, are not allowed to work, and are not permitted to be active independently in any way, is not seen by the ruling regime and the socially dominant forces as something deeply destructive and restrictive, as it is by the European Court of Justice, but rather as something normal and desirable. A woman's rebellion against this fate, on the other hand, would be seen as wrong, as disturbed, and could even be punished by death. In working with refugees, it is especially important for us to consider such aspects of the culture from which they come. But even beyond that, I find it significant to occasionally look out the window of our treatment rooms at the surrounding society and its influences on us and our patients.

Example

My patient Uwe, whom I already wrote about in Sect. 2.1.8, suffered from essential hypertension, a high blood pressure for which no organic causes can be identified. Alexander (1950, 1951) counted this illness among the Holy Seven, the seven major psychosomatic diseases. According to this, feelings of aggression and anger increase heart rate and blood pressure. If the aggression cannot be discharged, through words or actions, it remains constantly available, i.e., the blood pressure remains permanently elevated. Uwe had experienced strict prohibitions against all forms of aggression in his upbringing and therefore associated these feelings with intense guilt. If he became annoyed with colleagues or his wife, his blood pressure would rise, without him feeling anger, let alone saying or doing anything. As a result, he only felt physical tension but no aggression, so he did not suffer from feelings of guilt. This was his primary gain from his illness. The secondary external gain was that everyone considered him nice and easygoing, which he experienced as significant, as it was the complete opposite of the image his parents usually had of him. Among his colleagues and his wife, he was well regarded because he never showed anger and let everything happen to him. At work, others could burden him with unpleasant tasks, which he carried out without complaint to their delight. He experienced his marriage as conflict-free and harmonious. His wife worked as a strict teacher in a school in a troubled district, where she dealt daily with defiant and aggressive children, so she enjoyed encountering no opposition at home and being able to control and dominate everything, which was the tertiary gain from his illness. After Uwe twice cautiously tried to engage in a discussion about changing one or two details in their marriage—spending more time together and talking more often—she panicked, as if she would now have to deal with a sulky, headstrong person at home as well. She threatened him with divorce if he did not go with her to a psychiatrist, with whom she had already made an appointment. There, only she spoke about his sudden changes after 20 years of harmonious marriage. The psychiatrist suspected a manic episode and prescribed him amitriptyline, a common antidepressant, presumably because it also has a sedating, sleep-inducing effect. I had clearly underestimated the strong impact of Uwe's developments in group therapy toward more expressions of his own will and autonomy on his wife. Through conversations with Uwe, couple sessions with his wife, and contact with the psychiatrist, the medication could be discontinued and his wife could be brought along with the changes, because she understood that it was not just about a struggle, but much more about an improvement, redesign, and intensification of their marriage, which she herself had actually wished for in some respects for a long time. As a quaternary gain from illness, I would like to mention that Uwe grew up under the authoritarian regime of the GDR, where his parents were mid-level, highly conformist officials, for whom Uwe found the following joke characteristic: "What do the GDR and a mushroom farm have in common? As soon as a head sticks out, it gets cut off." Wishes for autonomy and expressions of one's own will were very dangerous for his parents both professionally and privately. In this respect, therapeutic changes in his family and in the GDR toward more constructive aggression and more self-assertion would have gotten Uwe into trouble. ◀

Structure-Specific Resistances

8

▶ There are no ideal, perfect, or error-free parents, families, or environments for children. In their psychological development, especially during the first seven years of life, some wishes and needs are met optimally or at least well enough, while others are met suboptimally, inadequately, or not at all. When essentially normal wishes—similarly pronounced in all children—are frustrated, forbidden, or shamed, lifelong conflicts often arise that significantly shape the personality, even of psychologically healthy individuals. As adults, we are all driven by something: some want to create order, others want to be on stage and show themselves, still others want to take care of other people. All of this is related to central relational wishes, or to central themes of relational conflict, as Luborsky (1988) has called them.

In Sect. 3.1 the early childhood developmental phases were already briefly mentioned; further below, they are described in more detail. Individual character structures arise from inadequately resolved conflicts during these phases. In contrast to the concept of character structures, which goes back to Freud (1908), Rudolf (1993) and others speak of structures that refer more to the developmental level and the good, moderate, poor, or disorganized level of integration of a personality. This sometimes leads to some confusion regarding the concept of structure. Here, I refer to the former concept of character structures.

The names of the character structures sound somewhat pathological, although they apply to all people, including those who never develop a mental illness. However, if a person with a particular unresolved conflict encounters a triggering situation that is problematic for them, the psychological disorders often arise that are echoed in the names of the character structures. Riemann (1961, pp. 17 f.) refers to the four personality structures as four basic fears, as "four ways of being in the world":

T. Abel, *Resistance in Psychotherapy*, https://doi.org/10.1007/978-3-662-72663-1_8

> "The four personality structures are initially normal structures with certain accentuations. However, if the accentuation becomes pronounced one-sidedness, it reaches limits that are to be understood as distortions or extreme variants of the four normal basic structures. In this way, we encounter the neurotic variants of the structural types, as described by psychotherapy and depth psychology in the four major forms of neurosis: schizoid, depressive, obsessive-compulsive, and hysterical. These neurotic personalities thus each reflect, in a pointed or extreme form, universally human modes of existence that we all know."

König (1993, 1998, 2004) has examined the different structures from various perspectives. Based on this, we can distinguish the following variants:

1. In the early symbiotic phase up to the 6th month of life, the focus is on the first steps of separation, the distinction between self and other, along with the associated fears. Suboptimally resolved conflicts lead to schizoid character structures, in more pronounced form to schizoid personality disorders, and in extreme cases to schizophrenia.
2. Disturbances in the oral phase up to the 12th month, which centers on nursing, on being soothed—in the literal sense, being quiet, no longer crying out in fear or hunger—lead to depressive characters, depressive personality disorders, or also to depression as a mental illness.
3. If the development of autonomy, personal will, control and power, as well as aggression in the anal phase up to the 4th year of life is met by parents with prohibitions and accusations of guilt, this leads to compulsive character traits, obsessive-compulsive personality disorders, or in extreme cases to an obsessive-compulsive disorder. If, on the other hand, parents respond more with fear to steps toward autonomy, expressions of will, or aggression by their child, phobic characters, anxious-avoidant personality disorders, or manifest anxiety disorders develop.
4. If wishes for admiration of one's own body, for recognition in one's own sexuality, or for winning competitions in the phallic phase are associated with strong feelings of shame or fear, histrionic characters, histrionic personality disorders, or disorders such as functional or conversion disorders develop.

Mentzos (2009) emphasizes that this is often the case, but of course depressive character structures can also develop obsessive-compulsive disorders, just as compulsive personalities can sometimes also develop depression. In this respect, this is a guideline, but not a rigid, exclusive assignment of characters to mental disorders. Most people have a character composed of several of these personality components. For example, they are people with depressive-compulsive structures or compulsive-histrionic personalities. Having several components does indicate more inadequately resolved conflicts, but it also brings more defense mechanisms, abilities, and desired aspirations. In this respect, it is more problematic if someone has only one of the mentioned structural components in their personality, that is, is only schizoid or only compulsive.

Conclusion
According to König (1995), the central relational wishes and fears of individual character or personality structures give rise to very specific, different resistances in psychotherapy, which are described in the following sections.

8.1 Resistances of Schizoid Personality Structures

▶ Schizoid character structures develop from conflicts surrounding the emergence of identity through differentiation, the separation of the self from the early object, often the mother, with whom an infant initially lives in a psychologically fused state, a symbiosis.

If the baby is subjected to too much separation too early, it experiences existential fears of an objectless void, because at this early stage it has not yet internalized images of other people. It does not know that beyond the limits of what it can perceive, there are other people somewhere who will eventually return to it, and it cries out from a sense of mortal threat. As adults, they avoid all situations of loneliness and being alone in order not to feel again the early abandonment anxieties, which are experienced with an intensity that many others cannot empathize with. Conversely, if separation is prevented, the child remains far too long in a close, symbiotic bond with the mother, so that it develops neither a well-defined own identity nor differentiated images of other people. As adults, they both wish for and fear slipping back into a symbiotic fusion with someone else, so they strongly avoid closeness to others.

The term symbiosis was coined by the botanist de Bary (1879) to characterize the coexistence of different species for mutual benefit, as opposed to parasitism, where only one benefits. Fromm (1941) introduced the term into psychoanalysis. Mahler (1972, p. 14) described the symbiotic phase of the dual unity of infant and mother as pre-objectal:

> "It precedes the differentiation between self and object. The infant vaguely perceives that the source of satisfaction of its needs lies outside its own self, in the sense that the object is not yet something specific and distinctly other, but only a vague sense arises that there is something else, still undefined, out there."

According to Mahler (1972), the symbiotic phase is followed by four subphases of separation and individuation up to the end of the third year of life. This process goes far beyond the symbiotic phase, which ends in the sixth month, even though particularly crucial developments take place during it. The rapprochement phase from the 18th to 24th month is still considered significant for the development of borderline personality organization. In the third year of life, object constancy is achieved, i.e., stable representations of important attachment figures in the child's mind, even when they are not physically present for extended periods. Only now, at age four, does a representational self with an autobiographical memory emerge (see Fonagy & Target, 2015). Most people locate their earliest life memories in this period. Being held in or expelled from symbiosis is therefore not pictorially remembered by anyone, but is stored as a purely emotional experience in implicit memory. Schizoid-structured individuals therefore have no words or memories for the formative conflicts of this early time.

They have permeable, often fragile ego boundaries inward, toward the world of feelings, but also outward, toward the environment. They long for closeness, but fear fusion and the loss of their identity so much that they prefer to maintain greater distance from others. For example, they like to work in a library, where they can sort the archive alone. Others are present by the hundreds in the form of books, into which they can emotionally immerse themselves without losing their identity. When they do enter into real relationships with others, it is only with people who seem completely identical to them, like one twin to another, which is why Kohut (2016) coined the term "twin transference." They only stay with a therapist whom they experience as psychologically completely identical to themselves, because then it is safe if the ego boundaries open and both come too close. Then their own identity is overwritten by another identity that is identical to their own down to the last detail.

Schizoid patients often fall silent already in the first sessions of therapy, because they assume the therapist understands them wordlessly and knows how they are feeling. Kohut (2016) therefore recommended avoiding empathic ruptures. However, this is not achievable in the long term. Even a question often frightens schizoid patients, because it shows that the therapist does not understand something wordlessly, i.e., is not identical with them. It is even more frightening for these patients when they tell a story, but we do not understand some details or do not understand them correctly. For the therapist, it is important to develop a sense for the patient's existential fear here, in order to enable her to remain in therapy by learning to tolerate that the therapist is another person and not a twin. This is where what Erikson (1970, p. 222) called identity resistance arises:

> "Identity resistance, in its milder and more frequent form, consists in the patient's fear that the analyst, due to his particular personality, milieu, or worldview, might carelessly or deliberately destroy the weak core of the patient's identity and replace it with his own."

König (1995, p. 69) put it this way: "Schizoids experience the influence of the therapist as an invasion of their self."

Example

After I had asked my patient Yvonne, in light of an extension of her health insurance coverage, to reflect on what she had achieved in therapy so far, she brought the following dream to the 144th session: "You and I are together in a new house. We live there together and are just having coffee. You go to my closet, from which you take an embroidery hoop that I have already half embroidered with a gray-blue pattern. But you use completely different thread, much more colorful than mine—orange, pink, green, neon bright. With it, you finish the pattern, which at first totally outrages me, but then, as I watch, I agree with it. After that, you move glasses and cups on the table using only mental powers. I am envious because you are so much further along with energy work than I am." The embroidery hoop first reminded her of her great-grandmother, whom she loved very much. She would have embroidered everything. But the embroidery also creates a picture; it could also stand for patterns of thought that have changed in therapy. Especially in the first year, she had been torn back and forth. Her parents were always very preoccupied with themselves and never had any idea of how she should be or become. She was allowed to do a lot, but that was also associated with indifference and absence on the part of her parents. That is why she enjoyed it when she had the impression that I had an idea of how she should be or become. At the same time, it frightened her that I might implant a foreign personality in her. The weak identity is expressed in the dream by the rather colorless embroidery pattern of the patient. I embroider over this colorless, meager personality pattern with something more beautiful, more lively. The wish that there might finally be someone who knows what and how she should become, as well as the fear that the core of her identity could be replaced by something foreign, were vividly illustrated by this dream. The power she attributed to me was expressed in the dream in the scene with the moving of the glasses. The patient had never actually engaged in moving glasses and did not want to be able to do so. In this respect, this scene rather contains the attribution of magical abilities, through which I naturally become even more dangerous for her as a kind of magician. Whoever can move glasses might also be able to bewitch another. The attribution of magical abilities, especially through the changes that patients notice in their perception and experience, makes the therapist a powerful, and therefore also dangerous, figure. By becoming aware of these connections, the patient was also better able to endure separations from me, such as my two-week vacation. Unlike before, she was not afraid that I might die, but my inner image in her mind remained stable. She was active. She even felt as if she were in love, by which she meant a good feeling toward herself and what she was doing. ◀

8.2 Resistances of Depressive Personality Structures

▶ The oral phase is assigned to the first year of life, especially the 7th to 12th month.

The baby has taken its first steps toward separation, is beginning to distinguish itself from the mother, and thus can also differentiate its own needs from the object that satisfies them. The child is called an infant because nourishing sucking at and drinking from the mother's breast is central, closely linked with being cared for, comforted, soothed, calmed, protected, sheltered, held, and cleaned. Breastfeeding refers to the satisfaction of needs, but also to the calming of the baby, who initially cries for a variety of reasons. If about 90% of the baby's needs are correctly recognized and promptly met, it can leave this phase with a basic trust—first, in itself, namely that it can correctly perceive and express its needs, and second, in others, the primary objects, that they will largely decode and satisfy these needs correctly.

Oral conflicts in this phase, which can lead to a depressive character structure if not corrected in later developmental stages, arise under various circumstances:

1. If the baby cries out of fear, sadness, or anger, but is immediately put to the breast and fed because the primary objects cannot distinguish between the different types of crying or do not know how else to deal with the baby's feelings, the baby internalizes that oral intake of liquid nourishment is good for everything distressing in life, whether it is hunger or tormenting emotions. Later in adult life, this person will be at risk of developing an addiction, because they will consume food, smoke cigarettes, drink alcohol, use drugs, or engage in compulsive sexuality not only in response to hunger or thirst, but also to a wide range of feelings such as fear, sadness, shame, or anger. Needs for comfort, consolation, or the expression of anger are displaced onto addictive substances.
2. If the primary objects, such as the mother, are very preoccupied with themselves—because they are depressed, have to work a lot, are often absent either physically or emotionally, frequently have conflicts in their partnership or with their own parents, or are unable to perceive the needs of others, including their baby—the infant is often left unattended for long periods. Not a few parents also acted, sometimes against their own feelings, under the influence of books, such as the parenting guide by Haarer (1934), first published in 1934, which after World War II was only stripped of its most blatant National Socialist statements and continued to be published until 1987. It shaped generations of West German parents. It recommended feeding, changing, and washing babies at set times of day. If they dawdled, breastfeeding was to be stopped after 20 minutes at the latest. Outside these times, mothers were advised to let their infants cry, preferably in a room where they were alone. Under all these circumstances, the emotional basic attitude remains in the implicit, non-consciously recallable memory that needs for nourishment and care are too much, overwhelm others excessively, and are thus associated with early, intense feelings of anxiety and shame, and later also with guilt. Adults shaped in this way experience these feelings of shame, guilt, disgust, or fear whenever they sense even the smallest inner wishes for comfort or care. They often develop eating disorders, such as anorexia, in which they become almost euphoric after days without food, or bulimia, in which they secretly devour food greedily, only to vomit it up again out of feelings of shame, guilt, or fear, terrified of retaining even the smallest crumb inside themselves.

3. A child who encounters very needy parents who are very depressed, often sad or anxious, will learn early on to suppress its own needs for nourishment and care, and instead try to cheer up, soothe, or comfort the parents—by smiling, being cheerful, content, holding back its own needs, and later by taking care of them. As adults, they often become helpers who see their own wishes for comfort and care in others, thus altruistically transferring these wishes to others.

Depressive individuals can often enter therapy quite well, because it is paid for by health insurance or by themselves. They do not have to feel as guilty about receiving comfort, security, and care from the therapist, because they can offset the guilt internally associated with oral wishes by paying money. They can cry and unburden themselves during the preliminary sessions. But soon a feeling arises, which Zafar (2000) already names in her book title: "You can't flow if your money doesn't flow." Whenever it becomes clear that there is no private relationship with the therapist, but that she, like a prostitute, only provides comfort as long as she is paid for it, anger begins to grow in the patients—at the therapist, who does not seem to mean it sincerely, but also at themselves, because the patient feels dependent on such an arrangement. König (1995, pp. 68 f.) puts it this way:

> "Every therapeutic progress that the patient could promote through their own disclosures reminds them of the goals of therapy and thus of its time limitation. When the therapist acts in their role as therapist, the depressive patient must realize that it is a professional, indeed personal, but not private relationship. The professional relationship between therapist and patient in psychoanalytic therapy is characterized, among other things, by the fact that it will end once the goal is reached. Private relationships, however, are generally not ended when goals have been achieved. … Depressive individuals suffer from the feeling of having to be eternally grateful if the therapist successfully exerts influence."

It is important to address the patient's feelings of anger as justified, so that the aggression is not turned inward in the form of depression against the self. Instead, the origin of the oral anger should be explored, such as the repeated frustration that the family of origin did not fulfill normal, childlike oral wishes for comfort and security, branded them as excessive, or stuffed the child's mouth with food and drink. If the anger is directed outward and recognized as justified, depressive symptoms decrease and the patient gradually learns to assert the fulfillment of her oral wishes in her current real relationships through the power of constructive aggression. If this resistance is not discussed, she either makes no progress in therapy or cannot transfer these changes into her everyday relationships, but can only fulfill oral wishes in therapy—just as other forbidden sexual wishes can only be satisfied with prostitutes, without ever being able to integrate them into their partnerships. The fairy tale "The Girl Without Hands" from the Brothers Grimm collection may help patients understand that even oral wishes fulfilled by a therapist leave something lasting behind. In this tale, the hungry girl comes to a garden but cannot pick an apple from the tree because she has no hands, so the prince must give her a fruit. This remains the case even in the royal couple's marriage. Only when an old anger from the girl's past resurfaces and leads to conflicts with her husband does she withdraw for seven years to the house of a white maiden, who not only restores her innocence—removing pathogenic, oral feelings of guilt for being too greedy—but also allows her hands to grow back, so that she can take things for herself in the world. She leaves the maiden, who was a companion and helper in her self-development for a time, but takes important things with her for her future life. This can help to soothe the anger of our patients with depressive structures, that we are only there for them for a while and professionally, dressed in white, and to comfort the sadness of having to part from us one day.

Example

A wealthy patient who wanted to pay for his treatment with me himself transferred 4000 € to me, unannounced, even before the first session, thus opening the hour. I was to email his secretary when the money was running low, and she would immediately transfer the next installment. In this way, he wanted to ensure that he owed me nothing, so that he could devote himself to his feelings without guilt. When I responded, somewhat surprised, that the money would cover 30 therapy sessions, he replied that this was perfectly fine—even if he only attended 10 sessions, I would not need to refund anything. This way, he could speak freely here. He was unsettled when I declined this approach and told him that I would send him an invoice at the end of each month, not to his secretary. He was used to buying many things with money, by giving gifts and inviting people with whom he wanted to be friends, so that he could confide in them and leave his sorrows, but also women, to whom he repeatedly gave precious gifts, even though they told and showed him that they loved him as he was. It frightened him that I did not want to be bought in the way he was accustomed, but only a little, for what to him were very minimal fees. He experienced the setting of the financial framework by me as annoying, which reminded him of the anger toward his parents, who, even when he was a small child, often left him alone, but showered him with expensive toys and luxurious events so that he would be quiet. Accessing this old anger was a relief for him, but also shameful, because he had to admit to himself that he was fobbing others off with money in the same way his parents had done to him and his wishes for security and comfort. Gradually, he managed to demand something emotionally important from me and later from other people as well. He tested how long women would remain affectionate toward him if he did not shower them with precious gifts, and was surprised by the new kinds of relationships. Of course, there were also phases in therapy in which old oral guilt feelings kept him from opening up and feeling secure. I mirrored his wearying statements during these times as chewing on something hard, in order to start a conversation about the resistance to the underlying oral wishes. In this way, the guilt feelings became increasingly conscious—being too much for others, like his parents, with his childish, naive wishes, because the parents were so busy with adult matters and with earning a lot of money for him. Without addressing the excessive advance payment and later his feelings of guilt, these would have formed an almost insurmountable resistance to the regrowth of his hands, even if he had stayed with me for 7 years. ◀

8.3 Resistances of Obsessive and Phobic Character Structures

▶ In the anal phase, which dominates the development of the toddler from the second to the fourth year of life, in addition to the development of cleanliness, the child's wishes for autonomy—to do things alone, to be able to—are especially important, as are issues of power, control, who decides what, who dominates whom, and the question of how much aggression is possible and helpful in relationships.

At the end of the first year of life, the baby first learns to crawl, and later to walk. Full of drive, it moves—at first with wobbly steps, then increasingly confidently—away from the mother and conquers its environment. As Mahler (1972) calls it, the child almost euphorically enjoys its growing strength, which means it no longer has to be carried through the world by its mother, completely dependent on her. Now it is independent and wants to do everything by itself. The words "I" for autonomy, to do something oneself, and "no" for "not you," that is, for setting boundaries and asserting one's own will, are favorite words at this age. The phase is also called the defiant phase to express these phenomena, but also the aggression that becomes noticeable to those around during this time. The word aggression comes from the Latin "aggredī" and means to move toward something or someone, to approach, to come near, or to attack. The latter can be hostile, but can also be understood as "to tackle something," "to take something on," for example, to begin an unpleasant but necessary task, or to overcome one's fear in order to address something important in a relationship, to approach the other person to clarify something, to express criticism, or to set a boundary. In the third phase of the development of drive theory from 1915 to 1920, Freud named aggression as the second central drive, alongside libido. Animals also have aggression, to defend or gain resources, as well as to cope with dangerous situations, within their own species or outside, toward animals of another species. In mammals, intraspecific aggression serves to defend territory and for competition, but only in extremely rare cases does it lead to killing a conspecific. In humans, unfortunately, this biological limitation of behavior has been lifted, so that we kill each other by the millions, which is why Freud, after the First World War, spoke of the death drive from 1920 onward. He assigned this regulatory function to the superego, the conscience, which is innate in other mammals, knowing that in each of us there is a very different, moral instance that has a very different degree of influence on our actions. Winnicott (1965) spoke of constructive aggression, which is aimed at making contact and setting boundaries, not at destruction. Aggression becomes destructive only when it is too strongly suppressed or punished in the child, or not limited at all, and when the child's superego cannot sufficiently keep it in check.

From the rapprochement phase described by Mahler (1972), we know that there is another side: toddlers venture boldly out into the world, but again and again they feel fear, their smallness, their powerlessness, so they look back or run back to their mother to sit on her lap. Here, longings for dependence, support, and submission to the mother's power and strength arise. Similar to wishes for autonomy, these too can be frustrated, shamed, or associated with feelings of fear or guilt by the family. As a result, conflicted structures remain in the character of the growing child. König (2004) distinguishes the following two character structures in this area of conflict:

1. In compulsively structured personality parts, wishes for autonomy, power, and control, expressions of one's own will, as well as aggressive impulses have been forbidden and suppressed, so that the toddler has already early on associated them with feelings of guilt or shame for being a defiant, naughty child. Later in life, these people, who appear well-adjusted, have no inner access to aggressive feelings, so they do not defend themselves, do not express their will, do not set boundaries, cannot negotiate compromises in relationships, but instead quickly submit, allow themselves to be controlled, become dependent, and adapt. Since autonomy is important for showing one's own feelings, which may differ from those of others, these individuals often appear very affectless, rational, intellectualizing, or pragmatic. To superiors, colleagues, but also people in their private environment, these characters are often very pleasant, because they do not cause trouble, but obediently subordinate themselves and do what they are told. If they develop psychological disorders, these are often compulsive control behaviors. For example, they may have to check twenty times whether they really turned off the stove, or whether a spark of their aggression might have slipped out unnoticed and blown up the whole house, in which so many things have already annoyed them. In psychotherapy, they show resistance because they cannot say: "I would like to talk about these experiences today." Or: "This experience is on my mind today." Instead, they look closely at the therapist to guess whether what they say is right or wrong, whether she wants to hear it or not. Some find it a little easier to talk about themselves and their feelings by lying on the couch and not having to see the therapist, but for most, the fear of doing something wrong and angering the therapist only increases. Therefore, it is important, beyond the content the patient brings up, to address the resistance, to talk independently of the therapist's imagined expectations about oneself and the currently dominant affects. Through the patient's fear, which she then communicates to us—of being yelled at, beaten, judged, or punished with withdrawal of love if she does not guess and fulfill our expectations—we often quickly reach early, painful experiences that have shaped her, but are now dysfunctional. When these patients are able to reduce their structure-specific resistance and stay more with themselves, we have already made a very significant step forward with them.
2. In phobically structured people, the family of origin tended to react with great fear to even the smallest steps toward autonomy. One patient recalled how her mother

would immediately run over and pick her up if she got dirty on the playground or even stumbled and fell. The mother would then say, “It’s terrible here, we’re never coming back!” So, outside of mother’s arms, the world is full of dangers and dirt. According to König (2004), mothers like these become controlling objects for the growing child. They spend their lives seeking people to take the mother’s place, to control and direct everything they do, so that nothing bad can possibly happen to them. If they develop psychological disorders, these are mainly phobias—fears associated with places or actions, such as crowds, large squares, or elevators that might get stuck. In psychotherapy, the therapist naturally becomes a controlling object. She is supposed to specify what the patient can talk about safely and which inner playgrounds she should avoid in order not to experience anxiety. Patients with these personality structure components usually say one or two sentences and then look expectantly at the therapist, so that she can tell them where to direct their thoughts next. To engage them in active participation, we must address these structure-specific resistances, encouraging patients to take more and more steps in their thinking independently, without our explicit approval. If it becomes too much autonomy for them, they can return to us emotionally, and then set out again into the world of their inner self. We should have them describe all the feelings of this back and forth, so that patients gradually give up their resistance to independent—and one might say “self-willed”—thinking and feeling.

Example

Uwe, a 54-year-old, compulsively structured civil engineer, suffered not only from essential hypertension but also from compulsive control behaviors. At home, in the apartment he shared with his equally compulsively structured wife, he had to check the stove for several minutes before leaving to make sure it was really turned off, so the house wouldn’t explode if a mail carrier rang the bell and ignited the leaked gas. In his office, he had to unplug all the sockets so that a spark wouldn’t blow up the building if a plug wasn’t properly seated. While he otherwise could not name feelings or describe situations, he had very intense images and above all feelings of fear about these explosions. When he spoke in the therapy group, it was a very systematic, orderly, purely rational presentation, isolated from all affects and all context—initially even read from a note—which tired the other group members. Often, however, he remained silent for long periods, saying nothing to others. Instead, he would jot down individual letters and numbers on a small slip of paper, his face turning red. When another group member asked what he was writing, he said, holding up his pen: “These are the speaking times of the individual group members.” When asked why he was recording them, he explained, again red in the face but with a very calm voice, that it was very clear from this that all the others here had received more than twice as much speaking time as he had, so he assumed he would soon be allotted 32 minutes. In one session, we understood that he could not feel the anger about being shortchanged here, but that it was expressed solely through his elevated blood pressure and the color of his face. Since he had no access to his constructive aggression, he could neither feel nor express the wish to say something himself. Only through numbers could he calculate a justification for himself. His fear was that he might explode inside, lose control of his anger, which had built up over many years, if he ever allowed himself to feel even a spark of annoyance. Then what he feared in his compulsive fantasies would happen—everything would blow up. Step by step, he was able to reduce his structure-specific resistance and more spontaneously risk showing something of himself, without knowing how the others would react. Others addressed his red face more often; sometimes he replied that he was just warm, but more and more often he was able to name anger at someone in the group or outside, along with the feelings of guilt that experiencing this anger brought him. I had already described in the section on tertiary gain from illness that it was initially not easy for his wife when he began to show feelings of anger and expressions of his own will outside the therapy group as well, and what different kinds of resistance this led to. ◀

8.4 Resistances of Histrionic and Narcissistic Structures

▶ The phallic phase, from the fifth to the seventh year of life, falls into a period in which children have developed a representational self (see Fonagy & Target, 2015). They possess a differentiated image of their psychological self, their body, and important other people. They can distinguish between different genders and begin to engage with their own sexuality, which gives the phase its name.

König (2004) distinguishes two subphases:

1. The phallic phase in the narrower sense, which concerns the competition between same-sex children, such as five-year-old boys competing to see who can urinate the farthest or girls of a similar age comparing their dresses. The children focus on their appearance, their bodies, and their genitals, and compare themselves to others. This comparison can occur in two ways: competition comes from the Latin word "concurrere," meaning to run together in a race, or contest. The destructive variant, rivalry, on the other hand, derives from the Latin "rivalis," a person who is allowed to use a "rivus," a stream or brook, for example, to irrigate their field, but who takes more than their share, depriving others or even cutting them off from the water entirely. Thus, there are joyful, developmentally stimulating forms of competition, but also destructive, exploitative, and castrating variants. Which one a child learns depends on their family, but also on the surrounding society. If children are discriminated against because of their skin color, gender, physical disabilities, or other factors, this can

sometimes leave them with lifelong feelings of inferiority. Something similar happens if they repeatedly lose in a competition that is actually meant to be joyful and fair, and are not comforted or encouraged to find their strengths in another area. They are then left, symbolically speaking, with the feeling of having too small a phallus, for which they must be ashamed, which they should not show for fear of being laughed at by their peers. They then believe they are not pretty, not intelligent, not athletic enough to be accepted and liked by others. Narcissistic character traits develop, and in the case of illness, narcissistic disorders. Freud derived this term from the Greek mythology of Narcissus (Latin: Narcissus): Narcissus was a rejected child of rape, who at 16 was very beautiful, desired by many lovers of both sexes, but who himself loved no one. In a body of water, he saw his reflection, without realizing that the beautiful youth there was himself. He fell in love with the image, but it immediately blurred and dissolved whenever his tears fell into the water or his hands tried to grasp what he saw. In trying to jump into the water to finally catch the youth, he drowned, and a narcissus flower grew on the bank, which still reminds us of him today. Even though, within and now also outside psychoanalysis, narcissism is associated with a person having withdrawn their libido from others and directed it entirely at themselves—thus appearing self-absorbed and egotistical—we should not forget the second part of the story. People with narcissistic character traits intensely seek admiration and recognition, but are unable to accept or retain it. Their preoccupation with themselves is a desperate, often futile attempt to understand who they really are. One patient described, for example, how a man of the same age looked at her admiringly. She turned around, confused, to see if there was a beautiful woman behind her. But when she saw no one, she turned back and gave the man a contemptuous look, thinking he must be quite crazy and disturbed to look at someone like her with such admiration. She could not connect the reflection in his eyes with herself, even though she longed for such a reflection again and again. In psychotherapy, these people will present themselves well-dressed, tell very intelligent and entertaining stories, but are unable to truly perceive or accept our recognition and admiration. Another form of resistance appears in that they turn us into the cursed nymph Echo, who in the myth can only repeat the last words of another as an echo, never formulating anything of her own. They talk the entire session. If we at some point feel we should make a comment or ask a question, they feel disturbed and quickly return to their original monologue. Kohut (2016) recommends avoiding such interruptions and instead listening empathically for a long time. I consider it more useful to address the structure-specific resistance as early as possible by mirroring what is happening in the session, especially that the patient cannot hear or accept anything from us, perhaps with the help of the story of Narcissus and Echo. We can expect the same brusque rejection and anger that Echo experienced when she finally reached Narcissus. However, the anger also forms a bridge between us. The patient's question as to whether we consider her a narcissist may contain some hurt, but it also opens a conversation about how we perceive and experience her, what images we might have of her. We become the body of water, whose reflection does not blur so quickly, but can be emotionally understood and embraced.

2. For the Oedipal phase, Freud referred to the drama "King Oedipus" by Sophocles, in which Oedipus kills his father, King Laius of Thebes, and has incestuous sexual relations with his mother Jocasta, fathering children. However, Oedipus does not know for a long time that they are his parents, because they abandoned him as a newborn and he only survived because he was found and raised by another king. Laius and Jocasta, fearing an oracle's prophecy, did exactly what later happened, so that a triangular relationship between the two of them and their son seemed impossible—something that is important in the Oedipal phase. In this phase, children enter into competition or rivalry with their parents. They first identify with the same-sex parent, provided they admire them and see them as a role model. They want to be as beautiful and strong as that parent. Only afterwards do they enter into competition with them for the favor of the other parent. Ideally, a triangulation has developed between the two parents and the child: from three dyads, that is, two-person relationships, a triangle has formed, with the child C, the mother M, and the father F as its vertices. The triangle is never isosceles; sometimes C and M are closer, then M and F, perhaps in the evening in the bedroom, so that C is farther away in the children's room. This is painful, because the lines from C to M and C to F are much longer than between M and F. But if triangulation is successful, the child knows that soon they will be closer to M or F again than the other parent. However, many conflicts can arise, for example, if the family is more characterized by rivalry than competition. Any approach of C to M, for example, will be experienced by F as if one side of the triangle is being cut, so that F feels jealousy, hatred, and exclusion, and tries to destroy the connection between C and M. The child senses the father's anger and jealousy and internalizes it as Oedipal guilt. The boy internalizes the fear of being punished—Freud would say castrated—if he succeeds in winning the mother's favor and admiration. He experiences himself as beautiful and lovable, but is not allowed to be, or at least no third party should see it, otherwise tormenting feelings of guilt arise for something so deeply desired. As a histrionically structured adult, he will seduce women, but after the first kiss leave them, develop erectile dysfunction, or only have secret affairs with married women. As soon as these women consider leaving their husbands for him, he—panicked by Oedipal guilt—will end the affair and seek the next secret love. Another variant is that the mother no longer loves the father and has lost all erotic interest in him, but has not yet wanted to separate. If the father feels the same, he will not react with jealousy to his son's advances, so the son can run into the mother's open arms. However, he will internalize that beautiful women only love boys, not adult men, so that even as an adult he retains a childlike, boyish aura. He will associate all things masculine with Oedipal shame, the fantasy that men are unattractive and disgusting, as the father once was for the mother. There are many more variants that could be explored here. Benjamin (2020) has described the Oedipal triad in great detail for girls. In single-parent, separated, same-sex, transgender par-

ents, and all other constellations possible in our liberal society today, we find many developmental possibilities as well as somewhat different courses of Oedipal development. In psychotherapy, we will try to empathize with the early triads of our histrionically structured female patients in order to understand what traces they have left in them. When choosing a therapist, the Oedipally desired parent may be chosen, which is more favorable in order to encounter and work through the Oedipal conflict within the transference relationship. The patient will then try very hard to please us and to be admired by us for her beauty or charm. If she succeeds, she either does not notice it and experiences us as uninterested and grumpy when she comes, or she does notice it and reacts with fear and guilt. A patient once asked me, quite startled, why I was smiling when I opened the door for her, and almost ran away. We were able to discuss the Oedipal guilt feelings about seeing something she had actually longed for and had never previously perceived in me. If the patient's failure to perceive friendly or approving reactions from the therapist, as well as her Oedipal fears and guilt feelings, are not discussed, they lead to a structure-specific resistance.

Two remarks are still important to me in this context: First, in histrionic character structures or disorders, the incest barrier has always been maintained by the parents. If they have not observed the incest taboo—the legal and, for most people, internalized prohibition of sexual acts between blood relatives—and have sexually abused their children, this results in severe, complex post-traumatic impairments of the entire personality, which burden the lives of the growing children with deep anxiety, mistrust instead of trust, and much more. This group of people, who today can fortunately be treated very well psychotherapeutically, is not meant here, because they have to cope with completely different conflicts, mostly concerning separation, and to process traumatic experiences, that is, experiences that are actually unmanageable for people.

Second, the term "hysterical" has been controversial in recent decades. It derives from the ancient Greek "hystéra" for uterus, because, among others, Plato assumed that it was a kind of living being of its own, which, after childbirth, desires and, if this desire is not fulfilled, wanders through the body, where it causes behavioral abnormalities or complaints such as palpitations, paralysis, blindness, or deafness, without any organic causes. These disorders were formerly called hysteria and today fall under somatoform disorders. The behaviors mentioned were mainly anxiety attacks, egocentricity, and a craving for attention. By associating it with the uterus, hysterical behaviors and illnesses were at times seen by some authors as purely female diseases, though by many others not: In 1618, Charles Lepois already described hysteria as a nervous, i.e., neurologically based illness that has nothing to do with the uterus. Georges Gilles de la Tourette assigned it to the brain in 1821. Jean-Martin Charcot even believed that hysteria affected men more than women. Christian Buddenbrook suffers from a globus hystericus in Thomas Mann's novel *Buddenbrooks*. Sigmund Freud described both hysterical phenomena and phallic conflicts in women and men alike. The terms phallic and hysterical refer to sexual organs, which, however, are not the cause, but rather a symbol for something conflictual, as I outlined in the previous two sections—conflicts that have to do with becoming aware of and accepting one's own body and gender. However, since hysteria was repeatedly used by some men as an explanation for phenomena they found puzzling and inexplicable in women, but also to control, devalue, and oppress women, feminists found it discriminatory. For this reason, since the 1980s, it has been replaced in the diagnostic manuals DSM and ICD, as well as in parts of the specialist literature, by histrionic. The adjective comes from the Latin noun "histrio," which in ancient Rome referred to an actor. Histrionic, or in English "histrionic," means theatrical, dramatic, and affected, thus describing part of the phenomena associated with the Oedipal conflict in people's experience. However, in some quotations in the book, the earlier term hysterical still appears.

Example

Several examples have already been mentioned in the preceding text, so I will forgo another one here for reasons of space. ◀

9 Countertransference Resistances

> Countertransference encompasses all the therapist's mental, emotional, imaginal, physical, and behavioral reactions that are triggered by the patient through her way of shaping the relationship, that is, through her transference. On the one hand, these are reactions set in motion by the patient's stories, feelings, and behavior in the empathic therapist, who contains the patient's feelings and senses the roles assigned to her. On the other hand, they are the therapist's very own internal reactions to the patient, as a subject with her own personal life and relationship experiences, her current life situation, her age, gender, social status, and with all her own feelings of love, joy, fear, anger, shame, and guilt, entering the therapeutic encounter. Both halves are equally important and will therefore be presented in detail in two separate sections.

The term countertransference was coined by Sigmund Freud in 1909 in correspondence with Carl Gustav Jung. From 1908 to 1909, Jung had a sexual relationship with Sabina Spielrein, who had been his patient since 1904, initially due to a psychotic episode at the Burghölzli psychiatric university clinic in Zurich, and later in his outpatient practice. He subsequently had further sexual relationships with his patients, such as Antonia Wolff (see Krutzenbichler & Essler, 2002). Both Sabina Spielrein and Jung's wife, Emma Jung, turned to Freud to inform him about the love affair, to which he reacted with shock. He introduced the concept of countertransference, by which he meant all feelings and impulses triggered in the psychoanalyst by his patients. Thus, countertransference represented the opposite of Freud's concept that the psychoanalyst should be a pure mirror for the patients, reflecting only their experience, while remaining completely unemotional, i.e., abstinent, feeling nothing of his own, let alone showing it. Therefore, he should not believe that feelings of love from patients are directed at him, because these are feelings that actually relate to their parents, such as their father. They are only transferred onto him because the patient sees not the psychoanalyst as a person and man in the mirror, but

T. Abel, *Resistance in Psychotherapy*, https://doi.org/10.1007/978-3-662-72663-1_9

her father. Freud (1915, p. 308) admonished his colleagues not to be too flattered by a patient's infatuation:

> "For the doctor, it is a valuable clarification and a good warning against any countertransference that may be lying in wait for him. He must recognize that the patient's falling in love is forced by the analytic situation and cannot be attributed to the merits of his own person, so he has no reason to be proud of such a 'conquest,' as it would be called outside of analysis."

Anyone who is nevertheless proud or even develops feelings of their own is experiencing countertransference, which must absolutely be avoided or worked through and resolved in the psychoanalyst's own analysis. In this context, the idea of a mandatory training analysis for aspiring psychoanalysts first emerged, to prevent the development of countertransference as much as possible in advance. After the above quote, Freud did not mention countertransference again, even though other close confidants of his, such as Sandor Ferenczi, also entered into love relationships with patients. It was not until 1949 that Paula Heimann gave a lecture on countertransference at the International Psychoanalytic Congress in Zurich and developed the understanding of it over many years (see Heimann, 2016). König (1993) provides an overview of other authors who made important contributions to countertransference. Abel (2023) also presents the modern, mostly American, intersubjective approaches, which go a step further in that they describe the therapist as a subject who is a unique part of the therapeutic interaction, rather than an anonymous, imperceptible, abstinent object. Otherwise, artificial intelligence could take over our work. In digital health applications, it already does so, for example as an app for patients with panic disorders or social phobia, who receive behavioral instructions and record their experiences in the app, on which the next interventions depend.

The basic rule we set for our patients in therapy—that they may feel, say, and physically express anything in the therapeutic space, but that physical violence or any kind of transgressive behavior is not permitted—naturally applies to us as well. Entering into a sexual relationship with a patient or hitting her would be a violation of ethical guidelines and professional regulations. In Germany, a compromise has been negotiated between different therapeutic schools, according to which a romantic relationship between a therapist and her patient is permitted two years after the end of psychotherapy. Behavioral therapy associations had argued in the debate for it to be allowed immediately after the end of therapy, while psychoanalytic organizations did not want to allow it at all. The experiences in the history of psychoanalysis show that such love relationships usually end quickly and disappointingly—not only in the cases of Jung or Ferenczi, who, during his love affair with his patient, also had a sexual relationship with her daughter, but also, for example, in the case of Frieda Reichmann, who married her analysand Erich Fromm in 1926. Even though they occasionally worked together after their separation in 1931, and even though Frieda Fromm-Reichmann never gave up her married name, the relationship was a disappointment for both. The deception inherent in this word is explained by the folk tale "Godfather Death," recorded by the Brothers Grimm (see Drewermann, 1992; Abel, 2005): In it, a doctor falls in love with a terminally ill princess whom he wishes to marry before she recovers—before he can experience what kind of person she really is when she is not pale and barely speaking on her deathbed. Likewise, she does not know what his good and dark sides are when he takes off his doctor's coat. Nevertheless, she also wants him as a man. Countertransference that gets out of control thus existed in doctor-patient relationships even before Carl Gustav Jung and psychoanalysis, or else it would not have found its way into a folk tale. Likewise, there is no wedding in the tale, so the experience that such things do not end well is also an old one. In a psychotherapeutic treatment, therapist and patient get to know each other very intensively, but only to a certain extent. If they meet in everyday life, it is no longer an asymmetrical but a symmetrical, equal relationship. The patient is not only weak, terminally ill, and pale, but perhaps a passionate dancer who attracts many glances. The doctor is not only a powerful savior and helper, but may also reveal insecure and malicious sides in everyday relationship life. The image of the other, which had attracted both at the sickbed, turns out to be an illusion. Beyond all ethical boundaries, it is therefore not a good idea, even after two years, to try to form a romantic relationship out of a countertransference that has not subsided. It would be better for both sides if the therapist dealt with her countertransference feelings—whether alone, in supervision, or in self-experience—in order to understand what has happened, which feelings come from the patient, which from herself, and how she can use this for therapeutic progress.

Conclusion

The understanding of countertransference has fundamentally changed to this day: Whereas it was once considered an emotional misstep to be avoided, we now perceive and take seriously all aspects of what patients trigger in us. This greatly intensifies the therapeutic process. Today, psychotherapists of all orientations are required to get to know themselves internally through self-experience as part of their training or further education, in order to be better prepared for perceiving and dealing with countertransference.

9.1 Therapist's Resistance to Empathy and Role Adoption

► One half of the resistance on the therapist's side has to do with what she internally receives from what the patient communicates and conveys emotionally. This concerns disturbances in empathizing and feeling with the patient, in containing the patient's strong affects, as well as the willingness to take on roles that the patient transfers or communicates.

Freud (1912) compared the psychotherapist to the receiver of a telephone, which receives and deciphers signals that have been encoded and sent on their way through a wire by the microphone of the speaking person. Without decoding the signals, no conversation, no understanding would be possible. The psychotherapist picks up many verbal and nonverbal signals from her patient and resonates with them internally. Problems in the receiver lead to misunderstanding or lack of understanding, and thus become a resistance to the progress of therapy. The therapist should pay close attention to and examine these, just as we would take apart a crackling telephone receiver to search for the reception problem, to stay with Freud's vivid image.

In psychodynamic approaches, the therapist becomes the receiver by entering a state of free or evenly suspended attention. She takes in all the patient's verbal and nonverbal communications without prejudice, giving them internal space by allowing images, feelings, bodily sensations, and thoughts to arise completely freely, without judging them as important, trivial, pleasant, embarrassing, disturbing, or pleasurable, and perhaps even rejecting them. She does not let herself be guided by abstract, theoretical concepts, nor by expectations of what the patient might or should talk about today. The synthetic work takes place only in the second part of the session, in which the psychotherapist tries, together with the patient, to establish connections. The better the patient succeeds in free association and the therapist in evenly suspended attention, the more a therapeutic conversation differs from everyday communication, which follows certain rules and connections. This difference is one of the most important active factors in psychotherapy. Often, a patient will talk with a friend over a glass of wine about the same topics as with her psychotherapist, but in that context, she is not allowed to jump seemingly randomly from one topic to another, but must first work through one subject before moving on to something else. Through the highly modified conversational technique, which both patient and therapist must first learn, different insights and deeper understanding emerge in therapy. Resistance arises here, on the one hand, among beginners who are nervous in their first treatment sessions, want to be helpful and active, not make mistakes, and not miss anything important. Out of fear, they cling to theoretical concepts, just like the second group, namely compulsively structured therapists. In the previous Sect. 8.3 I described that compulsive personality structures are very interested in control and power, have difficulty tolerating ignorance, chaos, and uncertainty, and therefore quickly fall back on rationality and theories. Both groups are therefore unable to surrender to "free floating attention," as it is called in English, so that already here there is static in the receiver, i.e., a resistance to evenly suspended attention on the part of the therapist.

Once the therapist has resolved her reception problems, the next step is empathy, a word derived from Ancient Greek, composed of "pathos" for suffering or passion and the prefix "em" for in, at, or on, thus meaning "feeling into." Here, we can imagine what is going on inside the other person, but without emotionally resonating ourselves. That happens with sympathy, also from an ancient Greek word, "sympátheia," meaning compassion. Here, we feel or suffer along with someone else, perhaps sensing in a weakened form the patient's sadness, anger, joy, or excitement within ourselves. If we are not even capable of empathy, but have the impression that the patient is making a serious effort to communicate her experience, therapeutic communication is, of course, severely impaired. For us, resistance to understanding the patient arises if we do not take the empathy problem seriously or too quickly see it as our own problem. If we take it seriously, no resistance arises on our part, because we will soon understand that we cannot empathize with something that is not there. Fonagy et al. (2004) have compiled findings from current infant and toddler research and outlined five phases of mental development. Only in phase four, in the second year of life, does the child become an intentional agent, internally representing their own feelings, intentions, and motives, as well as those of others. Children at this age sense what their mother wants or does not want, even if she does not say so, because they have a first, still vague model in their mind of how their mother thinks and feels, what intentions she has. In all earlier phases, such internal images do not yet exist. In the third, the teleological phase, other people can at least be assessed by their outwardly visible actions, and the child can communicate through actions. Autistic and other patients often have not reached phase four, but instead try to calm themselves and communicate with others through stereotypical actions. They have no internal representations of themselves or others to draw upon. That is what I meant when I said that there is nothing in them for us to empathize with. In this way, they are already conveying their central problem to us. Before we can work with them therapeutically in the usual way, mentalization-based interventions according to Fonagy and Target (2015) are necessary, as well as fostering symbolization abilities, so that patients gradually reach stages four and five of mental development, have representations of self and objects in their minds, into which we can then also empathize. In Sect. 2.1.11 I wrote about the autistic patient Antonia, who had no images of herself or others in her mind, but at best could describe their actions. In a clinic, she was given infusions of ketamine, a hallucinogenic drug, as a kind of desperate attempt by doctors to provide her with internal images, even if only hallucinations. But not even ketamine could evoke anything in this imageless inner emptiness. The resistance of the clinic colleagues to admitting that they could not empathize with the patient because there was only emptiness inside her led to this futile treatment attempt. It would have been better to understand the emptiness in the therapist's mind while listening as an inability to empathize, despite the best efforts of both patient and therapist, and to draw the above-mentioned conclusions from this.

If we succeed in empathizing, so that we sense what images, thoughts, and feelings the patient has in her mind, but are not sympathetic, not compassionate, cannot emotionally resonate with her even a little, this is often also due to the way the patient communicates, provided we know we are not just having a bad day and have indeed felt compassion with previous patients. We should take the lack of compassion seriously, because it would be resistance to ignore it, just to avoid feeling emotionally numb or inexperienced, because with this patient we simply cannot feel anything. Taking it seriously would mean asking ourselves why the patient is telling us something important to her without triggering anything in us. Often, we can infer a rationalization by the patient, who only communicates explanatory thoughts about her experience, but wards off feelings, i.e., does not feel them. Our lack of feeling in the countertransference would then be a feeling with the patient's lack of feeling. If she shows feelings, such as sadness, but we do not notice the slightest sadness in ourselves, this can be a sign of affect isolation, so that the patient would say the sadness has nothing to do with the story. She then isolates us from the sadness, just as she has isolated herself from it. Or a sadness that cannot be empathized with is the result of the patient's affectualization, who is actually angry inside but does not dare to show the anger outwardly, preferring to cry instead. We do not feel the sadness with her because it is not the true feeling the patient connects with the content. We could ask whether there are other feelings hidden within the patient besides sadness, so that she can indicate that she sometimes also feels anger when she thinks about the topic. All these and many other reasons can lead to the patient not allowing us to feel with her. Some also do not want to be pitied. We will only be able to understand the respective reasons if we take our lack of compassion seriously and perceive it, otherwise it will become resistance on our part.

Depending on the therapist's personality structure, resistances to feeling with the patient may arise, which every therapist should know about herself or discover in her own self-experience. Schizoid therapists are usually very sensitive and also sense what is unspoken in the other person. However, they have difficulty empathizing with or feeling with something that is very different from their own experience. Here, they may encounter empathy or sympathy resistance, so that the patient cannot reach them with her experiences. Compulsive therapists cannot tolerate too many feelings from the patient, so they soothe rather than empathize. From a sober perspective, everything is not so bad after all. They quickly categorize the patient's feelings into rational, theoretical categories before they can even unfold. Phobically structured therapists are afraid of their patients' aggression and therefore cannot feel with them well in these areas. Depressive therapists want to be needed and caring, so their patients' wishes for autonomy seem threatening, because then the patient might soon manage on her own, without her therapist. Histrionic therapists can often feel with the patient quickly and intensely, so that they themselves are moved to tears when the patient cries. For some patients, this would be frightening, so they would rather not cry anymore, for example, to avoid being pitied again. Narcissistic therapists want their patients to feel significantly better soon and to admire their therapist for it. If the patient's emotional litanies repeat, they become bored or internally devalue the patient for not changing, not making an effort, not appreciating how much the therapist is helping her. Everyone should know her individual reasons that sometimes make it difficult to empathize and feel with the patient, and which can thus become resistance to therapeutic progress.

If we are able to empathize and feel with our patients, differentiated and immature thoughts, feelings, images, impulses, and longings reach us, into our container, as Bion (1962) called it. Especially when dealing with strong, unprocessed feelings and impulses, the alpha function falls to us—a preliminary processing of primitive beta elements, that is, undigested, diffuse affects, which we then return to the patient in small, manageable doses. Containing is a particularly important element of our work with early-disturbed patients and their primitive, intense affects. However, our container is not always the same size or equally stable. When we are going through life transitions, have much of our own to process, or are plagued by illness, we should tune in to ourselves to sense how much can currently fit into our container, and perhaps refer an early-disturbed patient, whom we would otherwise gladly have taken on, to a colleague. During the recovery phase after an encephalitis, I initially began working just two hours a day. I had no difficulties in everyday life and could exercise for hours. It was only when I wanted to use my brain, my container, that I developed headaches, even before I could clearly feel and distinguish the feelings conveyed to me in my container. I became painfully aware, in the truest sense of the word, of how much from our patients is initially communicated subliminally, unconsciously, before we notice what has accumulated in our internal waste bin. I could not resume therapy with all patients at the same time, so I started with the most unstable and sickest. That was certainly a mistake, because they are the ones who need the most containing, for which my wounded brain was not yet well equipped. Some I had to refer to colleagues for a few weeks until I was able to withstand the onslaught of their affects again. If we overestimate our container, this constitutes a resistance on our part to the therapy, because the patients are then left sitting on part of their unprocessed affects, perhaps even losing hope that anyone could help them with this at all.

The last and certainly most delicate aspect in this area is what Sandler (1976) described in his groundbreaking work "Countertransference and role responsiveness" as the most important part of countertransference: the evenly suspended readiness to echo, that is, the willingness to take on roles that our patients unconsciously assign to us at any given moment. At every moment, the patient unconsciously assumes a role and assigns her therapist a complementary role. For example, she may experience herself as a four-year-old who wants to fight with her mother for her own will, autonomy, and power. The therapist would then be assigned the role of the strict, prohibitive mother. As long as the therapist sits in her chair, nodding kindly and listening patiently to the patient, it would be a transference if the patient were to say she experiences the therapist as strict and rejecting of everything she wants to share. The therapist could ask how the patient comes to this impression, to which the patient might reply that although the therapist looks at her kindly and permissively, she suspects that behind the facade the therapist is annoyed and impatient. Here it would be clear that the patient is seeing something on the "therapist" screen that is not actually there, so a transference interpretation would soon be possible and easily comprehensible for the patient. But what if the therapist actually becomes annoyed and impatient, thinking that everything the patient is saying is unimportant, and that she would rather talk about another, truly important topic? Then she would be in the role assigned to her by the patient. Whether she just looks a bit annoyed, shifts restlessly in her chair, or makes somewhat impatient interventions, the patient will notice. A transference interpretation would not only be useless but actually wrong, because the patient is not seeing something that is not there, but rather, is seeing something that is there: a prohibitive person who does not want the patient to talk about what is important to her at that moment, who wants to control her and restrict her autonomy. If we ask the patient how she experiences us, she will usually be able to name quite a few details about our impatience. We do not deny our patients' accurate perceptions, but rather confirm them. We can partially share our countertransference by saying that she sometimes makes us impatient, that we sometimes think she should talk about something else. She will probably recall many scenes with her mother, but also from her current life with others who also take on the mother's former role. Ultimately, she will have a part within herself that is often impatient with her, especially when there is no other impatient person nearby to whom she could assign this role. This makes it clearer what has happened between us. The externalized conflict between patient and therapist once again becomes an internal conflict between a self that is fighting for autonomy and a prohibitive mother object.

The second variant is that we are assigned the role of a part of the self. My patient Bea told rather long-winded stories about various people in her current life from whom she did not feel well treated, but whom she excused or at least internally defended, saying that they actually meant well by her. Within me, impatience grew, and later even anger. When Bea asked me in a sing-song voice whether something was making me angry, I confirmed that a feeling of that sort had indeed spread in me, without my knowing why. She nodded in surprisingly understanding fashion and told me that she sometimes also became very angry, for example, when she wanted to buy something for a bulimic episode but it took forever at the checkout because other customers and the cashiers were endlessly fumbling around. She would then secretly clench her fists in her jacket and could scream out loud why it was taking so long. At the same time, she was frightened by the enormous anger inside her and felt like a sweating monster. In her real-life relationships, she had never been able to talk about the monster, which originated from the time with her mentally ill mother, who often lamented about herself and her suffering without ever being interested in her daughter's needs. Only in complete secrecy, during vomiting, did the monster express in drastic terms how much it found everything disgusting. My impatience and anger quickly disappeared as we talked about the role of the angry child that she had assigned to me, while she had slipped into the role of her lamenting mother. In addition to interpreting this role assignment, I was able to convey my joy and relief that she had, in this way, allowed me to feel how much anger at everything she had experienced was still inside her, which encouraged her to make further role assignments.

However, the roles that are offered to us are very often associated with very intense feelings—of hatred, deep sadness, fear, but also intense love, sexual desire, and great longing. Feelings are evoked in us that we have never experienced with such intensity in everyday life or in our own self-exploration. Many therapists have inner aversions to one or another group of these roles and do not accept them for a long time or only very reluctantly. This is the resistance in countertransference to the assignment of roles, which hinders us from working through the intense inner conflicts of our patients.

9.2 Resistance through the Therapist's Co-Transference

▶ The second half of countertransference concerns the therapist's experience, which is not primarily related to the patient and what she radiates and communicates, but rather primarily to the therapist herself, her life history, and personality.

Donna Orange (2004, p. 87) proposed the term co-transference for this, essentially the therapist's transference, and describes the significance of her biographical background for her work as a therapist as follows:

> "I grew up as the oldest of ten children. Everything was scarce, both economically and emotionally. So I was raised to be a giver, not a receiver of care. I could value myself mainly for the sheer number of tasks I accomplished to keep the family going. In my earliest memories, I am folding diapers and being held responsible for the misbehavior of my younger siblings or for the damage they caused. This story, and much more that I do not wish to recount in detail, actually forms my experience as a clinician. With my intellectual and clinical training, this story filters, informs, and organizes both my ideas and my responsiveness to patients, whether they are the oldest, youngest, or middle children, or only children. An intersubjective approach to psychoanalytic understanding must take into account the subjective world of the analyst, including his or her theory, personality, emotional history, and pre-reflective organizing principles. Co-transference refers primarily to the analyst's contribution to the intersubjective field in psychoanalytic treatment."

As already discussed under the framework resistances in Sect. 2.1.1, a patient should only decide to undergo psychotherapy with a therapist if she feels comfortable and understood during the initial contact; otherwise, she should continue searching. Likewise, a therapist should only take on a patient if she can empathize with her, finds her likable and interesting. In the next step, we explore the question of why we chose to treat this particular patient and not another, what we see in her, what we want to make of her—that is, what kind of development we envision for her and perhaps also what we do not envision.

With transference resistances, the focus was on what the patient sees in the therapist—whether she projects her mother, father, a sibling, or her partner onto the therapist. She may also project onto the therapist an accepted or rejected part of herself. Very similar questions arise for the therapist. Despite all the differences, entering into a therapeutic relationship can certainly be compared to starting a partnership, perhaps even to having children. Parents often have an image of their child before or during pregnancy—how they hope the child will be, how it should never be, what it might become, and much more. For example, a socially anxious and insecure patient named his daughter Lilith, after Adam's first wife, before Eve, who refused to submit to Adam sexually and therefore left him (see Hurwitz, 1980). Even before she was born, she was meant to become a strong, independent woman who would not let anyone push her around—thus embodying the patient's ego ideal, from which he always felt very distant and which he was only able to approach more and more through analytic group therapy. Another example is Oedipus, whose parents, even before his conception, feared something murderous, incestuous that their child might one day develop, so they abandoned him immediately after birth. Emotionally, they rejected their child even before its existence, thereby bringing about exactly what they feared but did not recognize in themselves and instead projected onto their future child (see also Wirth, 2015). Richter (1963, 1970) describes in many of his works the tasks, goals, and burdens—conscious or unconscious—that parents place on their children as they set out in life. Of course, our patients are not our children, but we certainly do sometimes have fantasies about what or how they should become, for example, something we ourselves have not yet achieved. A therapist who sometimes regrets not having had children may be especially attentive to a patient with ambivalent feelings about having children, and may subconsciously hope that the patient will fulfill her wish for a child and not deny herself as the therapist did. The resistance on the therapist's side could consist in not sufficiently attending to the feelings that speak against having a child for the patient. I myself actually wanted to become a writer, but in the GDR I had to choose a course of study, as everyone was expected to pursue vocational training or higher education. I chose psychology. Certainly, I have published academic works, but no novels. With patients, I notice how delighted I am when they discover their artistic side and consider quitting their jobs to write books or paint pictures somewhere on the stormy Baltic Sea. I would love to tell them what a good idea that is, so that they do something I have not yet dared to do myself. The countertransference resistance in me, which I must continually monitor, would lead me to overestimate the importance of my patients' artistic aspirations and to overlook their fears and feelings of guilt associated with this step. These are just two of many possible ways in which we might, for our own reasons, encourage or block something in our patients that has nothing to do with therapeutic techniques. In self-experience as part of psychotherapeutic training, we reflect on our first treatments and will certainly become aware of some of these aspects. But throughout our professional lives, it is wise to keep this part of our countertransference in view, so that it does not become a resistance—or if it already has. The exciting thing about our profession is that in every treatment, in every new relationship with a patient, we also learn a little more about ourselves, if we pay attention to resistances in countertransference.

What we can see in children, partners, therapists, or indeed in patients, Freud (1914) described with his two types of object choice: Either we seek in another person a part of our own self, or an internalized object, usually from our family of origin. Both the self-image and the internal image of another, an object, are projected onto the other person, just as a projector casts an image onto a screen. If it is the image of an object, we speak of transference. Whether the projected image still reveals anything of the screen, of the other person, varies greatly from person to person, but it is beneficial for both us and our patients to occasionally rub our eyes and see that it is indeed our child, our partner, our therapist, or our patient sitting before us—and not our mother or what we dislike in ourselves. The following possible projections onto our patients can be distinguished, following the considerations on partner choice by Richter (1963, 1970) and Wirth (2007, 2015):

1. If the patient embodies the image of the therapist's own self, then she is supposed to become as the therapist sees herself. The therapist's countertransference resistance is then directed against everything in the patient that is her own, where the patient wants to become or be different. The therapy would then produce a being like the cloned child in the film "Blueprint" by Rolf Schübel or the novel of the same name by Charlotte Kerner. It tells the story of a gifted pianist, Iris, who, faced with the onset of multiple sclerosis, has herself cloned so that her musical talent will not be lost through her daughter Siri. Our patient, or those who undergo self-experience with us, would then become a blueprint, a copy of ourselves. This can also concern certain aspects of our self. For example, this is the case for me with patients who are visually impaired or blind. I myself became blind at 19 and, thanks to our free society with its many opportunities for development and thanks to modern computers and smartphones with speech and Braille output, I lead an independent, included, and fulfilling life. When patients come to me whose vision is deteriorating, I can empathize well and offer various opportunities for identification. On the other hand, I sometimes become uneasy when, despite good progress in coping with their visual impairment, they fail to take advantage of opportunities to try new paths, acquire aids, and instead remain in dependencies that are actually unnecessary. Here I am faced with the question of whether it is a resistance on the part of the patient—against granting herself more autonomy, freeing herself from dependencies beyond the eye condition—or whether it is my wish that she do everything as I did, in a way that was good and suitable for me. The latter would be a blueprint of my own way of coping with my handicap. Therapists with schizoid personality traits are, of course, also more often preoccupied with seeing something identical to themselves in the other. If they then work with a schizoid patient who has a twin transference onto the therapist, both see themselves in the other. This can facilitate understanding, but also lead to resistance if one of the twins grows tired of being a blueprint and would like to assume their own identity. Then the therapist should distinguish between the patient's fear of separation and her own fear that the patient will now become more and more different from her.
2. If the patient is the substitute for the therapist's ideal self, she is supposed to fulfill the therapist's unfulfilled wishes and ideals. I have already mentioned two examples above: the childless therapist and myself with my artistic ego ideal.
3. If the therapist projects her own negative self-aspect, which she rejects in herself, onto the patient, the patient is assigned the role of acting out, on behalf of the therapist, the forbidden wishes, weaknesses, fears, malice, and feelings of inferiority of her practitioner. The therapist will then encourage the patient to acknowledge her fears and weaknesses by openly displaying them, but will subsequently attempt to combat or civilize what has been projected onto the patient.

3.1. Therapists with schizoid character structure components may perceive in their patient a part of themselves that longs for very close, boundless, symbiotic fusion. They may then offer the patient an increased session frequency of two, three, four, or five hours per week, or double sessions. They will not be able to end therapy sessions on time, because every separation is too frightening for the childlike self-aspect projected onto the patient. They will not be able to understand well if their patient is late or makes other attempts to set boundaries, and will interpret this as resistance on the part of the patient, even though these are actually quite normal boundary-setting behaviors of a patient who does not have such great needs for closeness as the projected self-aspect of her therapist.

3.2. Most therapists have depressive structural components in their personality. In their patient, they care for a needy part of themselves that longs for security, motherliness, and emotional nurturing, because within themselves it is not accepted—due to prohibitions or out of shame for being too greedy—to wish for too much care. Especially in the early phase of therapy, the patient will also gladly and, after working through her resistances, extensively allow herself to be mothered, which the therapist also enjoys doing. However, once the patient is emotionally satisfied, she wants to turn to other feelings and areas of life, thereby depriving the therapist of the opportunity to fulfill, altruistically through the patient, those wishes she has relinquished. The therapist can express her resistance to the patient's further development in various ways. She may end the therapy with the justification that the patient is now doing well and no longer needs treatment, and stick to this decision even if the patient objects that she would still like to make progress in one area or another. Or she may accompany all further development with a certain disinterest, suspecting that the patient does not want to deal with the truly important oral wishes for care out of resistance. She might then encourage regressive processes and undo development that has already taken place, for example into the anal phase, so that the patient gives up what she has achieved and must be mothered again. We would describe these courses as malignant regression, i.e., pathological regression. These are tragic and ethically very questionable therapy courses, which we can prevent by recognizing our own countertransference resistance.

3.3. Compulsively structured therapists reject aggressive self-aspects in themselves, such as the defiant, stubborn four-year-old child they once were, because this is internally linked with the prohibitive, punitive father figure in a mixture of fear and anger. Its flare-up in experience leads to feelings of guilt or shame. If they now see this four-year-old, forbidden, and therefore projected self-aspect in the patient, they first try to encourage it in her. Either they want the forbidden part in themselves to be lived out by the patient, so that they turn the patient into a quick-tempered person who can hardly find compromises. Or they take on the father's role and limit the patient's aggressive impulses as soon as she expresses them. Both would make it more difficult for the patient to develop her own way of dealing with aggression and expressing her will.

3.4. Phobically structured therapists see in their patients the courageous part of themselves that they have rejected. They initially encourage and support it. But soon they become like their own mother, who, figuratively speaking, takes the patient onto her lap as soon as she has fallen and scraped her knee on the playground of life. Similar to the mother of the phobic patient from Sect. 8.3, the therapist might now say: "We will never go to this playground again! It's just too dangerous here!" This would succinctly capture the structure-specific countertransference resistance of phobic therapists. If unrecognized, it would block any further development of the patient, because this is not possible without scrapes. The patient would also be unable to develop self-confidence, since the word "confidence" contains "to confide" or "to dare," i.e., the courage needed to face the dangers of the world.

3.5. Narcissistically structured therapists recognize in their patient what they do not perceive in themselves, and what Narcissus does not see in the reflection of the water—namely, the beauty in themselves. They will acknowledge, admire, and encourage this in the patient, which can be very beneficial for patients with low self-confidence, provided they do not themselves have narcissistic conflicts about

3.6. Therapists with a histrionic personality structure experience the childlike part in themselves as negative, the part that so desperately wishes for the admiration of a parent but does not receive it, because wishing is already oedipally forbidden or because such wishes could only be fulfilled in secret if they were not to be punished. In the patient, they encourage the awareness of such wishes and initially fulfill them by giving the admiration they themselves always longed for. At some point, however, the situation shifts and the therapist feels that the patient has already received so much admiration but still demands more, so she stops admiring and points out to the patient the excessiveness of her wishes, thereby doing to her what the desired parent did to herself. Or everything goes well as long as the patient only wants to be admired by the therapist in therapy. Only when she is admired by others outside and enjoys it even more than the recognition from her therapist might the therapist lose patience and introduce prohibitions. This would then be a resistance against transferring something learned in therapy—namely, to allow oneself to receive admiration—into the outside world, where it would suddenly no longer be permitted.

4. The patient can become a substitute partner for the therapist if the latter has just separated or divorced from a romantic relationship. The therapist then turns very intensively to her patients, or to a single one, because she has lost her partner or the relationship has become stale. In the introductory section to Chap.9,I wrote about this, for example about Carl Gustav Jung, who was dissatisfied with his marriage and entered into sexual relationships with several patients, such as Sabina Spielrein. It was even more extreme with Sandor Ferenczi, who first entered into a romantic relationship with his patient, then analyzed her daughter and also had a sexual relationship with her. Unfortunately, such sexual abuses still occur in psychotherapy today, but are now increasingly strictly prosecuted both professionally

and criminally. If the desire for a partnership substitute remains in the therapist's fantasy, she will take intensive care of the patient, enjoy meeting her, spending time with her, talking with her, which initially helps the patient because she can feel accepted and important. However, even here the therapist has very specific ideas, both conscious and unconscious, about how the patient should and should not be, so that the patient's scope for development remains limited. In addition, the therapist has resistances regarding the transfer of what has been achieved into real relationships, especially if the patient enters into a romantic relationship outside. Then the therapist becomes the witch in Rapunzel, when she discovers that something new is growing in her, a baby that is not from the witch but must come from someone outside. For the witch, it feels like a betrayal, so she banishes Rapunzel with a curse. Only after a long period of weeping in the desert, reminiscent of a severe depression, does Rapunzel finally find her way back to life.

5. The therapist perceives in the patient a significant member of her primary family, a parent, a sibling, a grandparent, or aspects thereof.

5.1. Therapists with schizoid personality traits may then experience the patient as an emotionally engulfing mother who accepts no boundaries, no separation. They feel overwhelmed by the patient, extend the sessions because they do not dare or are unable to set a temporal boundary, and are left after the session overflowing with emotions. They will have great difficulty processing what they have absorbed during the sessions and will be unable to carry out clear interventions, since even empathizing, mirroring, or especially containing presupposes the ability to distinguish between their own feelings and those of the patient and to perceive them as separate. Often, they can only regain the necessary emotional distance with the help of a third party, such as a supervisor or a peer supervision group. If, on the other hand, schizoid therapists experience in their patient a mother who is too strongly and rigidly separated, they will feel lonely and isolated in the interaction and will develop neither empathy nor sympathy. They will listen to the patient in a state of inner emptiness. Here, too, it is important to recognize the countertransference resistance, namely, that it is not primarily due to the patient that they experience her as overwhelming or distant, but rather due to their own maternal transference onto the patient.

5.2. Therapists with depressive structures might rediscover in a depressive patient their own depressive, withdrawn, energyless mother, who in their early childhood was unable or only insufficiently able to care for them. As they once did for their mother, they will care for the patient, hoping that she will soon feel better. But if the patient remains needy and hungry, a rage will gradually arise in the therapist, as towards the constantly dissatisfied mother whom they had to care for instead of being cared for by her. As in the Grimm fairy tale "Hansel and Gretel," she will symbolically, full of rage, push the patient into the oven, as Gretel did with the witch, for example by abruptly ending the therapy or bluntly declaring the patient's wishes as unattainable.

5.3. Obsessive therapists might discover in a patient who frequently rejects their interventions, interpretations, or suggestions, their harsh father who suppressed all their expressions of will, rejected their ideas, and punished aggressive impulses. They would react with fear or feelings of guilt and become increasingly hesitant to use therapeutic techniques, perhaps limiting themselves to a nod of approval. They would be unable to clarify why, or from what resistances, the patient often rejects their interventions, nor to engage in a constructive discussion about the therapeutic approach. The therapy would soon be paralyzed by this countertransference resistance.

5.4. Phobically structured therapists are in any case very cautious and reserved with their interventions. Should the patient react with surprise or even fright, the therapist may experience her as the constricting mother who would quickly take her onto her lap, who reacted anxiously to every step the therapist took as a child, especially if it looked a bit unsteady. The therapist will then hold back therapeutically and will not address the patient's contradictions or resistances for a long time, which then manifests as a considerable countertransference resistance.

5.5. Therapists with narcissistic traits might see in their patients something like "Big Daddy" from the play "Cat on a Hot Tin Roof" by Tennessee Williams and experience themselves as the eternally sidelined and, despite all efforts, rejected son Gooper. Like him, they will engage in therapy and give everything they have to offer. Nevertheless, their patients will apparently always behave like "Big Daddy" and long for the beloved and favored son Brick, for example when they rave about how much a self-paid hypnotherapist or body therapy has helped them, while with the Gooper-therapist they can only talk sensibly but cannot change anything. Instead of addressing the patient's displacement resistances, such situations wound them so deeply that it becomes a countertransference resistance and blocks the treatment.

5.6. Histrionically structured therapists find themselves in an inner dilemma when they re-experience in the patient an oedipally admired parent, such as their mother. They will initially strive to gain her erotic admiration, or at least her general recognition, by flattering her, positively mirroring her strengths and abilities, perhaps even commenting on her good looks. Should they succeed in gaining the patient's attention and admiration, oedipal guilt feelings will arise, causing them to withdraw. The tin roof gets hot. As Brick in the play feels disgust when he achieves "Big Daddy's" full attention and recognition, when his father even sends everyone else away to speak with him alone, the therapist suddenly feels aversive, rejecting feelings toward her patient due to oedipal guilt and shame, even or especially because the patient admires her. In Tennessee Williams' play, Brick manages to talk to "Big Daddy" about his previously unacknowledged love for him as well as his homoerotic love for his childhood friend Skipper. Since the therapist cannot talk to her patient about her oedipal dilemma, she should have addressed and worked through it in her own self-experience during psychotherapeutic training, so that later, in her work with her patient, she notices similarities instead of developing a countertransference resistance.

Conclusion

If, through her self-experience during psychotherapeutic training, the therapist has become aware of her own character structure and the types of countertransference resistance to which she is prone, then the phenomena described can already be noticed in their early stages, so that she does not block the treatment or allow it to take a problematic course.

9.3 Training and Parenthood as Reasons for Resistance

▶ The co-transference of the therapist can be influenced by certain specific circumstances in her life situation, two examples of which will be mentioned here: namely, the psychotherapeutic training and the parenthood of the therapist.

During their psychotherapeutic training, trainee psychotherapists conduct their first treatments. The conditions under which they work vary greatly. At some training institutes, patients are assigned to them by the outpatient clinic, so they cannot select them from several preliminary interviews or files. In some cases, they are only allowed to refuse to take on a treatment in rare exceptional cases. Therapist and patient must then work together, for better or worse, whether or not they find each other sympathetic. If not, the effectiveness of the therapy is severely hampered from the outset, especially in the form of a good working relationship that does not develop or develops inadequately, as well as transference, countertransference, and co-transference resistances. Patients may lose hope that they can be helped as a result of such often unsatisfactory treatments and become chronic. Therapists develop doubts about their ability to conduct good, helpful psychotherapeutic treatments. That is why I support supervisees at such institutes by engaging with the outpatient clinic to enable free choice of the therapeutic pair. But even at institutes where trainees can first select from files and then, in trial sessions together with the patient, decide for or against therapy, trainee therapists sometimes feel guilty about rejecting a patient who would like to see them, because they feel they cannot do that to her, that they should not send yet another patient back to the outpatient clinic, or for other reasons of guilt. Here, close supervisory support is important to recognize transference and co-transference resistances from the outset and to teach the therapist how to sensitively and kindly explain to the patient the referral to a colleague. If it is relevant, the therapist could cautiously name a co-transference. She could say that the patient reminds her of a person with whom she had a very conflictual relationship, which she may not always be able to keep out of her contact with the patient. By revealing the co-transference, the patient knows that it is not her fault that she is being sent away, not because she is unlovable, too difficult, or repulsive, but because there are reasons in the therapist's experience, in her history, that prevent collaboration. This is relieving and not as rejecting as sending someone away without giving reasons or with false, pretextual explanations, such as the therapist suddenly having no free times after all. Within the outpatient clinic, referral to a colleague is then quite possible, especially if the therapist asks her colleagues who could take over the patient.

A typical co-transference in training treatments is characterized by the fear that the patient might terminate the therapy. In Germany, there are maximum quotas of 800 hours, or in the case of combined training in depth psychology-based and analytic therapy, 1600 hours, as well as minimum numbers of long-term treatments with certain minimum hours. If a patient terminates therapy after, say, 200 hours, which the trainee needs as one of two required long-term cases of 250 hours in analytic therapy training, she must start from scratch with the next patient and hope that at least this one will make it to 250 hours. Several terminations of long-term therapies make it increasingly difficult to collect the required long-term cases without exceeding the upper limits of 800 or 1600 hours. Therefore, trainees avoid interventions that they fear might destabilize or even anger their patients. The first intervention step, clarification, is still quite possible. At the second step, confrontation with contradictory aspects, or even the third step, interpretation of repressed, shame-laden aspects, therapists often become afraid of frightening or angering the patient, so that she might terminate therapy. Interventions that would actually make sense and occur to the therapist are then omitted as a form of co-transference resistance. This greatly slows down the therapy. Sometimes, precisely what the therapist fears then happens: patients terminate treatment precisely because the therapist avoids addressing and questioning sensitive issues. As a result, the patient gains no new insights, even in areas where she would be willing to face them. The therapy brings too little that is new, and the patient ultimately terminates for this reason.

Even though we should treat our patients as gently as possible, we cannot entirely avoid the fact that insights about oneself and important objects can sometimes be painful. It is therefore helpful not only for trainees but for all therapists to point this out at the beginning of therapy. In the trial sessions, we can explain to patients that some insights may trigger painful or unsettling feelings, that they may sometimes be angry with us, or may often feel misunderstood, but that they should still come to the next session instead of terminating therapy, in order to try to discuss what happened with us. I have often experienced patients telling me that they only came to the therapy session today, instead of quitting, because I had made it clear to them at the beginning that they might sometimes feel very angry with me and that it would be good to at least try to talk to me about it. These always turned out to be very important sessions. It is similar with misunderstanding: I announce already in the preliminary sessions that patients often tell me that I have not quite understood them at a certain point. They then explain what they said again, perhaps from a slightly different perspective, until I understand it. If we did not say this at the beginning, some patients would give up talking about certain topics because they believe it makes no sense to bring them up if even we, as trained experts, do not understand. The topics then remain outside, or the patients terminate the treatment. Trainees sometimes do not like to show that they have not understood something, or are shocked when the patient feels misunderstood, because this could make the patient doubt their competence. Misunderstanding then does not become a source for deepening a topic, but a resistance.

Another co-transference resistance can arise from the supervision required for trainees. During my own psychotherapeutic training and further education, I chose my supervisors so that, in my view, their personal style and theoretical focus matched the respective patients I wanted to take on. Therefore, I never felt that I was being pushed by the supervisor in a technical direction I did not actually want. Sometimes, however, this does happen, either because the supervisors at a training institute are very busy, so the trainee has to take whichever supervisor she can get, or because the trainee does not dare to contradict the supervisor's technical recommendations. She will then carry out interventions with which she cannot really identify, or she will secretly, with feelings of guilt, do something in therapy that she would never report to the supervisor. This can lead to co-transference resistances in trainees and throw the treatments off balance. In this respect, we supervisors do well to repeatedly ask whether the supervisee can identify with what we have worked out in supervision, or whether she would like to contradict us on some points.

Parenthood is something intimate, fascinating, but also frightening, especially for psychotherapists. Among the many reasons for choosing this profession, alongside wishes for transformative power over others, altruism, and curiosity, there is often a sense of one's own psychological woundedness, usually by one's parents. We then want to do better with our patients, and even more so with our own children, than our parents did with us. The ego ideal of being a good mother or father then accompanies us daily, especially when we become parents ourselves. A supervisee of mine became a father during therapy with a patient who had had a very bad father. Before and after the birth of his son, he was very preoccupied with the question of whether he would be a good father to his child, and imagined all the things he could do wrong. With regard to his patient, he repeatedly said that the therapy should be a corrective emotional experience for him, a "re-parenting" with himself as an only good father. Because of this co-transference resistance, he overlooked for some time very clear negative father transferences from his patient, who repeatedly saw in him bad or disparaging sides of his father, fought against them, or was frightened. Only when we talked about his co-transference, his need to prove himself to the patient as a good father, was he able to perceive and work through the negative father transferences. In the end, he understood that a corrective experience alone is not enough to permanently change internalized shame, guilt, fears, or destructive tendencies.

References

Abel, T. (2005). Gevatter Tod: Gefahren einer gemeinsamen Abwehr von Ohnmachtserfahrungen in der Psychotherapie. In A. Springer, A. U. Gerlach, & A. M. Schlösser (Eds.), *Macht und Ohnmacht* (pp. 247–256). Psychosozial.

Abel, T. (2011a). Zigeunermädchen: Der fremde Bürger als Massenphänomen. *Zeitschrift für Individualpsychologie, 36*, 162–173.

Abel, T. (2011b). Wir können nicht nicht kommunizieren: Über die Unmöglichkeit, nicht intersubjektiv zu arbeiten. *Zeitschrift für Individualpsychologie, 36*, 270–274.

Abel, T. (2013). Widerstandsanalyse anhand von Träumen. In B. Janta, B. Unruh, & S. Walz-Pawlita (Eds.), *Der Traum* (pp. 147–162). Psychosozial.

Abel, T. (2020a). Das achte Leben – Konflikte um Generativität in der psychoanalytischen Bewegung am Beispiel der Geschichte der Objektbeziehungspsychologie. In I. Moeslein-Teising, G. Schäfer, & R. Martin (Eds.), *Generativität* (pp. 231–242). Psychosozial.

Abel, T. (2020b). Von inneren Bildern zu Objektrepräsentanzen – Lebensstilanalyse und „Zentrales Beziehungskonfliktthema". In P. Wahl (Eds.), *Bildung und innere Bilder* (pp. 120–133). Vandenhoeck & Ruprecht.

Abel, T. (2023). *Handbuch der Objektbeziehungspsychologie*. Psychosozial.

Adler, A. (1912). *Über den nervösen Charakter: Grundzüge einer vergleichenden Individualpsychologie und Psychotherapie. 1997*. Vandenhoeck & Ruprecht.

Adler, A. (1933). *Der Sinn des Lebens. 1992*. Fischer-Taschenbuch.

Adler, K. (2020). *Ida*. Rowohlt Taschenbuch.

Alexander, F. (1950). *Psychosomatic medicine. Its principles and applications*. Norton.

Alexander, F. (1951). *Psychosomatische Medizin: Grundlagen und Anwendungsgebiete*. De Gruyter.

Back, M., Echterhoff, G., Müller, O., Pollack, D., & Schlipphak, B. (2024). *Working Report: Von Verteidigern und Entdeckern: Ein Identitätskonflikt um Zugehörigkeit und Bedrohung*. Studie Universität Münster. https://doi.org/10.17879/97049506223.

Bary, H. A. de. (1879). *Die Erscheinung der Symbiose*. Trübner

Benjamin, J. (2019). *Anerkennung, Zeugenschaft und Moral: soziale Traumata in psychoanalytischer Perspektive*. Psychosozial.

Benjamin, J. (2020). *Die Fesseln der Liebe. Psychoanalyse, Feminismus und das Problem der Macht*. Vittorio Klostermann.

Bion, W. R. (1962). *Lernen durch Erfahrung. 1997*. Suhrkamp.

Bion, W. R. (1990). *Erfahrungen in Gruppen*. Suhrkamp.

T. Abel, *Resistance in Psychotherapy*, https://doi.org/10.1007/978-3-662-72663-1

Bisson, J. I., Ehlers, A., Matthews, R., Pilling, S., Richards, D., & Turner, S. (2007). Psychological treatments for chronic post-traumatic stress disorder: Systematic review and meta-analysis. *British Journal of Psychiatry, 190*, 97–104. https://doi.org/10.1192/bjp.bp.106.021402.

Clarkin, J. F., Yeomans, F. E., & Kernberg, O. F. (2008). *Psychotherapie der Borderline-Persönlichkeit – Manual zur psychodynamischen Therapie*. Schattauer.

Crepaldi, G. (2022). *Containing*. Psychosozial.

Dettmering, P. (Eds.). (1999). *Kinder- und Hausmarchen der Bruder Grimm. Erstdruckfassung 1812–1815*. Klotz.

Deutscher Bundestag. (2023). *Drucksache 20/8860: Antrag der Fraktion der CDU/CSU – Versorgung von Menschen in psychischen Krisen und mit psychischen Erkrankungen stärken*. https://t1p.de/h3svt. Accessed: 25. Apr. 2025.

Drewermann, E. (1992). *Der Herr Gevatter. Der Gevatter Tod. Fundevogel*. Walter.

Erikson, E. H. (1970). *Jugend und Krise. Die Psychodynamik im sozialen Wandel*. Klett.

Ermann, M. (2012). *Psychoanalyse in den Jahren nach Freud. Entwicklungen 1940–1975*. Kohlhammer.

Ferenczi, S. (1910). *Introjektion und Übertragung. Jahrbuch für Psychoanalyse und Psychopathologische Forschungen II*. Franz Deuticke.

Ferenczi, S. (1933). Sprachverwirrung zwischen den Erwachsenen und dem Kind. *Internationale Zeitschrift für Psychoanalyse, 19*(1/2), 5–15.

Fonagy, P. (2003). *Bindungstheorie und Psychoanalyse*. Klett Cotta.

Fonagy, P., & Target, M. (2015). *Psychoanalyse und die Psychopathologie der Entwicklung*. Klett-Cotta.

Fonagy, P., Gergely, G., Jurist, E. L., & Target, M. (2004). *Affektregulierung, Mentalisierung und die Entwicklung des Selbst*. Klett Cotta.

Freud, A. (1936). *Das Ich und die Abwehrmechanismen. 2021*. Fischer.

Freud, S. (1895). *Studien zur Hysterie. GW I* (pp. 75–312). Fischer.

Freud, S. (1904). *Drei Abhandlungen zur Sexualtheorie. GW V* (pp. 27–146). Fischer.

Freud, S. (1905). *Bruchstück einer Hysterie-Analyse. GW V, S* (pp. 161–286). Fischer.

Freud, S. (1908). *Charakter und Analerotik. GW VII* (pp. 200–209). Fischer.

Freud, S. (1912). *Ratschläge für den Arzt bei der psychoanalytischen Behandlung. GW VIII* (pp. 367–387). Fischer.

Freud, S. (1913). *Einleitung der Behandlung. GW VIII* (pp. 453–478). Fischer.

Freud, S. (1914). *Zur Einführung des Narzißmus. GW* (Vol. X, pp. 137–170). Fischer.

Freud, S. (1915). *Bemerkungen über die Übertragungsliebe. GW X* (pp. 306–323). Fischer.

Freud, S. (1916). *Die Fehlleistungen. GW XI* (pp. 7–78). Fischer.

Freud, S. (1917). *Trauer und Melancholie. GW X* (pp. 428–446). Fischer.

Freud, S. (1923). *Das Ich und das Es. GW XIII* (pp. 235–289). Fischer.

Freud, S. (1926). *Hemmung, Symptom und Angst. GW XIV* (pp. 111–205). Fischer.

Freud, S. (1927). *Die Zukunft einer Illusion. GW, XIV* (pp. 323–380). Fischer.

Fromm, E. (1941). *Die Flucht vor der Freiheit*. Europäische Verlagsanstalt.

Glover, E. (1955). *The technique of psychoanalysis*. Bailliere Tindall & Cox.

Greenson, R. R. (1973). *Technik und Praxis der Psychoanalyse* (Vol. 1). Klett.

Greenson, R. R. (1982). Das Problem des Durcharbeitens. In R. R. Greenson (Eds.), *Psychoanalytische Erkundungen* (pp. 178–221). Klett-Cotta.

Gruen, A. (2000). *Der Fremde in uns*. Klett-Cotta.

Haan, N. (1977). *Coping and defending. Processes of self-environment organization*. Academic Press.

Haarer, J. (1934). *Die deutsche Mutter und ihr erstes Kind*. Lehmanns.

Haas, W. (2005). *Familienstellen – Therapie oder Okkultismus?* Asanger.

Haible-Baer, N., & Kirsch, P. (2024). Die Diagnose der ADHS im Erwachsenenalter – Eine Aufgabe für Psychologische Psychotherapeutinnen und -therapeuten? *Psychotherapeutenjournal, 23*(2), 159–166.

Härter, M., Loh, A., & Spies, C. (Eds.). (2005). *Gemeinsam entscheiden – erfolgreich behandeln*. Deutscher Ärzte-Verlag.

Heimann, P. (2016). *Gegenübertragung und andere Schriften zur Psychoanalyse*. Klett-Cotta.

Hirsch, M. (2002). *Schuld und Schuldgefühl: zur Psychoanalyse von Trauma und Introjekt*. Vandenhoeck & Ruprecht.

Hirsch, M. (2018). *Psychoanalytische Traumatologie – das Trauma in der Familie: psychoanalytische Theorie und Therapie schwerer Persönlichkeitsstörungen*. Schattauer.

Hurwitz, S. (1980). *Lilith – die erste Eva. Eine Studie über dunkle Aspekte des Weiblichen*. Daimon.

Jacobi, F., Höfler, M., Strehle, J., Mack, S., Gerschler, A., Scholl, L., Busch, M. A., Maske, U., Hapke, U., Gaebel, W., Maier, W., Wagner, M., Zielasek, J., & Wittchen, H. U. (2014). Psychische Störungen in der Allgemeinbevölkerung. Studie zur Gesundheit Erwachsener in Deutschland und ihr Zusatzmodul „Psychische Gesundheit" (DEGS1MH). *Nervenarzt, 85*, 77–87.

Kaleta, M., Leutner, M., Thurner, S., Endel, G., Kiss, N., Robausch, M., Klimek, P., & Kautzky-Willer, A. (2023). Trends in diabetes incidence in Austria 2013–2017. *Scientific Reports, 13*. https://www.nature.com/articles/s41598-023-35806-0. Accessed: 25. Apr. 2025.

Klein, M. (1946). Notes on some schizoid mechanisms. *International Journal of Psycho-Analysis, 27*, 99–110.

Klein, M. (1957). *Neid und Dankbarkeit. Eine Untersuchung unbewußter Quellen. Gesammelte Schriften, Band III: Schriften 1946–1963* (pp. 283–367). Frommann-Holzboog.

Klovert, H. (2024). *Herointod mit 19 Jahren. Unser Sohn, der Süchtige. DER SPIEGEL 32/2024* (pp. 34–38). Spiegel-Verlag Rudolf Augstein.

Kohut, H. (2016). *Gesammelte Werke*. Psychosozial.

König, K. (1993). *Gegenübertragungsanalyse*. Vandenhoeck & Ruprecht.

König, K. (1995). *Widerstandsanalyse*. Vandenhoeck & Ruprecht.

König, K. (1997). *Abwehrmechanismen*. Vandenhoeck & Ruprecht.

König, K. (1998). *Übertragungsanalyse*. Vandenhoeck & Ruprecht.

König, K. (2004). *Charakter, Persönlichkeit und Persönlichkeitsstörung*. Klett-Cotta.

Krutzenbichler, H. S., & Essers, H. (2002). *Muß denn Liebe Sünde sein? Zur Psychoanalyse der Übertragungs- und Gegenübertragungsliebe*. Psychosozial.

Kübler-Ross, E. (2014). *Interviews mit Sterbenden*. Kreuz.

Lazarus, R. S. (1991). *Emotion and adaptation*. Oxford University Press.

Linehan, M. M. (2008). *Dialektisch-Behaviorale Therapie (DBT) der Borderline-Persönlichkeitsstörung*. Psychosozial.

Luborsky, L. (1984). *Principles of psychoanalytic psychotherapy. A manual for supportive-expressive psychotherapy*. Basic Books.

Luborsky, L. (1988). *Einführung in die analytische Psychotherapie*. Springer.

Maaz, H. J. (1990). *Der Gefühlsstau. Ein Psychogramm der DDR*. Argon.

Maaz, H. J. (2012). *Die narzisstische Gesellschaft. Ein Psychogramm*. Beck.

Mahler, M. (1972). *Symbiose und Individuation. Bd. 1. Psychosen im frühen Kindesalter*. Klett-Cotta.

Mentzos, S. (2009). *Lehrbuch der Psychodynamik: Die Funktion der Dysfunktionalität psychischer Störungen*. Vandenhoeck & Ruprecht.

Nissen, B. (2015). Zur psychoanalytischen Konzeptualisierung und Behandlung von Störungen aus dem autistischen und autistoiden Spektrum. *Psychotherapeutenjournal, 14*(2), 110–119.

Orange, D. M. (2004). *Emotionales Verständnis und Intersubjektivität: Beiträge zu einer psychoanalytischen Epistemologie*. Brandes & Apsel.

Plass, D., Vos, T., & Hornberg, C. (2014). Entwicklung der Krankheitslast in Deutschland. *Deutsches Ärzteblatt, 111*, 629–638.

Rank, O. (1927). *Grundzüge einer genetischen Psychologie*. Deuticke.

Reddemann, L. (2021). *Psychodynamisch Imaginative Traumatherapie – PITT. Ein Mitgefühls- und Ressourcen-orientierter Ansatz in der Psychotraumatologie*. Klett-Cotta.

Reich, G. (2015). *Ess-Störungen*. TRIAS.

Reich, G. (2017). *Hungern, um zu leben – die Paradoxie der Magersucht*. Psychosozial.

Reich, G. (2024). *Bulimia nervosa*. Hogrefe.

Reich, W. (1933). *Charakteranalyse*. Selbstverlag.

Reuter, E. (2005). *Gehirn-Wäsche. Macht und Willkür in der „systemischen Psychotherapie" nach Bert Hellinger*. Lehmann, Antipsychiatrieverlag.

Richter, H. E. (1963). *Eltern, Kind und Neurose. Zur Psychoanalyse der kindlichen Rolle in der Familie*. Rowohlt.

Richter, H. E. (1970). *Patient Familie. Entstehung, Struktur und Therapie von Konflikten in Ehe und Familie. 2012*. Psychosozial.

Riemann, F. (1961). *Grundformen der Angst: eine tiefenpsychologische Studie*. Reinhardt.

Röhr, H. P. (1996). *Weg aus dem Chaos: Das Hans-mein-Igel-Syndrom oder Die Borderline-Störung verstehen*. Walter.

Rudolf, G. (1993). *Psychotherapeutische Medizin und Psychosomatik. Ein einführendes Lehrbuch auf psychodynamischer Grundlage*. Georg Thieme.

Ruge, W. (2012). *Gelobtes Land – Meine Jahre in Stalins Sowjetunion*. Rowohlt.

Sandler, J. (1976). Countertransference and Role Responsiveness. *International Review of Psychoanalysis, 3*, 43–47.

Sandler, J. (1999). *Innere Objektbeziehungen*. Klett-Cotta.

Sandler, J. (2001). *Die Grundbegriffe der psychoanalytischen Therapie*. Klett-Cotta.

Schneider, S., & Margraf, J. (2014). *Panik: Angstanfälle und ihre Behandlung*. Springer.

Schulte, D. (2014). *Therapiemotivation: Widerstände analysieren – Therapieziele klären – Motivation fördern*. Hogrefe.

Seiffge-Krenke, I. (2017). *Widerstand, Abwehr und Bewältigung*. Vandenhoeck & Ruprecht.

Steele, K. (2017). *Die Behandlung traumabasierter Dissoziation*. G.P. Probst.

Steinert, C., & Leichsenring, F. (2017). *Psychodynamische Psychotherapie in Zeiten evidenzbasierter Medizin: Bambi ist gesund und munter*. Vandenhoeck & Ruprecht.

Stroeken, H. (1992). *Freud und seine Patienten*. Fischer-Taschenbuch.

Thomä, H., & Kächele, H. (2006). *Lehrbuch der psychoanalytischen Therapie. Teil 1: Grundlagen*. Springer.

Uexküll, T. von. (1963). *Grundfragen der psychosomatischen Medizin*. Rowohlt.

Van der Kolk, B. A. (2000). Trauma und Gedächtnis. In B. A. van der Kolk, A. C. McFarlane, & L. Weisaeth (Eds.), *Traumatic Stress: Grundlagen und Behandlungsansätze* (pp. P221–P240). Junfermann.

Weiss, J. (1993). *How psychotherapy works. Process and technique*. Guilford Press.

Welwood, J. (2014). *Bewusst lieben – Ein Weg des Erwachens*. Arbor.

Wilczek, B. (2015). Erwachsene mit hochfunktionalem Autismus in der psychotherapeutischen Praxis – Herausforderungen und Chancen. *Psychotherapeutenjournal, 14*(2), 120–129.

Winnicott, D. (1965). *The maturational process and the facilitating environment*. Hogarth Press.

Winnicott, D. (1996). Übergangsobjekte und Übergangsphänomene. *Psyche, 23*(9), 666–682.

Wirth, H. J. (2007). Narzissmus und Machtmissbrauch in der Psychotherapie. *Psychoanalytische Familientherapie. Zeitschrift für Paar-, Familien- und Sozialtherapie, 14*(8), 85–98.

Wirth, H. J. (2015). Das Trauma der Geburt bei Ödipus und seine Bedeutung für die Psychoanalyse. *Psychoanalyse im Widerspruch, 27*(53), 63–82.

Yeomans, F. E., Clarkin, J. F., & Kernberg, O. F. (2017). *Übertragungsfokussierte Psychotherapie für Borderline-Patienten – Das Praxismanual.* Schattauer.

Zafar, H. (2000). *„Du kannst nicht fließen, wenn dein Geld nicht fließt": Macht und Mißbrauch in der Psychotherapie.* Rowohlt.

MIX
Papier aus verantwortungsvollen Quellen
Paper from responsible sources
FSC® C105338

If you have any concerns about our products,
you can contact us on
ProductSafety@springernature.com

In case Publisher is established outside the EU,
the EU authorized representative is:
Springer Nature Customer Service Center GmbH
Europaplatz 3, 69115 Heidelberg, Germany

Printed by Libri Plureos GmbH
in Hamburg, Germany